Contents

SECOND EDITION

Digital Wars
Apple, Google, Microsoft and the battle for the internet

CHARLES ARTHUR

KoganPage

LONDON PHILADELPHIA NEW DELHI

First published in Great Britain and the United States in 2012 by Kogan Page Limited
Second edition published 2014

2nd Floor, 45 Gee Street
London EC1V 3RS
United Kingdom
www.koganpage.com

1518 Walnut Street, Suite 1100
Philadelphia PA 19102
USA

4737/23 Ansari Road
Daryaganj
New Delhi 110002
India

© Charles Arthur, 2012, 2014

The right of Charles Arthur to be identified as the author of this work has been asserted by him in accordance with the Copyright, Designs and Patents Act 1988.

ISBN   978 0 7494 7203 0
E-ISBN   978 0 7494 7204 7

British Library Cataloguing-in-Publication Data

A CIP record for this book is available from the British Library.

Library of Congress Cataloging-in-Publication Data

Arthur, Charles, 1961-
     Digital wars : Apple, Google, Microsoft and the battle for the Internet / Charles Arthur. –
2nd ed.
         pages cm
         ISBN 978-0-7494-7203-0 (pbk.) – ISBN 978-0-7494-7204-7 (ebook)   1. Internet
industry–United States.   2. Apple Computer, Inc.   3. Google (Firm)   4. Microsoft
Corporation.   I. Title.
     HD9696.8.U62A78 2014
     338.4'70040973–dc23
                                                                                               2014001876

Typeset by Graphicraft Limited, Hong Kong
Print production managed by Jellyfish
Printed and bound by CPI Group (UK) Ltd, Croydon, CR0 4YY

Introduction: in the beginning

The world we experience is analogue: colours, sounds, smells, all merge and mix smoothly. The digital world ushered in by computers is different: binary, on or off, yes or no. The arrival of affordable personal computing beginning in the 1970s, followed by the addition in the 1990s of the internet, began to create entirely new businesses – such as Yahoo, a website that offered up-to-the-minute news, weather and free e-mail – and to overturn existing ones, such as the music industry, at a pace that multiplied geometrically with the number of computers connected to the network.

Into this maelstrom of change came three companies: Apple, Microsoft and Google. They were radically different from each other. By the time all three arrived on the digital battlefield, the glory days of one were apparently behind it; another stood atop the computing and business world; the third was barely more than a clever idea in the minds of two very clever students.

The companies would subsequently fight a series of pitched battles for control of different parts of the digital landscape. Their weapons would be hardware, software and advertising. At stake were their reputations – but, equally, our future. Does it matter which search engine most people use? Where we buy our digital music? Who makes the software that powers our mobile phone, or the tablet that we use while waiting for a train or meeting? Some think not: that the momentum of human intentions means we will always get the correct outcomes, no matter who is overseeing our experiences. Others say that the digital landscape is covered in tollgates, and that those who control them will always determine the shape of the future.

What is certain is that to control any of them is a golden opportunity to extract tolls from the millions and millions of people passing through. The reward for winning any of the digital wars is enormous wealth – and, often, the chance to use that to build a fresh set of tollgates on another part of the landscape, or displace an existing rival.

The first time that all three found themselves sharing the same digital space was 1998. They could not know of the battles to come. But those battles would be world-changing.

Chapter One
1998

Bill Gates and Microsoft

Late in 1998 the *New Yorker* writer Ken Auletta visited Bill Gates, then chief executive of Microsoft, at his offices in Redmond, Washington. It was, as you'd expect of a chief executive, a corner office, with trees on one side and buildings on another. Unassuming brown office chairs sat around polished pine furniture; Gates's desk emerged from the tree-side wall, looking more like a breakfast bar than the symbol of a powerful executive. On the desktop under the window facing the trees sat three 21-inch computer monitors. Gates could move documents around their entire expanse.

Microsoft's stock was roaring, making the company worth around $250 billion and Gates, then 43, the richest man in the world, based on his share of the business. Microsoft's Windows ran about 95 per cent of the PCs in the world, with 100 million being sold annually in a market that was growing by 15–20 per cent. A year earlier, a Microsoft press release had boasted about its new search engine, MSN.com, proclaiming that its goal wasn't just to be the best search site on the net: 'Our goal is to make MSN.com the number one site on the internet, period.' Its server operating system was winning contracts. So who, Auletta asked, did he fear? An existing rival such as Sun Microsystems, or database maker Oracle, or web browser company Netscape? No, none of those, said Gates: 'I fear someone in a garage who is devising something completely new.' Obviously, he didn't know where, or what, or who; as Auletta noted, 'He just knew that innovation was usually the enemy of established companies.'[1]

Why a garage? Because Silicon Valley garages are famous breeding grounds for innovative, disruptive companies that could react faster to conditions and use the newest technology, buoyed by venture capital funding and not burdened with bureaucracy and quarterly earnings reports.

Gates is the classic example of what the writer Malcolm Gladwell calls 'outliers':[2] people who have spent enormous amounts of time learning and then refining their skills – in Gates's case, programming. The clever workarounds that he used to program the very first versions of Basic that his company wrote are legendary among (older) programmers, who recall the days when a spare kilobyte of memory was as precious as water on a desert trek. By contrast with what Gates grew up with, today's programmers have endless reservoirs of storage and memory.

But Gates also brought an animal-sharp business sense and ability to unravel complex problems, while being able to spot the 'gotchas' (the little bugs that might come back to bite you). He had stamped his hard-driving personality on Microsoft, which was known as the 800-pound gorilla of software: if you were setting up a business in the late 1990s then your aim was either to be acquired by it or to steer well clear of anything it did, because it would crush smaller competitors pitilessly.

The tactics Microsoft used were often questionable; for example undercutting rivals on price, because it could, to drive them out of the market. That sort of approach had gained Microsoft another name around the technology industry: the Evil Empire.

In 1998 Microsoft was crushing yet another upstart – Netscape, which had had the temerity to suggest that the browser could become the basis for doing work anywhere, so that Windows itself would become irrelevant; all you'd need would be a computer that could run a browser, and you'd be able to do everything for which you presently needed a PC.

Steve Jobs and Apple

Microsoft had reached the pinnacle by besting Apple – the company co-founded by Steve Jobs, a charming, brilliant, tempestuous, iconoclastic, unique businessman who had been thrown out of it in 1985 but returned, triumphantly, at the end of 1996 when another company he had set up, NeXT Computer, was bought by the then ailing Apple, which was bleeding cash. He forced out the incumbent chief executive in July 1997 and became 'interim' chief executive that September – at which point the company had made a loss of a billion dollars for the financial year.

Jobs, in his early 40s (born, like Gates, in 1955), was no programmer. It's unlikely that any analysis would discover any Gladwell-qualifying immersion in a particular skill. His talents instead lay in his personal, design and social skills: he could discern the weaknesses and desires of the people across a negotiating table to navigate to a deal, and use a combination of excoriation, wheedling and charm to drive subordinates and even equals into producing better products than they ever expected they could. In Apple's earliest days he negotiated excellent deals on semiconductors because he could memorize entire price lists. Yet he could also scream at staff who he thought had done less than they could. Designers, meanwhile, found his constant demands for another little change maddening. (The designer of the Calculator application on the first Macintosh grew so weary of Jobs's constant demands for changes that he wrote a program that would let Jobs design it.)

Jobs's lust for design has no obvious roots; he was the adopted son of working parents. But he was able to enunciate it very clearly. 'Design is a funny word. Some people think design means how it looks', he said in an interview with *Wired* in 1995.[3] 'But of course if you dig deeper, it's really how it works... to design something really well, you have to *get* it. You have to really grok [deeply understand] what it's all about. It takes a passionate commitment to really, thoroughly, understand something, chew it up, not just quickly swallow it.' John Sculley, the former chief executive of Apple (who had been hired by Jobs and helped fire him), recounted in a separate interview with Leander Kahney how 'from the moment I met him [Steve] always loved beautiful products, especially hardware. He came to my house and he was fascinated because I had special hinges and locks designed for doors... Steve in particular felt that you had to begin design from the vantage point of the experience of the user.'[4]

Yet it was those negotiation skills that so often came in useful. Jobs was not strictly a salesperson, in that he wouldn't try to sell something he didn't completely believe in or use himself. However, when he needed something, his negotiating skills came to the fore. Not even Gates was immune from them. In 1997, and with the company (by his later admission) just 90 days from bankruptcy, Jobs spoke to Gates. Microsoft was infringing some of Apple's patents, and Apple needed money; more than that, it needed a commitment that Gates's company would keep making its Office suite available for the Mac. Otherwise businesses would abandon it, and that would be that: Apple could turn off the lights.

If Jobs had been confrontational, Gates could have let any legal battle over the patents stretch out and let Apple's weakening cash position drown it. But if he had been too weak, Gates might have ceded nothing, with the same result. Jobs knew this and acknowledged it to Gates, saying 'We need help.' But then he framed the situation not as confrontation, but cooperation. 'Bill,' he said, 'between us, we own 100 per cent of the desktop!' He made it sound as though Microsoft would be shaping the destiny of technology by investing in Apple's future. Gates wasn't taken in – though he did agree to buy $150 million of non-voting stock and to continue developing Office for the Mac. Afterwards, says Alan Deutschman, who recounted the tale in *The Second Coming of Steve Jobs*, about his return, Gates remarked: 'That guy is so amazing. He is a master at selling.'[5]

The Jobs who returned was completely unlike the one who had left. That one had been willing to spend huge amounts on trivial details that nobody would see, been unwilling to work inside a rigorous corporate framework, and hired someone – Sculley – who ended up unseating him. The Jobs who returned had seen NeXT Computer fail at making hardware because it couldn't get the volume to turn a profit, while Pixar, a company he bought from George Lucas, had sucked up huge amounts of the cash raised from selling his Apple shares, while requiring him to be a careful manager both of people – because they were that company's principal resource – and of money. He had learnt that it wasn't enough to offer great hardware; people needed a reason to really, really want it. Not enough of them had really wanted the NeXT Cube or the Pixar Image Computer.

The Jobs who returned, in short, already knew the truth that many businesspeople learn: you only get smart after you've gone bust three times. Jobs had flirted with it twice; the parlous state of the Apple he returned to made it three times. He brought a renewed focus and refreshed outlook.

Jobs began by killing surplus products in a bonfire of Apple's past vanities, such as the Newton – a futuristic touchscreen portable handheld computer created by Sculley. He later said the company had fallen into 'a coma' during his absence; it had chased profit instead of market share, and become greedy instead of focusing on its customers' desires. Many staff were fired and internal projects axed. Jobs justified that to worried developers in a 1997 speech: 'Focus is about saying no, and the result is going to be some really great products where the total is much greater than the sum of its parts.'[6]

A total of 350 products was cut to just 10. There were 15 different computers, with meaningless names such as the 6500 and 8600. The average person, who was meant to be Apple's prime market (since the business market had been conquered by Windows PCs), had no way to know which were desktops or laptops, high- or low-end. Jobs sliced the product line into a two-by-two matrix – consumer and business; and portable and desktop. Apple's teams would focus on producing a really good product in each category rather than spreading itself across an untenably wide range, each with its own upgrade cycle, user base, fans and flaws. 'If we have four great products, that's all we need,' he explained.[7] (The matrix for computers has remained almost unchanged since Jobs set it out in May 1998.)

Even so, Apple's destiny looked like a foregone conclusion. Why buy one of its products rather than a cheaper PC running Windows, which offered a broader range of software? In October 1997, Michael Dell, chief executive and founder of Dell Computer, was asked what he would do if he were in Jobs's position, leading a company that had just lost $1 billion on revenues of $7 billion. Dell could shrug off Apple's existence: his business was more than five times bigger, was based in Texas rather than Silicon Valley, spent comparatively little on research and development, was not known for innovation, and sold PCs using Windows. Dell was the anti-Apple, Michael Dell the anti-Jobs.

'What would I do? I'd shut it down and give the money back to the shareholders,' Dell replied bluntly.[8] The shareholders at the time would have received $5.49 per share – a total of $2.7 billion.

Dell's comment rankled with Jobs, who privately phoned him to remonstrate, calling his response disrespectful. Beating Dell – somehow, anyhow – became a minor obsession. In future speeches, Jobs would compare how many days' sales of computers Apple had in its warehouses against Dell's, and better it.

He set about Apple's dysfunctional supply chain, the part of a computer business that nobody sees, where factories build components that have to be ready for assembly at the right time, volume and price and run through quality assurance and shipped. As armies march on their stomachs, hardware businesses live or die on their supply chains.

The man who made that possible was recruited in March 1998. Tim Cook, who turned 38 in November that year, had previously spent four years at Compaq – then a ruthlessly effective PC manufacturer – and before that at IBM. Jobs and Cook clicked; the job interview simply worked where others had failed. Early on Cook held a meeting to try to sort out the many kinks in the supply chain in Asia. 'This is really bad,' he said in the meeting. 'Someone should be in China driving this.' Later in the same meeting, he looked over at Sabih Khan, then a key operations executive. 'Why are you still here?' he asked calmly. Khan got up, and headed for the airport.[9]

Cook's no-nonsense approach snapped Apple's manufacturing and supply chain into line. Inventory dropped from five weeks' worth of products to two days', as Cook shut factories and warehouses and tore up Apple's decade-old middleware. Its former method of quarterly ordering and building was abandoned: 'We plan weekly and execute daily,' he explained in 1999. 'I'm relentless on that.' He knew that the modern PC manufacturing business demanded the leanest possible operation; he saw inventory as 'fundamentally evil' – a drag on the company's balance sheet that falls in value by 1 to 2 per cent per week. 'In the business we're in, the product gets stale as fast as milk,' he said, adding that in a year or two 'I'd prefer to be able to talk inventories in terms of hours, not days.'[10]

Cook's effect on the company's balance sheet was immediate – and lasting. It began to accrue, instead of bleed, cash. But by June 1998 it was still a minnow, in computing terms, selling perhaps a couple of million computers a year.

Bill Gates and Steve Jobs

Gates and Jobs were long-time friends as well as rivals: a couple of decades earlier, they had taken girlfriends on double dates together. So what did Gates think of the threat from Cupertino? Speaking in June 1998 to another journalist, Mark Stephens (who writes under the more arresting moniker of Robert X Cringely), he grew ruminative. 'What I can't figure out is why he is even trying,' Gates said to Stephens. 'He knows he can't win.'[11]

(Typically, Gates was being accommodating; typically, Jobs wasn't. Stephens had been commissioned by *Vanity Fair* magazine to write an article about the relationship between Gates and Jobs. Jobs had insisted that Stephens talk to Gates first. He then never quite got around to his interview. The profile was never published.

The late Chris Gulker, who worked at Apple during its downslide and had some experience with Jobs, once told me that 'Steve basically regards the press as insects.')

Gates was absolutely right: there was no way that Jobs, or Apple, could win the war to be the dominant operating system on personal computers. Microsoft had won that years before. When Apple's previous set of executives had tried to mimic Microsoft, and licensed the Mac OS – the set of programs that makes a computer behave as it does, its binary DNA – to other computer makers, it had been as effective as slitting their wrists. The 'clones' undercut Apple's prices, taking revenue and profit from hardware sales; the revenue from software licences didn't cover the lost profits. Apple had begun losing money uncontrollably. Almost the first thing Jobs did on retaking the reins was to end the cloning deal, despite the lawsuits and costs it invited. Apple, he understood, couldn't survive by licensing its software. It was fine for Microsoft, which benefited from the scale of PC manufacturing. But Apple had to make physical things; it couldn't make money from selling software untethered from hardware.

Jobs anyway thought computing was in a sort of dead end too. 'The desktop computer industry is dead,' he said in 1995. 'Innovation has virtually ceased. Microsoft dominates with very little innovation. That's over. Apple lost. The desktop market has entered the dark ages, and it's going to be in the dark ages for the next 10 years, or certainly for the rest of this decade.'[12]

Why had Apple lost? Serried ranks of economists and management theorists were sure why: its model of 'vertical integration' – designing both the machines and the software – couldn't work in the computer industry. 'Vertically integrated companies can't compete! The oxymoron of "internal customers" is poison to a competitive culture. That is the lesson of the computer industry,' wrote Tom Evslin, an experienced tech entrepreneur.[13] Management and economic theory said that horizontal integration – PC makers building PCs, Microsoft writing the software – meant that the market optimum, of the maximum possible production volume and the lowest possible prices for consumers, would be reached much more quickly.[14]

While that's true, it overlooks other elements that are harder to quantify: user experience and collateral costs. Certainly Microsoft's brilliance and success at opening up the Windows platform by taking a standard hardware reference (created initially by IBM) and ensuring that its software would run on that platform, while making it easy for developers to write programs that would run on top of Windows, drove standardization and so drove down hardware prices. But it's hard to argue that Windows is optimal – that is, the best possible operating system that can be written for personal computers. People found it confusing, with mundane usability questions, such as why you would click on a button marked 'Start' when you want to turn the computer off (an observation that has become so hackneyed that it's only when you are explaining it to a first-time user that you notice its incongruity). Or why, having clicked that button, you're presented (in Windows Vista) with 15 routes (via physical buttons and menu items) to turn the machine off in four subtly different ways: sleep, hibernate, power off, suspend.

The collateral risk wasn't trivial either. Windows 95, 98, Me and XP had horrendous security holes; the latter had a protective firewall, but it was turned off by default, leaving domestic users (a particular target of its marketing) open to virus attacks – which came in huge numbers, as hackers had discovered that Windows was a happy hunting ground. The number and severity of the security holes would in 2002 force Microsoft to halt work in order to retrain its programmers in how to write more secure code, as part of a new 'Trustworthy Computing' initiative. The cost of the viruses and other malware to Windows users, plus the collateral damage in terms of bank accounts looted, runs to tens of billions of dollars.

Even so, by the time Gates met Auletta, the horizontal system was taken as business gospel, an immutable truth that might as well have been included as the 11th Commandment.

The idea that you could command a computing market by designing everything yourself – the hardware and the software – was simply laughable. Management theory said you couldn't. Windows was the proof.

Steve Jobs knew it, of course. As one former Apple employee told me, about being in a meeting with Cook: 'He said that, "If you've lost the battle, one way to win is to move to a new battlefield."' What Jobs needed was a new battlefield – or two – where he could restart the fight against Gates on different terms: ones that he would set.

Larry Page, Sergey Brin and Google

In 1998, around the time Cringely and Gates were meeting, things were happening in Silicon Valley – the 1,500 square miles stretching south-east of San Francisco bay, from Palo Alto at its northerly point down to Santa Clara. It was the dot-com boom, and two people who had recently decided to give up their postgraduate studies were running their company from a garage in Menlo Park. Larry Page and Sergey Brin, both 25 (both were born in 1973, 18 years after both Gates and Jobs), had become friends at Stanford University while doing their doctorates. They fitted Gladwell's template perfectly: brilliant thinkers who had honed their computing skills through endless hours of study. But that 18-year gap between them and Gates and Jobs meant they had come of age in a world where the internet was already a background hum, and computing resources and mobile connectivity were becoming ubiquitous. They were primed for a world where the internet would be as easy to come by as electricity from a socket, and where the idea that you might be contacted by anyone anywhere at any time via mobile phone was becoming normal. Their vision was of a very, very different world from the one in which Gates and Jobs had grown up. Their big idea was about finding stuff on the internet: together they had built a 'search engine'. They had wanted to call it 'Googol' (an enormous number – 10 to the hundredth power – to represent the vastness of the net, but also as a mathematical in-joke; Page and Brin love maths jokes). But that was taken. They settled on 'Google'.

Had Gates known about them, he might have worried, briefly. But there was no way Gates could have easily known about it – except by spending lots and lots of time surfing the web. The scientific paper describing how Google chose its results wasn't formally published until the end of December 1998; a paper describing how 'PageRank', the system used to determine what order the search results should be delivered in – with the 'most relevant' (as determined by the rest of the web) first – wasn't deposited with Stanford University's online publishing service until 1999.[15] The duo incorporated Google as a company on 4 September 1998, while they were renting space in the garage of Susan Wojcicki. They did that using a cheque written in August for $100,000 from Andy Bechtolsheim, co-founder of Sun Microsystems, made out to 'Google Inc'. (Page and Brin left it in a drawer in Stanford while they tried to get some more funding and figure out the mechanics of setting up the company that would be able to accept it. Bechtolsheim got about 1 per cent of the business.) At the time the site was answering about 10,000 queries a day; in September, around the time Gates and Stephens met, Page and Brin were just about to hire the company's first employee, Craig Silverstein. Like Apple, Google was a minnow compared to the leader in its field – the search engine AltaVista, which had earned $50 million in sponsorship revenue in 1997 and was receiving 80 million hits per day.

Even so, at the end of the year, Google was named one of the top 100 websites by *PC Magazine*. Given how few queries it was answering, that was a harbinger of things to come.

Internet search

At the time, despite its 1997 press release about MSN, internet search was not a high priority for Microsoft (or Apple, whose executives have never thought of it as a 'web' company). The idea of standalone search engines for internet content was obvious enough, but the internet was nascent, and it wasn't obvious how people would use it. Gates's view was that your computer – more specifically, your operating system – would direct how you used the internet: where you went, what you did. And, obviously, Microsoft would set what you saw and how you accessed the system; its Internet Explorer browser would determine how people experienced the web.

Yet Internet Explorer itself might have offered Gates a clue to the threats his company was facing. Microsoft's success grew from the contract it got in 1981 from IBM, then the biggest computing company the world had ever seen, to provide an operating system for its 'personal computer' project. IBM didn't have the code to do it, and needed to catch up with companies such as Apple, Atari and Commodore that were trailblazing the personal computer market; so it turned to Microsoft. IBM was almost destroyed, though, when the PC market, and the 'clones' using Microsoft's MS-DOS operating system, sucked profits from its mainframe and minicomputer business; it took a wholesale reorganization to put the company back on an even footing.

Internet Explorer, like IBM's PC, was a catch-up operation: Netscape had introduced the browser to an amazed public in 1994. Microsoft needed one urgently to offer on its blockbuster Windows 95 product – but the internet's rise had caught the company by surprise; Windows 95 didn't even have an in-built method to access the internet. Gates had been alerted to the internet's vast importance by a memo in 1994 from a young recruit called J Allard, then 25 (whom we'll meet again). Microsoft scrambled to produce its own browser, and ended up licensing code from a smaller company, Spyglass, in order to have something to offer the world. Just like IBM, it had been caught out by a new development. It quickly made that up by offering it as a free download, undercutting Netscape's business model, and then threatening PC makers that considered making Netscape the default browser on Windows systems.

But while Gates could feel comfortable that he had won the war with Jobs, and with Netscape, he had left the equivalent of a body under the patio. Within Microsoft, the determination not to let Netscape's upstart browser reduce Windows to an optional extra had driven its executives into a competitive fury. E-mails had flitted about on the tactics to be used; the plan was to 'cut off Netscape's air supply'. Those e-mails would soon surface as the US Justice Department reopened its antitrust investigation, accusing Microsoft of using its monopoly in the market for desktop operating systems to force computer makers not to install Netscape. (Having a monopoly in a market is legal in the United States; using that monopoly to win share in another market is not.)

For Google, though, it didn't matter what browser people were using. They had a quite different approach. To Brin and Page, the web and the internet promised entirely new ways of doing things – which didn't just mean finding information, but also running companies. Their company had a single, enormously ambitious aim: 'to organize the world's information and make it accessible'. Accessible from what? A desktop, laptop, mobile, something else? Certainly, all of those. They weren't particular. Not that there was any search market, or viable internet, for mobile phones, at that stage. Though some were thinking about it, the phones had barely any computing power, had tiny screens, and couldn't get data. The biggest manufacturer was a Finnish company called Nokia, whose chunky designs were famous. Nobody thought of mobile phones as internet devices, though. For that you needed a PC.

Capital thinking

Market capitalization is an oft-used measure of companies to indicate their business heft or importance, calculated by multiplying the company's stock price by the number of issued shares. When the share price rises or falls, so does the capitalization. While it has no effect on the internal processes of the company – it doesn't, say, indicate cash available to the company – it is a useful proxy for something else: the market's estimation of the total profit the company will make in its lifetime, adjusted to net present value.

Imagine a company with 1 million issued shares and a cash pile of £1 billion (in this book, 'billion' means 'thousand million'), but no other assets and no ongoing business. Clearly, a fair price for each of the company's shares would be £1,000. Next imagine a company with 1 million issued shares but no cash; however, it has a guaranteed income stream of £100 million (adjusted for inflation) for the next 10 years, after which its income will fall to zero. Over the 10 years, the company will acquire the equivalent of £1 billion in today's money. So, once more, the fair price for each share is £1,000. The dynamic, dramatic process that you hear about as stocks rise and fall is this calculation made visible. When share prices fall or rise on bad or good news about a business, it's an adjustment against the company's expected profit over its life.

Market capitalization tells you how important and profitable a company looks to the stock market. Inside a company, it generally means little, unless it's nudging zero, when the company will find it hard to raise cash (because banks and stockholders see that the market has no confidence in its prospects). The only times the external stock price matters inside the company are when it goes public (in which case stockholding employees usually become suddenly rich) or when stock options given to an employee mature, in which case the stock's value will make all the difference to whether the employee's previous years of work have been worthwhile or wasted.

As 1998 ended, Google's market capitalization – in theory – was $10 million, based on Bechtolsheim's $100,000 investment for 1 per cent. (Any 'capitalization' was theoretical; you'd have had to find someone prepared to buy the shares.) Apple was worth $5.54 billion. Microsoft was worth $344.6 billion. In all, the trio were worth $350.15 billion: Microsoft was 98 per cent of it.

Yet despite being so different – Microsoft dominant in personal computer software, Apple struggling to survive in the computer hardware business, and Google in the emerging field of internet search – their destinies would inevitably intertwine as four irresistible forces came into play: the falling price of computing power, faithfully following Moore's law and doubling every 12 to 18 months; the growing reach of the internet; the growth of mobile phones; and consumers' buying power.

But before that could happen, each would have to struggle with its own nemesis. For Google, it would be having no business model, while burning through up to a million dollars a month. For Apple, it was another brush with being snuffed out in the jaws of recession.

For Microsoft, it would be an existential threat to its very identity, at the hands of the US government in an antitrust case filed in May 1998, which opened in court that October. It was to shape Microsoft's thinking for the decade to come.

Chapter Two
Microsoft antitrust

If one firm controlled the licensing of all Intel-compatible PC operating systems world-wide, it could set the price of a license substantially above that which would be charged in a competitive market and leave the price there for a significant period of time without losing so many customers as to make the action unprofitable. Therefore, in determining the level of Microsoft's market power, the relevant market is the licensing of all Intel-compatible PC operating systems world-wide.

Findings of fact, *United States of America* v *Microsoft Corporation*, Civil Action 98-1232 (Issued November 1999) (the document is available in Adobe PDF, WordPerfect 5.1 and HTML formats, but no Microsoft-proprietary ones)

Steve Ballmer

Life changed at Microsoft in 2000. On 13 January Steve Ballmer, who in June 1980 had become its 30th employee, was promoted from heading its sales and support operations to chief executive. Bill Gates was still the chairman and 'chief software architect', with oversight of how the company should build its tools and products. He would still be involved in key decisions. But Ballmer took over day-to-day responsibility for the company; he would have to embody the qualities that the company now stood for to governments and businesses and individuals.

The change was like an earthquake on the sea floor far from land. On the surface, nothing seemed different at first. Gates and Ballmer had been close working partners for years. They are an interesting physical contrast: Gates, the slightly introverted engineer and software genius whose presence doesn't draw the eye, and Ballmer, the large, loud and physically imposing presence, a salesperson able to spot telltale details about a customer's frame of mind and find a contract to fit it. They made an excellent pairing, with Gates driving on the programmers and managers who made the products, while Ballmer marshalled the sales troops.

But, once in charge, Ballmer didn't bring the same software discipline as Gates. Though he graduated with a degree in maths and economics, he doesn't have the grounding in writing code. Developers at Microsoft knew that; the instinctive reaction of some was that the company had lost something essential. Although Gates's job meant he was still in charge of chewing out managers who fell behind, he was no longer at the centre of Microsoft's universe; he became a comet, spinning out and back as he spent more and more time on his charity aimed at curing preventable disease in the developing world.

The antitrust trial

By the time Ballmer took charge, the antitrust trial was over; the judge's findings of fact had been delivered. They were damning: Microsoft had abused its monopoly in Windows to extend its dominance to other areas. That was illegal. But no sentence had been delivered.

The trial, and especially the testimony and press coverage, had an enormous effect on the internal culture of Microsoft. The staff didn't stop thinking they were the best programmers in the world. But quite suddenly they couldn't attract the rest of the best programmers in the world. Partly that was because as the antitrust trial ground on through 1998 and 1999 the dot-com boom took off, promising enormous riches to smart coders who hitched a ride with the right company. 'Get your stock options cheaply, and when the business IPOs you'll be rich, just like those lucky guys at Netscape and Yahoo.' But there was also the feeling that to work for Microsoft was to compromise your ethics.

Inside Microsoft, there was soul-searching. An early example had come at the 1999 annual executive retreat, where Gates and Ballmer wanted to talk over the finances of the company, examine its performance and chart the next product lines – the 'roadmap'. The antitrust trial's findings of fact – the judge's established truth about the company – hadn't yet been published. But Microsoft had been hauled over the coals in court; Bill Gates in particular had been made to look evasive and arrogant in his videoed deposition with the prosecution's David Boies.

At the meeting, Orlando Ayala, then head of sales for Latin America and the South Pacific, told the top executives that he didn't want to talk about the roadmap. One participant recalls Ayala saying that 'We've got to talk about what our values are at this company. I can't work here any more if my brother [who didn't work for Microsoft] keeps challenging what I'm doing.' The attendee describes it as an example of 'stopping the normal company process of growth and business as usual, saying we have to change how this company does business.'

The attendee says: 'We said "No, we don't want to discuss that [roadmap], because we're in a crisis here and we need to address what we stand for as a company"... We've been called evil; most of us with outside friends and family are being questioned by them, asked why we're working for Microsoft if it's an evil company.'

The executive admits it was an 'uncomfortable' feeling: 'We all recognized the ability of Microsoft to build great software that would change the world.' The trouble was that, outside the company, it was simply thought of as acting like a gangster, threatening those who looked as though they might set up on a patch adjacent to its own ground. (The judge, Thomas Penfield Jackson, talking to journalists under embargo during the trial, suggested that Microsoft's actions *were* like those of drug traffickers or gangland killers.)

The court's findings of fact said Microsoft held a monopoly of PC operating systems; it could artificially set licence prices, safe in the knowledge that barely anyone would decline. Judge Jackson pointed to an internal Microsoft study, provided in evidence, which determined that charging $49 for the Windows 98 upgrade would earn a reasonable return on investment, but that charging $89 would maximize revenue, hitting the sweet spot of the demand curve beyond which too many would-be buyers would stick with what they had. Only a monopoly would have that pricing power.

Being a monopoly (generally defined as having 80 per cent or more of a market) is not illegal in the United States; nor does it necessarily attract sanctions. But using a monopoly in one field to extend or create one in another field is, and does, if it can be shown to have harmed consumers in either or both markets. By going after the Netscape browser, which had begun to set itself up as a platform of sorts (albeit one that almost always ran on Windows), and using its control of Windows first to deny Netscape access to some application program interfaces (APIs) it needed for Windows 95 and then to boost its own Internet Explorer by insisting on its inclusion – at the threat to original equipment manufacturer (OEM) PC makers of not getting Windows licences, which would kill their businesses – Microsoft crossed the line.

Among those also targeted for Microsoft's arm-twisting via Windows to try to crush other products in different fields, the trial heard, were Intel, Sun Microsystems, Real Networks, IBM – which was denied an OEM licence for Windows 95 until a quarter of an hour before its official launch, and so missed out on huge swathes of PC sales – and Apple. In particular, Apple was offered a deal: stop developing its own systems for playing music and films on Windows, and let Microsoft handle them using its DirectX system. If it did, Microsoft would stop putting obstacles in the way of Apple's QuickTime on Windows. Steve Jobs, who was at the meeting in June 1998, rejected the idea because it would limit the ability for third parties to develop content that would run on Windows PCs and Apple machines. (In retrospect, that decision may be one of the most significant to Apple's later success that Jobs ever made, since it meant that Microsoft could not control how Apple-encoded music was played on Windows.)

Internet Explorer was the focus of the trial, though: the number of Microsoft staff working on it had grown from a handful in early 1995 to more than a thousand in 1999. And Microsoft gave it away because reaching an effective monopoly share (50 per cent of the browser market would be good, 80 per cent and up ideal) was the target. Jackson completed the necessary trio needed for an antitrust conviction by pointing to harm not only for the companies affected, but also for consumers: tying Internet Explorer into Windows 'made it easier for malicious viruses that penetrate the system via Internet Explorer to infect non-browsing parts of the system'.

The stock market wasn't worried by the findings of fact; in the month after their publication, Microsoft's stock value actually jumped, and it reached its all-time peak market capitalization, $612.5 billion, on the last working day of December 1999. The rest of the market for technology stocks rose too – though one analysis suggested that this was because Jackson (a pro-business Republican) had cleared the way for other companies to begin competing effectively.

The outcome of the trial

Then in April 2000, with Ballmer four months into his new job, Jackson handed down his sentence: Microsoft should be split into two – one company making operating systems, one making applications.

Microsoft fought the order with all its might and wile. Jackson, it transpired, had compromised his supposedly impartial position by talking to the *New Yorker*'s Ken Auletta during the trial, for a book to be published immediately after it. In February 2001 a group of appeal judges declared that Jackson had violated judicial ethics with his conversations. (The real problem was that his remarks were published before the appeals process was exhausted, instead of when his verdict was published.) The break-up was halted over Jackson's 'perceived bias'. He railed that any bias was Microsoft's fault, because it 'proved, time and time again, to be inaccurate, misleading, evasive, and transparently false... Microsoft is a company with an institutional disdain for both the truth and for rules of law that lesser entities must respect. It is also a company whose senior management is not averse to offering specious testimony to support spurious defences to claims of its wrongdoing.'

Inside the company there was relief – and also a realization that it had dodged a bullet. Though the sentence had been set aside, the findings of fact, and conviction, had not been overturned. At the next annual worldwide sales conference – held in the Seattle Mariners stadium – Ballmer explained that the culture had to change: no longer could Microsoft use its advantage in one field to dominate another. (The European Commission was to follow with similar investigations, which rumbled on in parallel before coming out with demands for Microsoft to open up its software interfaces in 2003.) But it was the US case which reached down into the company's soul.

Joe Wilcox, at the time an analyst who followed Microsoft, says that the US and EU antitrust investigations 'hugely affected' its workings: 'Microsoft was unequivocally less aggressive following the November 2001 US settlement, even though the judge wouldn't ratify the agreement for another year. There was a lack of certainty and aggression in Microsoft's response to Apple or other companies.'[1]

Some inside the company felt they had already abandoned the practices for which they were being condemned. 'Arguably some of the things that we'd written in contracts were sailing a bit close to the wind', admits one former Microsoft employee. 'But frankly if you look now at other people's current contracts, whether it's Apple's around the iPhone, or Google's, or even Intel's, you'd say they were far more egregious than any of the contract terms that Microsoft signed up with Intel.' This misses the point: it wasn't the contracts that were bad, but the tactics, allied to Microsoft having a monopoly. Apple has no monopoly share of smartphones. Intel and Google arguably do in their own fields – and have both attracted attention (in Intel's case, to enormous cost) from antitrust investigators.

Microsoft avoided a break-up in the 2001 settlement, but had to agree that a three-strong outside panel would have full access to Microsoft's source code, records and systems. Another part of the settlement said that the divisions of Microsoft had to operate Chinese walls over their APIs (the programming 'hooks' that let products work; a typical API lets you query the operating system for details such as the system clock time or the location of a file, and return the present time in a set format, or a link to that file on a hard drive). The ruling said that, if one division opened up the APIs for a particular product to any other division within Microsoft, they had to be made publicly available. That would prevent the use of 'secret' or private APIs known only inside the company to enhance its own products at the expense of competitors. The settlement was to run for 10 years, until November 2011. (It was finally lifted in June 2011; Microsoft got time off for good behaviour.)

Pieter Knook, who worked for Microsoft through the period in its Asian business, says that the post-judgement process was exhaustive. 'Every executive officer, every year, had to go through antitrust training, certify they were in compliance with the terms of the [antitrust settlement] agreement – so there was this very strong understanding, and obligation that you felt to do the right thing.'

Everyone inside the company soon came to realize that just because they had got lucky once – with a judge who had spoken out of turn – it didn't mean they'd manage it again. The Jackson trial had been the company's second run-in with the Department of Justice (after a less bruising one in 1994). If there were a third one, it might not end so well.

'It had a big impact, and even a decade later it was still having an impact', says Mary Jo Foley, a journalist who has followed Microsoft for years.

> When they think about adding new features to different products or how they make sure their products work together, I think in the back of their minds is always this lingering kind of thought or checklist, like: 'If we do that, are we going to get sued by so and so for antitrust?' 'Are we going to get sued by so and so, or so and so?'[2]

When any feature was being thought about, that question kept coming up: will it break the antitrust ruling? 'I think it has almost had a chilling effect on the way they do product development,' Foley suggests.

With Microsoft suitably admonished, and now living under a new regime of oversight, the scene was set for Microsoft's next challenges: in search, digital music and mobile phones. First was a little start-up that was already becoming the talk of internet users, one that was to form its corporate thinking around a motto that tried to express a desire not to be Microsoft: 'Don't be evil.'

Chapter Three
Search: Google versus Microsoft

The weather in Brisbane for the 7th World Wide Web conference in May 1998 was dismal: 'It rained every day,' recalls Mike Bracken, one of the attendees. Among the many papers on the schedule for the conference, though largely unnoticed, was one by two Stanford undergraduates, entitled 'The anatomy of a large-scale hypertextual web search engine'.

Larry Page and Sergey Brin, then 25 and 24, were setting out their idea of a better search engine; given the rapidly growing number of pages and users on the world wide web (devised only six years earlier), it was the modern equivalent of building a better mousetrap. The idea was that the world would beat a path to their door – or click its way to their web page.

They weren't the first who had had the idea of how to index the web, nor the first to have thought about indexing it in the way that they did. But they were to do it by far the best. They created a system for searching the content of the net – hardly a new idea, since Yahoo and dozens of other companies were already doing exactly the same. The problem with those other companies' offerings was that either the companies weren't making much money from it or they were making enough money so that they didn't have any incentive to improve it.

The beginnings of search

At the time, pretty much all of Microsoft's top executives were blind to the benefits and the potential of online search, because they hadn't grown up surfing around the web. Arguably, few people anywhere truly understood those benefits. But it is not just hindsight that indicates the importance of search online. As soon as the world wide web went beyond a few hundred, thousand, tens of thousands of pages, it became impossible to navigate directly; the internet was not a TV set, but a field strewn with pages filled with potentially useful information for anyone who wanted it. That meant that search – really clever search – would become essential. Yahoo, which began as a tree-like directory of the web and in its early incarnation offered a human-chosen 'Site of the Day', rapidly capitulated in the face of exponential growth. And besides, databases with full-content indexing could do the tedious job of indexing the web. Just 'crawl' the pages – load each one, copy it, and index the occurrence of words – and stick the results in a database, and respond to searches for a word by finding the pages that indexed highest on those words. Internet search was simple.

Or so it seemed.

The race at first looked as though it would go to the swift and the large. Compaq took a lead with AltaVista, a search engine set up essentially to show off the power of the 64-bit Alpha chip it had acquired along with Digital Equipment Corporation. The chips could chomp through huge indexes; all AltaVista needed then was to crawl the web and index it, and it would dominate; and it could make money by selling advertisements on its opening search page.

That worked. But, as the web grew, the results it served up became polluted. Spam and porn sites began using 'invisible' text – white on a white background, or sized so small humans could not see it, but AltaVista's crawler could. The problems with spam became increasingly annoying for users. But AltaVista's revenues kept rising as more people came online. It wasn't because it had significantly improved the user experience or its search results; it was because advertisers were buying more and more advertising slots. In fact the advertisements made the user experience worse, because they made the page load more slowly on the dial-up connections used by the vast majority of people. But AltaVista was the best there was, for the moment.

In October 1997 Microsoft, which already ran one of the biggest sites on the net, made a bold proclamation: it would soon be launching its own search engine, code-named Yukon – except that the searching would be done by a separate company, Inktomi, which would provide access to an index of more than 75 million documents. Microsoft would have to figure out how to make money from the process. CNET's Janet Kornblum wrote at the time, 'A search engine is a natural for the software giant. For very little investment, Microsoft can start generating the kind of clicks that translate directly into advertising dollars by simply sending the many Netizens who log onto its Web site to the engine.'[1] The search engine wouldn't be behind the MSN paywall (of content provided exclusively to paying MSN subscribers), but accessible online free to anyone. 'Microsoft executives already are bragging that it will be "the freshest, most current index available to consumers" by starting with an expandable database and leveraging Inktomi's Web crawling technology,' noted Kornblum. David Peterschmidt, chief executive of Inktomi, told her that, 'Our focus is on providing consumers with the deepest, most powerful, and easiest product to help them find exactly what they want on the internet.'

Kornblum noted that it didn't necessarily have to be the best at finding things: mostly, she noted, 'it needs to do the bottom line: generate clicks'. Danny Sullivan, a search expert, wrote in November 1997 on his Search Engine Watch page – even then covering what seemed like a wide industry – 'Microsoft is not adding any special search technology to the mix. There is no killer search app that will be created. This may occur in the future, but at launch, it will remain more of the same.'[2]

Though there were plenty of search engines around in the late 1990s – Yahoo, AltaVista, Lycos, Excite, HotBot, Ask Jeeves, WebCrawler, Dogpile, AOL, Infoseek, Netscape, MetaCrawler, AlltheWeb – none dealt with the key problem of search. Their indexes all treated the web as though it were a flat field covered with pages filled with information, when in fact they all contained information about each other, encoded by how they linked to each other. Some pages had lots of incoming links; some had none. Logically, pages with many incoming links must have a higher reputation for whatever phrase was being linked to than those without. Not even Microsoft, with its overweening ambition, seemed to have grasped this.

Partly it was because, even if you did perceive that, you'd realize that it would take a hugely complex mathematical calculation, using vast amounts of computing power, to figure out what those links were telling you for each page, each phrase. You needed to have calculated how every page on the web ranked relative to the others – which would keep shifting, especially for the smaller ones, based on their links. Based on that ranking you'd then have to decide which pages on authoritative sites pointed to the text you wanted. And the ranking would vary based on the text. Something like this had to be done each time a query was entered.

Page and Brin had done that in 1996, with a system on a single PC at Stanford. They called the algorithm for ranking web pages 'PageRank' – a joke on Page's name. They would go on to develop a massively parallel computing system and software that could harness the power of hundreds, then thousands, and later hundreds of thousands of stripped-down PCs running a version of the free Linux operating system to do precisely this over and over again, millions of times a day. It would also hook into enormous amounts of storage where the crawled, indexed and compressed copy of the internet was held.

Google

Every universe has its creation myths, and cyberspace is no exception. One of the internet's is that the idea of PageRank sprang, Athena-like, from the brows of Page and Brin (but especially Page; hence the patent's name). In fact, others had the same idea of using 'reputation' to generate search results, such as Jonathan Kleinberg of Cornell University, who published a paper in May 1997 outlining almost exactly the same idea as the one that was later read out at the Brisbane conference.[3]

Page and Brin had tried to sell their idea to various companies in 1996, taking it to two of the biggest, Excite and Yahoo, and demonstrating how good it was at producing just the right result first time. The big sites accepted that it was a great product, but didn't see the need to buy a better search engine; they already had their own and, as Jerry Yang, the co-founder and chief executive at Yahoo, pointed out, if the right result was at the top on the first page people would just click that and leave the site – and Yahoo made its money from people clicking on pages on *its* site. Better search would be bad for business.

Page and Brin returned to Stanford, worked on it some more, and then got the entrepreneurial bug. They got venture capital funding and started in earnest. Now they were determined to make it into a really big business, because they had the vision that the internet would, in time, engulf everything. And if finding things was hard now, what was it going to be like once the internet got really big?

They published their paper on how to build a giant search engine that would be able to index the web and serve up the results in December 1998, followed in 1999 by the key paper explaining how PageRank worked to push the 'best' results to the top, rather than those that someone else had paid for or that simply used the search term repeatedly without being in any way informative. As an example of the latter, Page and Brin pointed in the second paper to the results of a search for 'Bill Clinton', the then US president: one search engine returned 'Bill Clinton Joke of the Day' as the top result. (The PageRank patent is owned by Stanford University, where it was developed; Google is the exclusive licensee.)

They became a classic Silicon Valley start-up in summer 1998, maxing out their credit cards to buy equipment, spending almost nothing on office furniture (the tables in their first offices at 232 Santa Margarita Avenue, Menlo Park were doors balanced on carpenters' timber-sawing stands), and operating in what is commonly known as 'stealth mode'. Renamed from 'BackRub', and almost named 'The Whatbox' (they decided it sounded a bit too much like 'wetbox', which sounded vaguely porn related), the Google web page first went live in August 1997.

They brought a particular focus to what they thought mattered about the experience of using their site. First, speed: the first page had to load quickly. Then, results had to load quickly. Being fast mattered as much as – perhaps more than – accuracy. Thus at a time when the quest for advertising revenue meant everyone else's search engine page looked very similar – banner advertisement at the top, tabs and vertical sectors such as white and yellow pages arrayed on the left-hand side – Google's search page was a breath of fresh air on an increasingly fetid web. It was boiled down to its simplest form: logo and input field. Here's where you are: Google. Here's the search box: get typing. Doug Edwards, who joined in November 1999 as 59th employee, recounts – with only some exaggeration – how 'Larry and Sergey would roll on the floor and speak in tongues if the engineers managed to speed up a page load by a nanosecond.'[4] So determined were they to leave it clean and uncluttered that in 2000 they turned down a $3 million offer from Visa for an advertising slot on the home page; it has never been used to advertise anything except Google products and approved projects such as Red Cross efforts. The obsession with how fast the home and results pages load drives Google's search engine team to this day.

Page and Brin, computer scientists both, brought that discipline's approach to their management method. Data would be the key determinant of decisions. If you used a particular set of words in a result, did more or fewer people click on the related link? If a staff member had an idea for investment, could you show that it would improve the user experience of using Google? They also believed firmly in hiring only people as smart as, or smarter than, them. This was a tough challenge, though having Stanford University just down the road helped.

While many dot-coms around them with millions in venture funding splashed out on expensive shiny top-line servers (often from Sun Microsystems), Google frugally built its own, using computer parts bought at rock-bottom prices and running a customized version of the free Linux operating system. Google never countenanced using Windows; the licensing costs alone for the hundreds of servers would have weighed down the company, and the inability to strip out unwanted code to create an optimized system would have made it worse. (Of the current top 10 web destinations, the only ones that use Windows for their servers are Microsoft, its Hotmail subsidiary and eBay.) They were then assembled into ad hoc server racks, and squashed into spaces in server farms, where 20 computers would be shoehorned into a volume that better-funded rivals such as eBay would use for one. Hardware redundancy was both a given and a necessity: often a third of the self-built servers didn't work, but that was good enough; the working ones could handle queries while the broken ones were fixed.

Yet the young Google had its own chef. Why? Because Page and Brin had, typically, reasoned it through: the best way to stop staff leaving the building to get meals (and so using valuable company time unproductively) was to have the very best food inside the building; the time saved would repay the cost.

Meanwhile, they focused on the user experience. And while Google, like rival search engines, also had its own teething troubles with porn and spam, the PageRank system, plus in 1999 a 'porn keyword' effort (to root out the words being used to point to pornographic spam, or that appeared in pages trying to piggyback on innocent searches) crowdsourced from its own engineers, quickly helped drive irrelevant porn links out of the key first page of results.

That helped, because the more people used Google the more they stuck to the first page of results, in contrast to the situation with other search engines, where people would often have to wade through two, three or even four pages to find something relevant. Less time spent searching equates to higher user satisfaction. (By 2006, the first two results on the first page were receiving 42 per cent of click-throughs, the third through to the tenth accumulated 47 per cent, and everything after the first page got just 11 per cent. That remained true in 2011.)

Word spread quickly. Almost as soon as it enlarged its index and made its site more visible, Google began winning plaudits from web users. In December 1998 Scott Rosenberg wrote approvingly at Salon.com that, 'Since discovering Google a few weeks ago, I've been so impressed with its usefulness and accuracy that I've made it my first search stop' – even though it was only an alpha version with 'only' 60 million pages indexed.[5] Google's early incarnation offered 'special searches' – but they were 'Stanford search' and 'Linux search' (for Red Hat, one of its first clients). Then there was its odd choice of options: 'Google Search' and 'I'm Feeling Lucky' – an expression of Google's confidence. 'In my book, Google itself is important', remarked Rosenberg, 'as a sign, amid the profusion of look-alike portals, that there's still plenty of room for improvement in the basic technologies we use on the Web every day.'

Google grew. In July 1999, it sealed a deal to provide the search function for Netscape, which was still fighting Microsoft in the courts. The morning the deal was announced – 6am Pacific time, 9am Eastern time – Google's traffic grew sevenfold within minutes, and the site had to be shut to non-Netscape users for two hours (a decision Page made to keep Netscape, as a partner, happy, even at the expense of other web users). The team learnt a key lesson: prepare for more, and keep partners happy. Apart from a brief glitch later that autumn, the site would never go down again.

Google was asked at the time whether it would offer free e-mail, as every other portal was doing. 'We wouldn't put free e-mail on our site unless we thought we could do a much better job,' Page replied carefully.[6] (Gmail, its free e-mail service, didn't appear for another four years.) By September 1999, Google had dropped its 'beta' label, and said it was dealing with 3.5 million searches per day. The data from Media Metrix said that Yahoo was the clear leader, with 38 million visitors, followed by MSN, which got about 28 million visitors per month.

The founders eschewed self-boosting advertising in favour of the occasional meeting with journalists (though Page found such interaction largely pointless; journalists didn't have interesting things to tell him) and word of mouth. And the word was good.

Search and Microsoft

At the same time, Microsoft's reputation was bring shredded in the courts as David Boies, the US prosecution counsel, took Bill Gates to task in the antitrust trial. For the early adopters who liked to try new stuff online, the fact that Google wasn't Microsoft turned out to be a big plus. And Microsoft didn't seem to be reacting as it was outdistanced. It didn't seem to notice, in fact.

'To understand how Microsoft missed the importance of search, you have to remember what was going on at the company at the time', says Steve Wildstrom, then technology editor for *BusinessWeek* magazine.

> First of all, Microsoft had never viewed search as central to its business. Microsoft management was focused on two things. One was surviving the Justice Department's antitrust suit intact and competitive – I think it's a serious mistake to underestimate the toll the case took on Microsoft, even though it ended up with no more than a slap on the wrist. The second was merging Windows 98 and Windows NT into a common platform for both business and consumers. This became Windows XP, launched in the fall of 2001.[7]

Search, he points out, lived off in the MSN group, out of the Microsoft mainstream.

But there was another thing, says Wildstrom: 'At the time, no one saw search as much of a way to make money.'

That's confirmed by one of the people who worked on Microsoft's search effort, who told me: 'In the early days, search was just seen as a cost centre. It wasn't a way to make money. Nobody had figured it out.'

Indeed, search engines seemed to contain an inherent contradiction: if you did it well, people would leave your site to go to the destination you'd served up – and, given the nature of search, that destination almost certainly wouldn't be a site you controlled (unless you tweaked the results, in which case you risked dissatisfying the user); there are more pages on the internet that aren't Yahoo.com or MSN.com or Askjeeves.com than those that are. That meant successful search engines lost the chance to serve up an advert. In pre-internet business terms, that's bad business.

Yet that's not how the internet always functions. Yang's 1996 decision to reject Google was predicated on the idea that people wouldn't seek out better solutions to their problems online. And it ignored the idea that you create customer loyalty by giving them the best experience possible and that, if people found what they wanted through one search engine and not on another, they'd probably keep coming back to the first and ignore the second.

While Microsoft struggled in the coils of the Justice Department trial, Google roared ahead.

Bust

By early 2000, Google was quickly becoming the search site of choice for aficionados. That rise coincided with the dot-com bust of March 2000, in which so many nascent internet emperors were shown to have no clothes. Some commentators thought that, as Google lacked a clear business model, it too would flail and disappear among the rubble of other overhyped stocks.

Inside Google itself, that wasn't a pressing concern. The staff had a monomaniac belief in the correctness of its vision, which was driven by Page and Brin, and driven downward by Urs Hölzle, its head of engineering, and Marissa Mayer, its head of user interaction. Google built quick and dirty, but fast. Edwards, who was its first head of marketing, explains in *I'm Feeling Lucky*, his memoir of his time at Google, that the focus was simply to get products and improvements out of the door that were 'good enough'.[8] Perfection be damned; the 'beta' label – used in desktop software to indicate a buggy, not-quite-ready-but-try-it-out-if-you're-brave version – would suffice for whatever new products it produced. Because it was software, it could be rewritten; because it was on the web, it could be updated; because Google controlled the site, it could update it at any time.

As Edwards makes clear in his recounting, Google then was a chaotically focused organism, where responsibilities and teams shifted according to business needs. Hölzle's one unbreakable rule about hiring engineering staff was that they must be at least as good as those already on the team: it was the only way you could guarantee to double your productivity. Hiring someone less good would suck resources out, as they required managing and mentoring. When hiring, experience counted for less than mental flexibility.

And, when making decisions, data counted for more than all of them. Edwards describes trying to get ideas and proposals past Page or Brin: he would suggest spending money on a marketing campaign, and Page (or Brin, or both) would shoot back: 'Wouldn't it be better to spend it on space tethers [connecting a ground point to an orbiting satellite to collect solar power]?' Once, Edwards went to Page and Brin and suggested the wording of some lines for the home page, explaining that 'they should drive repeat traffic by reaffirming our quality to first-time users. Here's the list.'

The founders pondered it for a bit, threw out some bizarre alternatives, and then Brin suggested: 'You know what we should do? We should make the homepage hot pink and see how many people come back.'

What they were really saying was: give us some hard data to support why this is a good idea. Edwards calls the experience of pitching ideas to them 'the reality abattoir'. Unsupported ideas simply got a bolt gun to the head.

The clearest example of this engineer-driven culture came some years later, though it could have happened at any time in Google's history; it's a good illustration of the contrast between its approach and that of Apple, with its visionary approach to product design, and Microsoft, with its market-led focus. It was known as '40 shades of blue'.

The aim was simple: find which shade of blue for a weblink is most likely to be clicked on. For long-forgotten reasons, Google Mail (introduced in 2003) used a very slightly different blue for its links than the main Google search page. One day much later Jamie Divine, one of the company's designers, picked a shade of blue for a product called the Google pages toolbar. He thought it looked good. Then a Google product manager (PM) – an engineer trained in empiricism – tried a different colour on users, using a method called 'A/B testing', where different people visiting the same page are randomly assigned different web outputs and their behaviour monitored. The PM showed that a blue with a touch more green worked better: more people clicked on it. And, at Google, data is power, and clicks are money. Divine and his team, however, disagreed: their blue was aesthetically better, they argued.

Mayer, an engineer who had studied artificial intelligence at university and who was by then head of search products, dived into the disagreement and offered a Solomonic solution: use a shade halfway between the two (calculated by 'hex value', which splits the colour spectrum into 65,536 possible values). But then Mayer reconsidered, and said the decision should be done scientifically. So the team generated 40 'blues' gradated across the range from the designer's to the product manager's, and carried out a more extensive A/B test in which visitors to Google Mail were segmented into 40 slices of 2.5 per cent. As they visited the pages on different days or times, they were served different colours and their click behaviour tracked. It was statistically rigorous, empirical, exhaustive.

It was also intensely annoying for the designers. Douglas Bowman, a designer who joined the company in 2006 having created advertisements, books, logos and web interfaces, was proud to have introduced the concept of visual design to Google – though, as he noted in a faintly exasperated leaving blogpost, by the time he came aboard the company was already seven years old: 'seven years is a long time to run a company without a classically trained designer'.[9] True – but, for an enterprise built by engineers whose focus is on making the engineering better, whose mantra is about algorithms, where the main page logo was designed by one of the founders trying his hand at Photoshop, it's not surprising.

Bowman found it frustrating:

> Without a person at (or near) the helm who thoroughly understands the principles of design, a company eventually runs out of reasons for designer decisions. With every new design decision, critics cry foul. Without conviction, doubt creeps in. Instincts fail. 'Is this the right move?' When a company is filled with engineers, it turns to engineering to solve problems. Reduce each decision to a simple logic problem. Remove all subjectivity and just look at the data. Data in your favour? Ok, launch it. Data shows negative effects? Back to the drawing board.

He cited the '40 shades of blue' episode, and recounted how 'I had a recent debate over whether a border [on a web element] should be 3, 4 or 5 pixels wide, and was asked to prove my case. I can't operate in an environment like that.'

It was the collision of art and science. Unfortunately art was on foot and science was driving a truck. 'I'll miss working with the incredibly smart and talented people I got to know there,' Bowman signed off. 'But I won't miss a design philosophy that lives or dies strictly by the sword of data.'

Google later calculated that the choice generated an extra $200 million in revenue annually. Inside Apple, Bowman would have been at home; the argument over the web border width would have been made on aesthetic grounds (and ultimately probably by Steve Jobs). But Google's aspiration is about scale: reaching the largest possible number of people as much of the time as possible. The mechanics of running a gigantic search engine that essentially contains a constantly updated copy of the internet mean that decisions have to be based around what will be most effective with the largest number of people. If a 5-pixel border can be shown to lead to more clicks than a 3-pixel one, then there is no room for discussion, because Page and Brin built their company around, and its ethos flows from, empiricism. Google borrowed its process from a method of ranking scientific papers, but imported the scientific method wholesale as a mode of problem solving.

Microsoft, meanwhile, also deals with huge numbers of people, through its main products – Windows and Office. But, as they are desktop software, they can be tweaked and added to endlessly, which has led over the years to a kitchen-sink approach in which no feature has been left out of either, especially not if a few key business users have demanded it. They are not stripped down at all – quite the opposite. Windows and Office can satisfy lots of people because they're almost guaranteed to include the feature you need – along with dozens that you don't, which might confuse you if you stray into them. Office began to be weighed down by the number of features, which led in 2007 to a radical redesign that replaced the menu system with a 'ribbon' (a change led by Steven Sinofsky, whose role in Microsoft's evolution was key). Many long-time users hated it – emphasizing the reality that Microsoft faces: any change it makes is sure to be inconvenient for someone. Yet the keep-it-all-in approach is antithetical to true design – and, arguably, to user experience. It doesn't satisfy Google's empirical test (since it's never, and can't be, made). And it doesn't satisfy the approach that Apple, taking its cue down the years from Jobs and its chief designer Jonathan Ive, takes, which is that design is about what you leave *out*, not what you keep in.

But, as well as ideas supported by data, Page and Brin also supported becoming profitable while not compromising their search quality, because as computer scientists they treasured above all else the idea that the search results would not be compromised by commercial thinking. They wouldn't allow pay-for-placement under any circumstances, and anyway some of their rivals were being criticized for doing exactly that. But nobody would pay to use a search engine directly, so they had either to charge people and companies that wanted to offer a search engine or to find some way to interest advertisers in their offering.

They spent a long time therefore pondering the best way to provide advertisements. All they knew was that they didn't want to do banner advertisements. As the dot-com bust deepened in April 2000 AltaVista, then still the biggest search engine on the web, cancelled a planned $300 million initial public offering that it had filed for the previous December.[10] The stock market didn't like dot-com stocks at all. Most of their business models were ruined.

But Google was gaining search share rapidly: queries grew at 8 per cent every week, from 8 million searches daily in the first week of May 2000 to 9 million two weeks later. That month it also landed the contract to provide search for Yahoo, as it had for Netscape. The contract would begin on 3 July. Fulfilling the Yahoo deal would mean an absolutely enormous spike in traffic. Google's team couldn't possibly deploy enough hardware in time. They needed to do something clever with software.

Fortuitously, the dot-com bust came at exactly the right time for Google. Suddenly server kit (one careful, bankrupt owner) was cheap. Space in server farms and offices became plentiful. And really good staff came on to the market. All those helped because, as Edwards explains, hitting Yahoo's July target date meant Google had to improve its index. That was ageing, because the software written by Page and Brin at Stanford to crawl the web had bugs that meant it would frequently fail as it travelled from page to page. If it did, all of the partial index it had collected would be lost. That had been overlooked for a few years, but now they also needed to improve the general quality of the software used to serve pages, control caches and update the index dynamically, at high speed. The crawler was rewritten in April to a month's deadline (removing, for example, any trace of the unhelpful error messages from the original Stanford code, which would indicate a crawl-killing error by outputting simply 'Whoa, horsey!'), while the index of pages was expanded enormously.

Yahoo's contract was Google's first Nietzschean moment: it would kill it, or make it much, much stronger. It would force it to be the best search engine with the fastest crawler and largest number of pages indexed, or into default on a number of the clauses of the contract drafted by Yahoo's chief scientist – who was a search specialist. Google was careering forward, running to stay upright.

One of the tweaks made by Jeff Dean and Sanjay Ghemawat, who worked on the crawler and indexing, was a simple one, Edwards notes: deleting 'the' from the search index. The crawler would just ignore it. As the most common word in the English language, it took up valuable bytes that could be used for 'signal' – real search information. That alone saved 1 per cent of disk space. (The only obvious collateral damage was to searches for the rock band The The.) A different tweak improved disk seek times (to find data on a disk so it could be read back) by between 30 and 40 per cent.

Even so, for the engineers trying to hike the search quality to meet Yahoo's demands, the deadline pressure was inhuman. But they were at Google and, as Edwards recalls one manager telling him, Google's trick was to hire incredibly bright yet insecure people who were then put under such pressure that they would never consider themselves to have succeeded. Staff worked as near to round the clock as was possible – and still didn't feel they were doing enough.

The Yahoo deal was sufficient pressure in itself, but even then Hölzle had another target: to index a billion web pages. There was no way to do them all successfully in time. Except the team did – with a week to spare. The deal wouldn't, however, generate much revenue. Rather, Google might make a loss on the contract, getting less from it than it cost to serve, because it generated so little advertising revenue – a few thousands per month, compared to outgoings nearing a million.

Link to money

Even if most search engines weren't thriving during the dot-com bust, the model devised by Bill Gross of Idealab was. He had come up with a very clever model for advertising: connect advertisers with the results of related queries. He saw that, if you got advertisers to bid for a spot in the list of results for a search – say, 'baby won't sleep' from some desperate parent – and then charged the advertiser for each time someone clicked on the advert, you could efficiently match searches to advertisers. His company GoTo.com basically ran a search engine where the results were advertisers' attempts to reach searchers. Input a search, and you'd see who most wanted your money for that search. Advertisers who bid more appeared higher up the results. As early as July 1998, Gross had some advertisers paying up to a dollar per click.

GoTo also provided an advertising back-end for sites including Yahoo and Microsoft's MSN: when people searched on those sites, GoTo would find advertisements matched against those search terms, which would appear alongside the results. (Its own page was a simple list of links to popular searches, and then to paid-for links.) The Google founders, struggling to find a method of monetization, were intrigued by Gross's model, but held back from adopting it. Gross approached Page and Brin repeatedly, but they didn't like the idea of 'polluting' their organic search results with paid ones. 'They were so pure about advertising,' Gross told John Battelle, author of *Search*, about Google's early days. 'We talked and talked but nothing came of it.'[11]

In July 2000, Microsoft put out a proud press release: MSN was now the top destination in the world, with 201 million visitors for the year.[12] But nobody thought of it as a search engine or a search destination. And that was even more the case by the end of the year.

Google began developing its own ad-serving model. Dubbed 'AdWords' (a name Edwards says he coined), it very closely resembled Gross's idea: just like GoTo, AdWords offered small text advertisements beside search results. Just as with GoTo, advertisers would bid against 'keywords' that would be entered in searches. Just as with GoTo, the highest bidder got top placement. It was introduced as a beta (inevitably) in September 2000. The first advertiser was a mail-order lobster company, Lively Lobster, in Rhode Island. It paid $83 to have its little text advertisement appear when people used 'lobster' in a search.

It was instantly popular with advertisers. But there were plenty of doubters. In September 2000, AltaVista was the 20th most visited portal, and Google the 48th, according to Media Metrix. 'There isn't really good evidence, frankly, that companies focused purely on search, as Google has been, can support themselves with that model,' said Northern Light chief technology officer Marc Krellenstein.[13]

The proof was in the numbers: Google's total revenues at the end of 2000 hit $24.5 million, compared to just $220,000 in 1999. It came from payments for providing custom search for around 100 co-branding partners, including Netscape and the *Washington Post*, which paid around $10 per thousand queries, plus up to $2,000 per month in licensing fees; the majority came from its deals with Red Hat and with router maker Cisco Systems. The key contract was the one with Yahoo, replacing Inktomi – which remained as the search provider for MSN.

Add in AdWords, and for the first time it turned an operating profit in December. By then it was doing 23 million searches per day, which the research company Gartner reckoned meant it had 25 per cent of the search market; Page said it was growing at 20 per cent per month. The staff had hit 100, and it was using around 6,000 computers in an array for search processing.

At the insistence of their venture capital backers, Page and Brin had also started a search for a chief executive. They lunched a series of big-name leaders from around Silicon Valley, in search of one who would be able to lead their small but fast-growing company to greatness. Eventually, they returned to their backers with some good news: they'd found the right person. Born in February 1955, he was a very experienced chief executive at a comparatively small company whose glory days were behind it and which was struggling to compete with Microsoft.

Yes, they explained to their backers: their choice was Steve Jobs. He, however, indicated non-availability. The search continued. Eventually it ended in March 2001 when they hired Eric Schmidt. Born in April 1955, he was very experienced, the former chief executive of Novell – a company whose glory days were behind it and which was struggling to compete with Microsoft. Page and Brin also liked him because he had been to the Burning Man festival, a meeting place for geeks. The venture capitalists liked him because he looked like, as Schmidt put it, 'adult supervision'.

Boom

With a business model in place, Google could expand aggressively. It started to benefit too from the network effect among advertisers. If you advertised on Google and you got business from it, then you'd probably point people back towards it. By automating the process of bidding for an advertisement based on any search term you liked, Google also made it possible for the tiniest business to get seen by the world in a way that previous search engines hadn't. And because the overwhelming majority of businesses are small, and because Google's advertising business could scale endlessly – since it was not relying on its own staff to input the advertisements or the contents of the web – it could grow really fast.

Its domination was so rapid and complete that by the end of 2000 it had entered the language. In the *Telegraph Herald* of Dubuque, Iowa, on 14 January 2001, Amy K Gilligan, its city editor, wrote: 'Have you been Googled yet? It's the latest thing. I was just sitting here Googling myself, in fact.'[14] Perhaps aware that older readers might be alarmed, she quickly added: 'Don't worry. It's not a euphemism. To Google someone means to gather information on them using the search engine Google. The most popular application is to Google a potential date.' (The article was entitled 'Googling is the newest date thing'.)

Porn might have been the downfall of the first generation of search engines, but sex – or the search for it – turned out to be the making of the next one. And, if the idea of 'Google' as not just a company or a brand but a verb had reached as far as the Midwestern state of Iowa, then it had already begun to win the battle to become a daily brand – one where its rival hadn't yet turned up on the field. That was amplified by an article by the venerable columnist Maureen Dowd in the *New York Times* near the end of August 2001, which noted that 'a thoroughly modern young lady [these days] might be found Paxiling herself, Googling her date, Bikramming her body and pondering The Offering' (ie taking a pill against social anxiety, checking her date's details, doing yoga and scheming to get out of paying half the dinner bill).[15]

Meanwhile the dot-com bust was deepening for search engines that relied on banner advertising from big companies, where marketing executives could cancel six-figure advertising spends on the basis of some projections about the economy. By contrast the businesses Google relied on weren't working on marketing projections; they were hawking for business right then and there. If you couldn't turn business that came your way from Google into sales, that wasn't Google's fault; it was your own. And nobody else seemed as good at driving traffic to sites. It was as Page and Brin had wanted: people came to the site and left it quickly. More and more, they exited via an advertisement.

According to Jupiter Media Metrix data, in January 2001 AltaVista had more than 10 million visitors, and Google just under 9 million. AltaVista's revenue however was collapsing, from $63 million in the quarter ending April 2000 to around $28 million in the three months to July 2001 (and at a thumping loss). A quarter of AltaVista's staff had been laid off in September 2000. As revenue plummeted, so did the visitors essential to attract advertising revenue, to below 8 million in June 2001.

In the same month, according to Media Metrix, Google had 13.4 million visitors. During the first half of 2001, it had become the busiest standalone search engine on the world wide web – a position it has held ever since.

That reputation was only enhanced on a day that turned out to be key in its history, and in so many people's: 11 September 2001. As people struggled to find and understand news about the attacks on New York and Washington, telephone networks overloaded, but internet connections stayed up. What people then needed was information – and many websites collapsed as demand rocketed. Google, however, proved resilient, and that day became an aggregator of news and links to information, reinforcing a reputation for solidity.

By the end of 2001, its revenues were $86.4 million and its profits $6.98 million.

At that point, many Silicon Valley companies of the past, seeing their revenues explode and profits blossom, would have been tempted to file for an initial public offering (IPO). But Page and Brin, advised by the endlessly patient Schmidt, chose another strategy: take a 'submarine' path and delay an IPO as long as they could. They were worried that Microsoft would spot the emerging market and its potential leader, and corner both. Page and Brin were familiar with Microsoft's reputation in the technology industry as a company that in the past had acquired, mimicked or (in the case of Stac Electronics and its compression system)[16] seen and then replicated competing technologies.

Auletta, who interviewed Schmidt, Page and Brin repeatedly for his 2009 book *Googled*,[17] describes their thinking: 'First, Brin and Page were part of a Valley culture that grew up fearing "the evil empire". They feared that if Microsoft knew what a good business search could be, they would enter it themselves and crush Google, as they had crushed Netscape.'

Brin and Page also thought that Microsoft's approach was 'too controlling, too bullying', Auletta says. That went against their personal philosophies that information should be freely available – indeed, their mission statement is to 'make the world's information available and organize it'. (Google itself relied on freely available information, of course; in effect, it made a copy of the entire web every time its crawler ran. This had dubious legality, so pushing 'open' and 'free' was also good for Google's business.)

Schmidt added an extra dimension when he took over. Novell and Sun Microsystems, his previous employers, had fought long-running (and generally losing) legal battles with Microsoft in the previous decade. 'He constantly warned the founders not to moon the giant, as Netscape had,' Auletta says. The founders echoed that too: Page once advised Edwards not to depict Google as a 'technology' company in some marketing material, concerned that Microsoft would spot it and think of its ambitions as being larger than search – which they were, but there were was no reason to bruit it around. Keeping out of Microsoft's sight for as long as possible was a key part of the company's strategy.

But they also knew that eventually the confrontation with Microsoft had to come: the giant would wake up, as much as anything because Bill Gates had declared the internet essential to his company's future back in May 1995. The only question was when – and how well prepared Google would be for the battle.

A key part of that was to have a really strong revenue stream. At the beginning of 2002, Google's engineers added a new wrinkle to AdWords: 'quality'. This turned AdWords from being a simple model based on cost per thousand (CPM – the 'M' stands for 'mille'), where advertisers paid to have their advertisement viewed a set number of times, or cost per click (CPC), where advertisers paid only if their advertisement was clicked on, into a hybrid of the two.

With the new system, Google ordered the advertisements according to how they performed in click-throughs, not on the CPM rate being paid. 'If advertisers are paying the same rate, the more relevant ad as judged by users will rise to the top', explained Omid Kordestani, Google's senior vice-president of worldwide business development and sales, at its launch. (Google initially called it 'AdWords Select', but the intention was to drop the second part of the name in time.) Advertisements with better CPC rates would rank higher in the list of text advertisements even if the advertiser had bid less than someone else. For new advertisements on new search word combinations, Google *predicted* how the advertisement would perform to rank it. (That alone implied substantial computing power.) The change passed more power to the advertisers, so that anyone, large or small, now had a fighting chance of winning business traffic if they could find the best wording for their advertisement. It was the data-driven approach that ruled inside Google, outsourced to the world of advertising. But it wasn't altruistic. Making advertisements with better click-through rates more prominent meant more clicks, and so more money, and fewer unclicked, wasted spots.

Better click-through rates also meant Kordestani's team could bid for really big contracts. While offering pure search results was nice, the real money was in offering a package – both the search *and* the advertisements – to the big 'billboards' of the web, such as Yahoo and AOL, which had huge numbers of users viewing their pages but no search engine of their own.

Typically such contracts worked on 'base payment plus revenue sharing': the search engine paid the billboard a fixed fee; then the billboard paid back money based on the number of searches, plus a revenue-sharing deal on every advertisement clicked. Such deals were a tightrope for the search provider: if too few people used the search or clicked on the advertisements, then the fixed fee payout would drain them of cash. Similarly, if the per-advertisement revenue share was too low, it wouldn't make a profit. But if you went into a contract negotiation with a billboard and demanded a higher cut per advertisement than rivals, you might lose the contract.

Early in 2002, Google signed a deal with the US internet service provider EarthLink to offer AdWords Select. With that, Kordestani got a foot in the door to negotiate to provide the search-related adverts for AOL, a potential billion-dollar contract that would come up for renewal in June, where Overture – as GoTo had renamed itself in October 2001 – was the incumbent.

Kordestani was confident of Google's technology prowess. And despite Overture being far larger than Google at the end of 2001 (54,000 advertisers compared to 1,000; $288 million of revenue versus $86.4 million), it perceived the threat from the upstart. Nor its directors were flattered by the imitation they saw in AdWords Select: in April 2002, as AOL was negotiating with the two companies, Overture filed a suit against Google alleging patent infringement. (The case was eventually settled out of court in August 2004: Google made no admission of wrongdoing but paid 2.7 million shares to Yahoo, and licensed Overture's technology.)

AOL suggested that it would go with Google in return for Google stock (then still privately held) and a minimum guaranteed payout from advertising revenue. When Schmidt saw the proposed terms, he worried – a lot. 'Google did not have enough cash to fulfil the guaranteed payout in the contract,' he explained in 2005 to the journalist Fred Vogelstein, then of *Wired*. 'Because the AOL people were very smart, and because Google was a new business, [AOL] negotiated very, very cleverly.'[18] The four Google executives – Schmidt, Page, Brin and Kordestani – and the negotiating team met to decide whether to accept the contract. If Google made it pay, it would be a bonanza. If not, extinction.

Schmidt was the most conservative; his start-up mantra was: 'Do not run out of cash.' Page and Brin, by contrast, were completely confident. The group argued and argued – heatedly. 'It was the closest point I ever saw literally [to] the company falling in two,' Schmidt later said. 'We would have gone bankrupt [if they couldn't meet the payout guarantee]. I was furious. This is as mad as I've ever gotten, because it was so obvious to me [that the deal was wrong].'[19]

In the absence of hard data, he stopped the meeting, to reconvene the next day. Then, the team figured out a different way to implement the cash flow; Schmidt was mollified. Not having lived through the company's first Nietzschean moment in the Netscape deal, he had been unprepared for Page and Brin's certainty in their team's abilities.

But Hölzle's insistence on only hiring the smartest and best paid off; and sometimes big changes flow from small ones. Edwards points to how one engineer, John Bauer, tweaked the code that displayed advertisements so the search keyword appeared in bold: it more than quadrupled click-throughs, and ensured that the AOL deal wouldn't kill Google. Gross had had the idea of advertisements targeted to searches first; but, as Wildstrom observes, 'Google did it better, and turned search advertising into the money machine that has funded everything else.'[20] The deal was signed in May 2002, and AOL became Google's own cash cow.

Brin also realized that the AdWords system had one unbeatable element. As an auction market, rivals couldn't undercut it: the price paid for an advertisement would be the lowest Google would accept, yet the highest the market could bear. If a rival reached as many people as Google, but its operating costs were no lower, then offering advertisement placement more cheaply would cut its own throat. Clearly, Google had to control its costs and retain its scale, but AdWords formed what the renowned investor Warren Buffett would call a 'moat' – a protective barrier against competitive attack – around Google's business model.

Now it was time to look at the competitive landscape, which would surely soon involve Microsoft. Another part of preparation for battle is to make sure your rival will have to fight on your choice of ground. Google had an obvious head start in that: it was a purely internet-based company that was agnostic about what sort of machines were used to access it. Microsoft could compete with that, but it started at a handicap. And the person who knows all about that is Joel Spolsky.

Random access

Joel Spolsky is something of a legend on the net, at least among the people who know Bill Gates's reputation as a wunderkind programmer. Gates could spot the flaws in programs or plans, would dismiss bad ideas or thinking as 'random', and if annoyed would add a smorgasbord of expletives for good measure.

In June 1991 Spolsky was working at Microsoft on 'a very specific and narrow problem' relating to the compatibility of the Excel spreadsheet program and the Visual Basic (VB) programming language. The two had to work together so that Excel could be programmed to carry out various tasks. Spreadsheets have to be good at calculating the difference between dates. Get it wrong, and you might end up miscalculating a mortgage or compound interest payment. Do it for lots of users – say across a multinational bank – and you might have cost it millions. One day, Gates was overseeing a meeting to review progress in getting Excel and VB to play nicely together. Such review meetings were the terror of the program managers and programmers called to them: they knew Gates would drill down and down and down into the detail until he hit the bottom of their knowledge. Then he would chip away at it. If he didn't like the answers, you could expect a very uncomfortable time. Nobody survived those meetings unscathed.

As the review on Excel was drawing towards its end, Gates asked casually: 'Is anyone really looking into all the details of how to do this? Like, all those date and time functions. Excel has so many date and time functions. Is Visual Basic going to have the same functions? Will they all work the same way?'

Spolsky spoke up and said yes, they'd all be fine – except for January and February 1900. They had some problems there he was working on.

'Huh. OK,' said Gates.

The meeting continued peacefully enough. But afterwards Spolsky's colleagues all marvelled at Gates's astonishingly calm demeanour. Spolsky says: 'I'm sure he swore at me, but I think he didn't use the F-word, or at least the count was zero, and I was told [afterwards] that that was the first time that had happened.'

None of the others knew about the bullet they had just dodged, but Spolsky did. Recalling the moment, he can't help grinning. 'That was sort of his hard question at the end of the test,' he says. 'I don't want to say that I was brilliant,' he adds. 'It was utter coincidence that the night before the review meeting I had been working on [the problem] that had to do with whether 1900 is a leap year.'[21] (He says the question of whether or not it is 'I will leave to your readers to argue about amongst themselves'.)

It turned out that there is ('or there was', Spolsky corrects) an inconsistency between the Visual Basic programming language when applied to Microsoft Excel about whether 1900 is a leap year. If you used VB to program Excel to calculate date differences going back to January or February 1900, you'd get errors. You wouldn't know they were there, but they would be. Neither set of software supported dates before 1900, so only those two months had the problem.

But if Spolsky had let the problem go by, a bank might have shifted its accounts relating to customers from years ago over and... who knows how much it might have cost? Perhaps nothing. Perhaps millions.

Except that would never have happened: Gates knew the problem was there, and would never have let Spolsky and his team forget it if they hadn't shown him that they knew it too during that meeting. And Spolsky knew Gates knew it.

He contrasts Gates – with his deep understanding of the detail of the technology – with Ballmer, at the time Gates's right-hand person, a Harvard graduate in economics and mathematics who was Microsoft's 30th employee. 'Steve Ballmer would never even know to ask a question like that,' Spolsky says. 'No offence to the present management of Microsoft. But it's just hard to conceive that he would even understand that question if you were in the room while it was asked. Which is unfortunate, and I think says something about where Microsoft has gone, in the last decade.'

Ballmer, he says:

> can manage a business – he has that MBA appreciation of how to keep the train running. But he's never going to be able to see his way to the next innovation. It's just not going to come out of his head. And when it doesn't come out of his head, the question is: can he even, does he even have the wherewithal to create an institution that allows those ideas, if they come from the field, to ever escape? I really don't think Microsoft is that kind of institution, and I don't know if that type of institution exists at that size, that size of company.

He points to Microsoft's late arrival to the internet. 'They were late to the game,' says Spolsky.

> And the reason they were late to the game because the people who were operating Microsoft did not have internet [connections] when they were in college – it hadn't made it to campuses. There was a whole generation of people who

graduated in 1991–1992 who were in Microsoft who had internet access on campus, and were aware of the benefits – it wasn't the world wide web at the time but there was Usenet and e-mail and FTP and there were famous FTP sites, and the value of the internet, kind of the way it worked – even just the value of e-mail and the value of networking – was well understood by the recent crop of college graduates, the one- and two-year veterans, even the four- and five-year veterans pretty well understood it, but there was nobody in any position of authority that had had internet access or e-mail – the people making decisions at Microsoft in the mid-to-late 90s literally did not have e-mail on campus, so they didn't understand what it was like to be a college student.

And that means, he suggests, that they didn't understand the internet. They weren't awake to the importance of search.

Google and the public consciousness

Google was. And it kept getting more search share – its own, plus Netscape's, plus Yahoo's, plus EarthLink's, plus AOL's. It became the funnel for more and more valuable data about what people were searching for online. It could follow how people's desires – what the writer John Battelle called 'the database of intentions'[22] – shifted. That was how it could determine the order for advertisements bought for the first time against search terms: it had seen so many already. The relevance of the searches and of the advertisements began to add to an aura of infallibility.

Google was also becoming embedded in the public consciousness. The first use of 'google' as a verb on US TV seems to have been in an episode of *Buffy the Vampire Slayer* that aired on 15 October 2002 ('Have you googled her yet?' asks one character. The other, outraged, replies 'She's 17!' 'It's a search engine,' responds the first, exasperated.) At the end of that year the American Dialect Society sought the Word (or phrase) of the Year from a pre-selected list. 'Weapons of mass destruction' received 38 of the 60 votes cast. In second place, with 11 votes, was 'google' – a verb whose given meaning was 'to search the Web using the search engine Google for information on a person or thing'. (In third place was 'blog', with 6 votes.) For 'most useful' word, 'google' won every one of the 60 votes.

The branding continued to spread. The writers of the hit prime-time TV series *ER* ('No strings attached', which first aired in February 2003) included a doctor going on a blind date; two colleagues decide to research the date, and are seen standing in front of a computer screen, typing.

'There's a Rick Kelly who's a wildlife artist,' says the first.

'Click on that other website,' says the second.

'You think it's the rock climber? How cute, especially with those tight shorts,' says the first.

The doctor passes by. 'What are you doing?' she asks.

'Googling your blind date,' says the first colleague.

'What? That is so rude,' says the doctor. 'If you wanna know anything about him, just ask me.'

'Why?' replies the second. 'You've never even met him.'

The exchange lasted just under 30 seconds, yet positioned Google at the heart of how people were now using the web – to search and find and dig into information that was pouring into online repositories from formerly paper-based systems disgorging themselves online, and from people creating their own identities, which – if you joined the dots – could be connected. That Google had vaulted from being just a brand into something you did, into a verb that could be thrown out in prime-time episodes of the most popular series on TV, without needing explanation, indicated that Microsoft already faced the most uphill of battles before it had even begun to fight in earnest.

But around the time that episode of *ER* was being filmed – in mid-2002 – Yusuf Mehdi realized that Google, and in particular the search business, needed to be taken seriously. Google didn't know it, but the giant had woken up. Mehdi was the head of Microsoft's MSN Search business.

Project Underdog

In February 2003, an audience of 25 of Microsoft's most senior management, including Gates and Ballmer, assembled in Building 36, on the east of Microsoft's Redmond campus. They were there to hear Christopher Payne, then 37 and the vice-president in charge of MSN, tell them about a serious business threat they had overlooked.

Payne had originally joined Microsoft in 1995, and then moved to Amazon in 1998 before rejoining MSN in 2001. In the middle of 2002 he had joined the team behind MSN Search, where he and Mehdi had looked at how Microsoft was doing in search, and realized it had a big problem.

It's easy for a 'webmaster' who controls a site to see where incoming traffic is coming from: any inbound browser will bring a 'referrer' link indicating which page sent it there. As the year wore on, Mehdi and Payne could see more and more traffic to MSN coming from Google. And they could also see that Google didn't seem to have any trouble finding advertisements (or 'inventory') to go with its searches.

MSN did. At the time MSN's search results were provided by Inktomi (which had indicated in December that it would be sold to Yahoo), while the advertisements came from Overture. All that MSN brought to the search party was its presence, and the servers that hosted the pages. Inktomi and Overture paid it depending on results, of course, but they also got to keep all the information about who clicked what, and what people were searching for. This was a burgeoning field in the hottest field of technology. Yet Microsoft, which prided itself on its ability to conquer software problems, was playing no part in it. It was a landlord watching as other businesses sold the hottest items in town through its front door.

Mehdi looked at the numbers: at the time, MSN Search was still allowing advertisers to buy link placement in search results, which meant that you might scroll through most of a page for a popular search before you found a 'real' result. Paid placement was worth around $30 million in revenues every quarter. But it was increasingly unpopular with searchers. And, compared to MSN's revenues of around $500 million per quarter (from both banner and search advertisements all over its network), it wasn't a lot. What Microsoft needed was its own search engine, with advertisements and search, to compete with Google.

Mehdi gave Payne the task of persuading the top brass that they should invest the hundreds of millions of dollars required. It was a daunting task. Payne, who had pushed out four versions of Microsoft Access (its database program), would have been familiar with the sort of reviews by Gates that Spolsky had survived. Building a search engine that would 'scale' as demand rose meant developing software to manage thousands of servers and storing and distributing a compressed version of the internet among them, and coming up with a new ranking algorithm. It also meant finding a new way to sell advertisements. Do all that, do it better than Google, and make it pay as well. That was the idea Payne had to sell.

Yet according to one person who was at the presentation – which went on for almost four hours – both Gates and Ballmer turned out to be eager to push forward and commit large sums. 'It wasn't about Google envy; that wasn't it,' said the attendee. 'In the presentations they saw the business opportunity, and the computer science challenge, and they really liked it.' The idea of buying Google was quickly dismissed; there wasn't much chance that it would be sold. Other potential acquisitions – including Overture – were discussed. Gates was against them. He was eager to take on the 'comp sci' challenge that search represented: huge databases! Random queries! Incredibly difficult remote machine control! Automatic updates! Geographically dispersed data being updated on a constant basis! It was meat and drink to the chief software architect.

Payne and Mehdi wound up asking for $100 million and 18 months and the chance to pull in smart people from other projects all over the company so they could build Microsoft's shining new rival to the upstart. Gates, Ballmer and the executives agreed.

Afterwards, a delighted Payne recruited Ken Moss, a hugely experienced and respected coder, a 16-year Microsoft veteran who had helped build Excel, and built a small but dedicated team. They settled on a name for the project: Underdog.

Mary Jo Foley, a journalist who has studied Microsoft for years, explains that the name was apt for a project to excite the team about the task ahead.

> Microsoft love to be the underdog – this is something that drives the culture at Microsoft more than anything else. They love nothing better than to be struggling, and coming up. It really fuels them. I've seen it over and over. I think they don't do as well when they're the dominant player; then they start losing share, like with Internet Explorer [which stagnated after Netscape was vanquished], for example. But when they are the ones in the losing seat it just fuels people there, and it makes them really crazy about gaining share and growing the market. I don't think they see it as problematic when they're the underdog. I think they kind of like it, actually.[23]

And Microsoft had started out as the underdog with Internet Explorer too, and look what had happened there: from nowhere to dominance in the course of a few years – as long as you ignored the antitrust methods and outcome. But, as became clear, nobody ignored that now.

Gates drove the project as far as he could: he was closely involved in the challenges that the team faced, which turned out to be considerable. Microsoft co-founder Paul Allen describes in his memoir how he would repeatedly complain to Gates about Microsoft's poor showing in search, only to be assured that 'we can catch up with them in six months'.[24] Search was a comp sci problem. Microsoft was a comp sci business – the best there was. Success was just a matter of time.

First they had to build a 'crawler' – the software to read the web pages, index the text and links, and copy them to a central store. Page and Brin had done this at Stanford; now Payne and Moss tried to do it again. Moss's target: index 5 billion websites. He later said it was 'the hardest thing I'd ever looked at, technology-wise'.

Having come through a technical glitch at the start of the year where their crawler took a week to index precisely 24 documents (Google was up to 4 billion), by summer 2003 they had indexed 500,000 pages. The crawler was working.

Now they faced three problems: how to deliver the most relevant results as quickly as possible; how to sell advertisements against them; and how to manage the technical problem of distributing the index and advertisements among multiple servers distributed around the United States, and eventually the world. The Underdog team enlisted the scientists at the Microsoft Research divisions (which normally do almost pure blue-skies research, rather than tightly product-focused work) to devise a ranking system to find 'relevant' results. Turning Project Underdog into a search engine that would truly challenge Google turned out to be like trying to repeat the Manhattan Project to build the first atomic bomb – while being banned from using uranium to create the chain reaction. 'This really was rocket science', one of the Underdog team told me.

They quickly discovered two things about building a search engine. First, indexing the internet is incredibly difficult. By the time the crawler hits a billion pages, you'd think the index would be stellar, because it must, surely, include the most commonly accessed pages. Instead, the Underdog crawler had been pulled into elephant traps of pornography and spam – pharmaceuticals, coupons, sex sites – by the links they plant all over the web; when the crawler blindly followed them, it would fall into black holes of sites tightly linked to each other but with no exit to the wider web. The crawler had to be tweaked repeatedly to dump the junk. (Google had already tackled this problem twice – the first time in creating BackRub at Stanford, and the second time when they expanded the index with their venture funding.)

Next, throwing back the best results to an impatient world was really, *really* difficult. You had to do it very fast, and you had to make the results relevant.

Doing it fast was hard enough. The index amounted to multiple hundreds of gigabytes of data, yet people wanted an answer less than two seconds after hitting the search button. That meant traversing the index and calculating and ordering the best results in milliseconds, and then sending the response back to the querying PC while dealing – hopefully – with millions of other queries at the same time.

That was hard, but being relevant was actually harder. The MSN search engine that was being replaced had worked on an 80:20 principle: 80 per cent of searches would be for 20 per cent of terms (in other words, most people would look for the same things), so if you optimized for the 80 per cent you'd do all right. The 80:20 principle was right, but the second assumption wasn't. The 'long tail' of queries is enormous, in both volume and unpredictability.

It turns out that people judge a search engine on the results not of common searches, but of *uncommon* ones: not 'White House website', but an explanation for the strange symptoms being exhibited by your cat, or putting in the name of a prospective date to see whether he goes rock climbing in tight shorts. If people don't find what they want in the long tail, they will often try another search engine – if they've heard of it. People had heard of Google, and when MSN failed to provide what they wanted they headed over there instead.

Preparing for battle

Google was ready to welcome disaffected MSN users. It had had years to optimize its systems for the task, with tens of thousands (and soon hundreds of thousands) of servers. Nor was it standing still. Early in 2003, at about the time Payne was making his pitch in Building 36, Google's engineers began developing Bigtable, 'a distributed storage system for managing structured data that is designed to scale to a very large size: petabytes of data across thousands of commodity servers'.[25] A petabyte is 1,000 terabytes, or a million gigabytes. Even on the technology front, Microsoft was starting from well behind.

Microsoft's internal politics also complicated the process of building and optimizing a new search engine. Pushing a completely new product to successful launch in Microsoft is like fighting a tank battle: success depends on how many divisions you have behind you. If you're outnumbered, then even the backing of the four-star generals may not be sufficient.

The set-up within Microsoft at the time dictated that executives were rewarded on the basis of their division's performance. This is, on its face, the perfect way to incentivize them: they were given stock options and, if their division contributed positively to the performance of the company, then they benefit. But, as we'll see, it can easily work against the wider interests of the company and its stockholders – including those executives.

The upshot was that the Underdog team could get something out of other divisions only if they could offer something in return, or get one of Gates and Ballmer to force the issue. One of their early requests was a special, stripped-down build of Windows Server to run the new search engine. The Windows team, which had begun to code the successor to Windows XP in earnest, didn't view the request as a priority, although one member of the team insisted to me that they got 'a lot of help' from the Windows division. It was just they had to wait a bit.

Viewed in one way – that business divisions can't just lavish their budgets on the rest of the business, that managers need to have and keep accountability – that approach makes perfect sense; viewed in another – that there are strategic, overarching aims that should be put ahead of divisional budgets – it doesn't. Even with Gates and Ballmer having indicated that search was an important field for Microsoft, the day-to-day process wouldn't go away; executives would still consider the impact of helping the Underdog group on their own work before Microsoft's.

Do it yourself

In the whole history of Microsoft's efforts in search, one particular choice stands out: the decision not to buy Overture, the company that had shown that pay-per-click advertising linked to search was a viable model.

In mid-2003, Overture came into play: Ted Meisel, who had taken over as its chief executive, was trying to get Yahoo and Microsoft, the two big companies to which he provided back-end advertising services, to bid against each other for his magical advertising system.

Overture had a problem: it had no destination site of its own, having given up GoTo.com to avoid conflict with its customers. That meant that the traffic acquisition costs (TACs) were rising. TAC is a key metric for an advertising-based engine: it measures how much is paid to get the advertisers' paid links in front of someone who might click them. In the first three months of 2003, Overture's revenues rose 57 per cent, but profits almost halved to $11 million. Other metrics – pay-per-click income (from people clicking on advertisements) and the average payment from advertisers – were heading up, but the TACs – paid to Yahoo and Microsoft – threatened to strangle it.

Google, being a site that people came to directly, had comparatively low TACs. Overture needed its own site again where people would come of their own volition to search: that would push down TACs and improve its profitability. But it also had to keep both MSN and Yahoo happy; if either dropped it, Wall Street would mark its shares down, and the other could pick it up for pennies.

Cleverly, Meisel snapped up the now-faded AltaVista and AlltheWeb, from Norway's FAST (which Google's engineers considered a potential search competitor), immediately giving Overture its own search presence. And he began talking to his potential suitors.

'The thing about Overture was that it was one of only a few players – Google was obviously the key one – who could drive down their TACs, and so offer adverts more cheaply to advertisers, and then price everyone else out of the market [by undercutting them on advertising cost],' explains one of the Underdog team. In an expanding market, Google might get so big it would shut others out. Yahoo and Microsoft, which both had large amounts of organic traffic (if not a successful search engine – yet), needed a place at the table. So now they both wanted Overture.

According to reports at the time, Payne suggested not long after the Building 36 meeting that Microsoft should buy Overture. A crucial meeting was called a couple of months later at which Gates and Ballmer were to decide, with the Underdog managers, whether to go ahead with the purchase, or leave it to Yahoo. Subsequent reports suggested that Gates vetoed the purchase because he was certain that Microsoft could build something better.

But those familiar with the details say it was different. Gates was prepared – after some typically aggressive interrogation – to go with the plan to buy Overture, for up to $2 billion. (That in itself was a bargain: Overture was on track to generate nearly $1 billion in revenues that year, and even unprofitable companies usually sell for five times their revenue or more.)

The obstacle was Steve Ballmer, who jumped on the idea of spending 'so much' money for a company whose model surely the Underdog team could replicate effectively. Why go to the trouble, he argued, of all the necessary due diligence required to acquire a publicly listed company (as Overture had been since 1998) and then integrating its perhaps disaffected staff, when Underdog already had programmers, scientists and sales teams who could do it all? 'His argument was, "what are you buying?"' one of the Underdog team says of a report of the meeting.

Ballmer seemed to have missed that Overture wasn't a software asset, but a marketing and advertiser relationship asset because it already had so many advertisers who were happy with its ability to link them with willing buyers. But, by the end of the meeting, he had pulled Gates around to his view. Underdog would have to build the search engine index, crawler and architecture and also an advertising network system, and persuade thousands of advertisers now with Overture to come over to Microsoft's as-yet unready search engine. Microsoft was going to reinvent the wheel – hub, spokes and axle.

Yahoo saw its chance and jumped in, buying Overture in July 2003 for $1.6 billion. 'I suspect in retrospect [Ballmer] would probably say that [letting Overture go] was a mistake,' says the Underdog team member, who is still bitter at the missed opportunity. It cost them months in effort, but years in terms of the race because so much had to be done from scratch.

Arguably, it was the key mistake that Microsoft made at an inflection point in the search business. But it's not even the worst part. Microsoft actually *already owned* an AdWords-style business exactly like Overture – one that arguably had inspired Overture in the first place. In November 1998, it had bought a company called LinkExchange for $265 million, because it liked its 'keywords' idea: small advertisers could bid for their names to appear next to search results, bidding against particular 'keywords'. Ali Partovi, who co-founded LinkExchange, and had tried for years to pitch the idea to Yahoo (then dominant in search traffic), hoped that, despite being owned by Microsoft, the idea could still be sold to other companies.

'As Microsoft employees, we continued pitching the Keywords deal not only to Yahoo, but also to the up-and-coming Google', Partovi recalled in 2010. 'I wasn't surprised to find that these companies were wary of partnering with Microsoft. My greater surprise was the seemingly insurmountable resistance we faced within Microsoft itself.'

He explained: 'After almost two years of fighting bureaucratic obstacles, we finally got the green light to launch "Keywords" as an MSN Search feature in 2000. It started growing rapidly, and the MSN Ad Sales division feared (correctly) that it would cannibalize banner ad revenue. They therefore decided (incorrectly) to shut down Keywords after a few months.' Partovi pleaded directly with Ballmer, who had just taken over as chief executive; Ballmer declined to intervene, saying he was trying to delegate more. So, just at the time that Google made AdWords live, Microsoft shut its own version down. Partovi left Microsoft in July 2000; he subsequently tried to interest Yahoo in the idea, but was turned down because Jerry Yang – then chief executive – thought it didn't 'fit well given our current set of strategies'.

Nobody at the 2003 meeting debating the purchase of Overture – including Gates and Ballmer – seems to have recalled that purchase. As Partovi later remarked, 'If Yahoo's demise [in search] stemmed in part from being ambivalent about technology, perhaps Microsoft's error stemmed in part from being ambivalent about ad sales: we couldn't get the senior execs interested enough to intervene.'[26]

So Microsoft continued reinventing the wheel – despite having bought it once and having had the chance to buy another.

Yet even while the Underdog team was making progress, Microsoft's managers didn't put their trust entirely in them. By October 2003, as talk of a Google flotation intensified, it emerged that senior executives at Microsoft had – despite Mehdi and Payne rejecting the idea at the start of the year – approached Google with the suggestion of a partnership or even acquisition. For Microsoft, a company with billions in the bank, it would be the fastest, simplest route to dominating search.

Page and Brin weren't interested. They were already preparing an initial public offering that could make multimillionaires of many of the employees and cement Google's position as the pre-eminent search business online. It would also give it the cash to move into new technologies, while determining its own destiny. Being acquired by Microsoft had a grim inevitability: absorption into the larger organization, bureaucracy, deceleration. The freewheeling engineering culture at Google, where engineers ruled and used their officially granted '20 per cent time' to develop new ideas – a sort of corporate-sponsored serendipity – would surely get quashed in Microsoft. Still, the submarine period was definitely over. Edwards describes the atmosphere within Google at the realization that Microsoft had woken up as 'fear, but not panic'.

Payne slogged on; reports at the time put his team at 500 strong. Google had about 1,100 employees by July 2003, having started the year with 680; it was adding about 30 per cent per quarter. Inside Microsoft, there was growing confidence that Google would be Netscape all over again, led by hubris to disaster.

However much Microsoft's executives might have wanted to believe that – for it is part of a company's culture to repeat to itself certain stories, especially of victory – Netscape and Google were very different products and companies. Netscape, nominally, charged for both the browser and the servers. The browser wasn't particularly well written – its ad hoc architecture made it increasingly difficult to improve. Most importantly of all, it wasn't pre-installed on PCs.

Microsoft won the battle with Netscape from the back as well as the front. It wrote a good, extensible piece of software in Internet Explorer, and got it installed by default on PCs. Windows Server was already available for the back end. And finally it undercut Netscape: Internet Explorer was free.

Google, however, couldn't be attacked on any of those fronts. Though Internet Explorer in Windows XP used MSN by default, it was easy to change. But the real difficulty was that Google was already free, so there was no way to undercut it. And its engineers were top-notch – as the trickle and then stream of departures from Microsoft to it began to show.

The only way to beat Google would be to do search better (because people judged on results) – and also to grab its traffic, because habit is a powerful beast online: once you've grown used to going to a certain site, you'll keep going there. (See Yahoo's continuing popularity as a destination for proof.) The problem for Microsoft was that Google remained popular. So how could Microsoft displace it?

Going public

On 29 April 2004 Google filed its S-1 document for an initial public offering that would raise $2.7 billion – more precisely, $2,718,281,828 (the first 10 digits of the mathematical unit e, also known as the exponential function; yet another mathematical joke). The flotation had been forced on the company: 29 April was the 120th day of 2004, and section 12(g) of the Securities Exchange Act of 1934 stipulates that 'a company must file financial and other information with the SEC 120 days after the close of the year in which the company reaches $10 million in assets and/or 500 shareholders, including people with stock options'. And all of Google's 1,900-odd employees at the time held stock. So it would have had to start filing public accounts whether it wanted to or not; an IPO would be a smart way to fill the company's coffers with cash now that the submarine was rising out of the water.

The S-1 began with the faintly shocking news – to the outside world, at least – that it had been profitable since 2001, and in the first three months of 2004 had a net income of $64 million on revenues of $389 million. Google was already a billion-dollar company, and doubling in size annually.

It was forced to cut its price closer to the flotation, on 19 August, and raised $1.2 billion through the sale of 14,142,135 (another maths joke referring to the square root of 2) of its shares for $85 each (other stockholders sold 5.4 million shares). The sale valued the entire company at $23 billion, while leaving more than 92 per cent of its shares within Google's control, and making many of its staff millionaires on paper.

The S-1 filing opened with a 'Letter from the Founders', authored by Page, which began by saying that 'Google is not a conventional company. We do not intend to become one... we have... emphasized an atmosphere of creativity and challenge, which has helped us provide unbiased, accurate and free access to information for those who rely on us around the world.' The founders explained that they had created a corporate structure 'that will protect Google's ability to innovate' (basically, to keep a lot of voting stock to themselves). The key was serving end users, which he said was 'at the heart of what we do and remains our number one priority'.

The comparisons with Apple are intriguing: that too is a company where the focus is always on the person who will be using its products, not on any of the intermediaries.

As is obligatory, the S-1 contained warnings for investors, though one reads in hindsight more like a memorandum:

> More individuals are using non-PC devices to access the Internet, and versions of our web search technology developed for these devices may not be widely adopted by users of these devices... If we are unable to attract and retain a substantial number of alternative device users to our web search services or if we are slow to develop products and technologies that are more compatible with non-PC communications devices, we will fail to capture a significant share of an increasingly important portion of the market for online services.

It also revealed – on close reading of Appendix F – that it had had $78 million worth of servers worldwide at the start of 2003, which had grown to $204 million by the end of it, and was set to double again in 2004; by March 2004 it was already up to $258 million. At a rough estimate, that meant it had more than a quarter of a million, and perhaps up to half a million, servers distributed around the world. Google was one of the five largest server manufacturers in the world. But it didn't sell them. It used them.

Payne might have thought he was being ambitious in early 2003 in seeking hundreds of millions to build a search engine. What he didn't realize was that that was just the table stake.

Competition

In July 2004, the month before Google's IPO, MSN unveiled a new page design for its search, free of links and clutter. In fact, some commented, it looked rather like Google's. But it wasn't yet using the new search engine.

Google knew that by going public it had finally broken free of the threat of being bought on the quiet by Microsoft, and broken free too of Windows – or, more precisely, of the desktop. Google lived on the internet, in the browser – the piece of software that had led to Microsoft's downfall. The artefact of Gates's triumph had turned into the new means of its usurpation. Google's managers also knew, through the people joining from Microsoft, precisely how it was viewed 700 miles away in Redmond.

Cultural differences

There were more and more hirings from Microsoft to Google; early in November 2004 Google opened a developer office in Seattle, just seven miles from Microsoft's Redmond headquarters. That made the job transfers – which were all one-way – simpler. For Microsoft refugees – who made up virtually all of the Seattle office within a couple of years – the culture shock was often dramatic. 'Google was a great culture,' says Gayle Laakmann, who has worked as an engineer at all of Microsoft, Google and Apple.[27]

> At Google the engineers were the ones really driving the products; we have very little interaction [from above] compared with Microsoft, where you would get what was called the 'spec' – specification – and I'd be told where to put every single pixel. At Google, we had a PM [product manager] and he was off doing things like meeting with AOL. In Google, when it came down to how to design a feature, if it was visual we might have a UI [user interface] designer come in and help us, but generally we were expected to make our own decisions, and expected that things were team decisions rather than those of an individual person. We as engineers would sit around and we'd talk and make a decision as a team.

Speaking in 2005, Schmidt suggested that the rigorous divisional structure of Microsoft just wouldn't work at Google. 'Flatness is not a function of reporting hierarchy,' he said. 'It's a function of information flow.'[28] Google was all about the free flow of information inside the company: there was a snippets database and project database, which were at the time open to all. Both pre-dated him.

The view of one ex-Microsoft employee was plain: 'Microsoft has to play Google's game to compete with Google.' But Microsoft wasn't comfortable doing that. And it couldn't create a Google culture inside Microsoft to compete.

Laakmann gives a picture inside Microsoft of something more like corporate salt mines: 'By and large Microsoft's products were just Windows and Office, with some exploration of other areas. But essentially it's all those two. So it's desktop software.' (She worked on Visual Studio, which third-party developers use to write programs for Windows.)

> And they've also got a lot of huge contracts, with computer manufacturers and government, so people's ability to take risks is much lower. They've a lot more people depending on what they ship. If they make any mistakes with Office or Windows, they can't just do what Google does and roll the web page back [to a previous version]. Whereas at Google, there are very few contracts, really. If you have a bug in your code and it's huge and it's screwed the product – no big deal. You just roll back to the version from a week earlier.

Microsoft's relaunched search engine

On 11 November 2004 Microsoft relaunched its search engine, now built on a heavily modified version of Windows Server, promising 'more useful answers to [consumers'] questions and more control over their search experience... The new MSN Search allows consumers to quickly receive relevant answers from a universe of more than 5 billion Web documents.'[29] Payne's efforts had finally borne fruit. His name wasn't on the press release; that honour went to Mehdi, grandly titled corporate vice-president for the MSN Information Services and Merchant Platform division. It was clear that the team had tried to think ahead to what people would want: the MSN beta index ('updated weekly or even daily') said it would be able to answer direct questions such as 'What is the capital of Turkey?' and get the answer (via Microsoft's fast-fading Encarta encyclopaedia brand), or content-specific searching, as well as geographically tailored search and 'search builder', which could build from various searches to create a new coherent one.

That was the theory. The practice was different, and didn't start auspiciously. The site crashed almost as soon as it went live. Would-be users only found an 'unavailable' page until the site was fixed later in the day. Jay Greene, writing for *BusinessWeek*, remarked that Microsoft had spent $100 million on MSN Search and 'trumpeted this test launch with a public-relations campaign to ensure that users around the world knew the service was ready for widespread use. So when MSN Search went down, a bit of Microsoft's credibility in the search-engine business went with it.'[30]

Still Payne slogged on. But Microsoft wasn't the cool place to work, and Google had begun to exert a gravitational pull on the world of software. By March 2005, when Microsoft finally launched its search-related advertising business – five years after Google and GoTo.com, seven years after buying Keywords – more than 100 Microsoft staff had left to work at Google, including Marc Lucovsky, one of the chief architects of Windows.

By May 2005, Microsoft had spent around $150 million on Project Underdog. And yet, if anything, it was even further behind. Abandoning the paid search placings in mid-2004 (a project internally called 'CIA', for 'clarity in advertising') had wiped out $50 million of revenues in a single quarter, and would cost more than $100 million in revenues in the next.

Google and Yahoo meanwhile kept pushing ahead – offering 'local' area search, maps, satellite photos, search inside video and even search on mobile phones, an area that Microsoft had thought it was going to own. Gates was certainly annoyed at not having got to search first. But he saw Google as a bigger threat: a threat to his company's very existence. Interviewed for *Fortune* early in 2005, he said: 'Google is interesting not just because of web search, but because they're going to try to take that and use it to get into other parts of software... If all there was was search, you really shouldn't care so much about it. It's because they are a software company.' Later in the interview, he added: 'In that sense, they are more like us than anyone else we have ever competed with.'[31]

Yet, even while he could see Google as the most important competitor, the importance was lost on other parts of the business, which focused tidily on their own numbers and could profitably ignore the rest. Laakmann explains: 'It's pretty divided. If you're in the Windows division, you don't really care that much about how Xbox or whatever product does. They're almost like different companies, a lot of fiefdoms, and it starts right from the top of the divisions down to the teams themselves.' Pieter Knook, who worked there for 18 years, ultimately running Windows Mobile, recalls the sort of opposition that he had faced while Windows Mobile was part of the Xbox division:

> The question that people got was: what did the Xbox have in common with Windows or with Office? Being in the Xbox division, I knew all about that because those guys [from Windows and Office] would say 'What are you [people in the division housing Xbox] doing for us? You're just eating up all our profit and you're spending all our money, and what for?'[32]

What for indeed? By mid-2005, the online advertising market was worth $5 billion and growing at 40 per cent. And the benefits were beginning to accrue to Google through a network effect: the more popular a marketplace destination is, the more it will grow compared to others because traders want to be at a place that maximizes their opportunity to trade. And Microsoft couldn't beat the auction model. Google's moat was repelling invaders.

But Microsoft could still use its dominance on the desktop and browsers to push its new web search to prominence, couldn't it? To those outside the business, the obvious threat was that future versions of its dominant Internet Explorer browser would make Microsoft's search engine the default. Then it would become the default search engine of millions of Windows machines, and hence the internet, surely?

A decade earlier, perhaps. But post-antitrust, everyone – including those inside the Underdog team – knew that making Microsoft's own property the default would carry huge antitrust risks. You couldn't just embed search in the browser.

The Underdog team realized that they could, however, embed their search in another product: Office. Since web search didn't exist as a feature in it already, adding it wouldn't have an antitrust implication. After all, it wasn't like using the platform (Windows) to push the product (Internet Explorer); it was using one product to offer another. It was a get-out-of-jail-free card, antitrust kryptonite, a brilliant scheme to make Microsoft Search whirl up the rankings.

They took the plan to the leader of the Office division. He turned them down flat. Office had a release schedule. It had user priorities. And none of those included, or was about to include, internet search.

In November 2005 Gates and his newly hired replacement as chief software architect, Ray Ozzie, had sent out a company-wide memo – one to add to the 'internet' and the 'security' memos that had previously gone out in 1995 and 2002. They wrote about the threats from the future, while couching it in the tones of opportunity. 'A new business model has emerged in the form of advertising-supported services and software,' the memo noted, adding: 'We knew that search would be important, but through Google's focus they've gained a tremendously strong position.'[33] (Whether Microsoft's actions indicate that its leaders really did always know that search would be important is arguable.) The whole memo can be read almost as a call to arms against Google's advertising-supported business.

One interpretation that Ballmer put on to it was that the Windows brand, the company's most widely known, needed to be emphasized. In September 2006 MSN Search was thus rebranded Windows Live Search, although it had nothing to do with the Windows division, certainly didn't live within it, and you didn't need to be a Windows user to use it (after all, you might be using a mobile phone to access it). The Underdog team hated it. Search needed to present an individual character, not to be subsumed into the monolith of Windows.

In December 2006, Steve Berkowitz, formerly chief executive of rival search engine Ask Jeeves but who had started at Microsoft the previous April, spoke to the *New York Times*, declaring his amazement at the size of the business: 'I'm used to being in companies where I am in a rowboat and I stick an oar in the water to change direction... Now I'm in a cruise ship and I have to call down "Hello, engine room!" Sometimes, the connections to the engine room aren't there.' Berkowitz thought Microsoft had become too enamoured with software for its own sake: 'A lot of decisions [about what to offer on the search engine] were driven by technology; they were not driven by the consumer. It isn't always the best technology that wins. It is the best experience.'[34] The Underdog team could have told him that they had tried to provide the best experience, and that they didn't have much choice but to focus on the technology; Gates liked the challenge, and Ballmer had vetoed their advertising acquisition.

And why 'Windows Live'? Kevin Johnson, in charge of the then 20,000-strong Windows team and, now, the online unit, argued that, once you had online software as well, 'it's a pretty logical thing that people would say, "Hey, I've got Windows and here's a set of Windows Live things that extend those services."'

Nobody outside Microsoft though had the faintest idea what 'Windows Live' indicated. Even Berkowitz echoed his team's uncertainty. 'I don't know if Live is the right name,' he mused. And so he kept the MSN name alive. He also added himself to the lengthening list of Microsoft executives declaring they were *eventually* going to catch Google: 'More and more [search engines] are getting the basics right. What Google has forgotten is how to take it to the next level of differentiation.' By this he meant the presentation of basic search results; at Ask Jeeves he had introduced the idea of giving a small preview of what the page would look like. (Google eventually did the same – in 2011.)

Payne left at the start of 2007 to join a start-up company – where, one must presume, it would be a lot simpler to make a decision. But the efforts of the Underdog team had not achieved their intended aim. Microsoft was still the underdog, by far: in fact its share of search had fallen compared to 2003.

In May 2009, less than three years after being renamed Windows Live Search and making absolutely no headway with either the public or opinion formers, it was renamed again, to Bing. (Wags quickly said this was an acronym for 'But It's Not Google'.) The Underdog team breathed a sigh of relief. Their progeny had escaped the shadow of Windows and been reborn with a zippy, consumer-focused name. It wasn't Office integration, but it was a lot better than nothing. Within Microsoft, 'Google Compete' had become a priority: 'Google's search and office apps [Docs and Spreadsheets, an online-only product costing $50 per person per year] were certainly on Microsoft's competitive radar', one former employee from the time told me, 'though there wasn't as much of a feeling that they'd taken off with the market as there was with Apple [and the iPod].'

Friends

The priority of 'Google Compete' meant that, when in 2007 Facebook began to emerge as a viable threat to Google, Microsoft didn't hesitate to court it. Facebook was different from almost every other site that preceded it. First, it was run by Mark Zuckerberg, a near-obsessive who stirred interest via clever tweaks: for example, each new college that wanted to join had to get a minimum number of recruits before being added to the system, which helped build excitement. But it also put all its content behind a wall. Google and other search engines were explicitly forbidden from 'crawling' many parts of the site by the contents of the 'robots.txt' file.

For web crawlers, the robots.txt file is the online equivalent of the fashionable disco's bouncer controlling the velvet rope. It says which search engines' spiders are allowed in and which directories they can (or more usually cannot) visit. The Googlebot was a VIP accustomed to walking to the head of the queue everywhere in town; Facebook put a meaty hand in its face.

This frustrated Google hugely, because it meant there was a whole section of web content that it was powerless to serve advertisements against. Ironically, it was the sort of personal data that had pushed it into public consciousness: millions of people posting constant 'status updates' about their daily activities to people they had identified as 'friends'.

Google made overtures, but Zuckerberg, who had grown up with the internet not just as a background hum, but as a fluid running through his veins, was wary. He viewed Google a little bit as Google had viewed Microsoft – as a company that had swallowed a whole industry sector, and that you should avoid being swallowed by. After long talks with Ballmer – who turned on all of his charm to seal the deal – Zuckerberg sold a 1.6 per cent holding in his company to Microsoft for $240 million, effectively valuing each of the 42 million members at the time at $357, and the company at $15 billion.

It was a win for Microsoft – but limited. Bing's search share did not grow appreciably in the United States or worldwide. Microsoft's problem was that nobody saw a reason to leave Google. It was good enough. Rather as Apple had found itself locked into a small slice of the PC market because Windows was good enough for most, Bing was locked into a small slice of the search market. The problem was that, while Apple could turn a profit from selling its PCs, only the size of Microsoft kept Bing afloat.

Search is not what John Sculley, the marketing man who was recruited by Steve Jobs from Pepsi to run Apple, would describe as a 'necktie thing'. Sculley's expertise was in a market where there was no truly appreciable difference between the two products. But you were seen drinking either Coca-Cola or Pepsi: you had to make a choice, and enunciate it, and it was visible. Sculley compared doing so to choosing a tie: you wore it, which meant that in a sense it branded you. Cool tie? Cool you. Expensive tie? Expensive you. Cheap, clashing tie? Cheap, tasteless you.

Search is none of that. You aren't judged to be cool based on which search engine you do or don't use; there isn't the public visibility of wearing white iPod earbuds while pulling a phone from your pocket. Search is utilitarian. AltaVista didn't succumb to Google because Google's site looked better (although a designer could argue that it does), but because the upstart did search, and then monetized search, better. Even while it has had its eyes on the bigger fish in the sea such as Microsoft, Google has also known that it is only through delivering better results for the user, or a better search experience, allied to – but never dominated by – better click-throughs for advertisers, that it will survive.

In fact few people know what search engine their friends use. (But they can guess. In North America and Europe, it's probably Google; in Russia, it's probably Yandex; in China, it's probably Baidu.) Both Google and Microsoft like to say that their competition is only a click away; but the dial has barely budged in the past five years on the search share, except through Microsoft's capture of Yahoo's search function. Brand may count for something in searching, but almost certainly habit counts for much more.

Microsoft's bid for Yahoo

For Microsoft, the competition meant nothing but pain. As 2008 began it made an audacious $45 billion bid for Yahoo, now the second-largest web property (after Google), offering a 62 per cent premium on the stock price. The logic behind the deal was straightforward enough: by powering its search, Microsoft could get the scale it needed to make Bing pay off. Yahoo was the biggest advertising billboard on the web, full of news content, offering e-mail, all opportunities for advertisements that could be driven through Bing.

The deal was poisoned, though, by Yahoo, which had cooked up a series of internal forecasts suggesting that the company would grow much bigger and be worth far more than a measly $45 billion. The forecasts were wildly wrong, predicated on levels of advertising growth that required the future to be just like the previous six years – only more so. Yahoo's executives, led by Jerry Yang, made the wrong call once again. This time, Yahoo failed to perceive that it was at the tail end of an enormous financial bubble, and repeatedly rejected Ballmer. When the credit crunch hit in the summer, big advertisers drastically cut back their marketing budgets, and Yahoo was suddenly left scrabbling for revenue. The bid collapsed, Yang was forced out, and in January 2009 Carol Bartz, a tough-talking Silicon Valley veteran, was offered the helm of Yahoo. She was more receptive to a simpler offer from Microsoft: that it would power Yahoo search and help serve advertisements. It seemed Ballmer had got what he wanted. (But even that soured: Facebook slurped up advertising revenue while Bartz slashed costs, so Yahoo's revenue fell while its profits rose, and the Bing deal wasn't profitable for either. The Yahoo board fired Bartz in September 2011 – and shocked Silicon Valley by hiring Mayer in July 2012.)

Google's identity

Inside Microsoft, the awareness that it wasn't winning in search became pervasive. In February 2009, a select set of employees was invited to a 'no holds barred' question-and-answer session with Steve Sinofsky, then the new head of the Windows division (who had moved over from the Office division). He was asked about the competitive threat to Office from Google's office apps.

'The cool kids may use Google apps, but we pretty much own the office app market,' Sinofsky replied. 'Now, ask yourself: would you rather be *big* or be *cool?*'

Someone else raised a hand, and asked: 'So when are we going to stop being *cool* in search?'

The answer was an extremely frosty silence.

Google has worked hard to create its external identity. What fonts official paper should use, how to present the company to users, and what words it's best to use (neutral when they need to be, humorous when there is room) took some time to emerge. In March 2009, Mayer explained to the *New York Times* the problems of a super-flat organization: you keep having to give the same advice repeatedly.[35] The guidelines (always 'Google' not 'we'; don't use italics, as their legibility is low on computer screens; avoid 'I', 'we', 'you'; simplify design by taking away a colour, an image or a font variation) had come from – of course – 'internal experiments' to measure users' preferences.

As the journalist and writer Nick Carr observed, Google thrives as the internet thrives:

> Google's protean appearance is not a reflection of its core business. Rather, it stems from the vast number of complements to its core business. Complements are, to put it simply, any products or services that tend be consumed together. Think hot dogs and mustard, or houses and mortgages. For Google, literally everything that happens on the internet is a complement to its main business. The more things that people and companies do online, the more ads they see and the more money Google makes. In addition, as internet activity increases, Google collects more data on consumers' needs and behaviour and can tailor its ads more precisely, strengthening its competitive advantage and further increasing its income. As more and more products and services are delivered digitally over computer networks – entertainment, news, software programs, financial transactions – Google's range of complements is expanding into ever more industry sectors.[36]

And yet despite that expansion its internal identity remains consistent: a place in which engineering, and empiricism, rules supreme. Sometimes empiricism is also allied to pragmatism: if you can't get it done, well, you can't, and that's the end of it. Yet Google is also able to throw enormous resources at problems where it thinks those will make a difference. Equally, it knows the value of keeping projects and teams small and focused. The Bigtable project that replaced its original indexing and storage system in 2005 (while Microsoft was lauding its brand new crawler-based MSN Search) was begun in 2003 and completed in 2004; in the paper describing it, the authors airily say that it took 'seven person-years'.[37] For a system that fundamentally rebuilt how the world's biggest search engine was configured, it is a shockingly small number – but it indicates just how small the team was. (The paper has nine joint authors.)

Being engineer-driven meant that Google could see further and, because of its youth, move more quickly than so many rivals. It saw the potential of online video long before others, and snapped up YouTube for what seemed like an insane amount, $1.6 billion, in October 2006 because it could see that video would become prevalent and that users' stored content – home video clips on camcorders and (ignoring copyright, as Google is wont to do) all those copyrighted films – was what had made its original search engine so powerful, and that it would be better to hold it close than to let someone else (Microsoft?) throw a walled garden around it. For Google the web was the ecosystem, a perfectly uplifting software form. For the first half-decade of its life the hardware didn't matter because the web hadn't broken free of the desktop and laptop computer and the tyranny of immobile connections: if you wanted to access the web, generally you had to be sitting in front of a computer.

By the end of 2007 Google's primacy on the web had become an obsession within Microsoft. Though the Facebook advertising deal positioned it within the ramparts of the social citadel that Google had most wanted to conquer, it wasn't enough; its rival remained miles ahead in everything that mattered – share of search, share of advertising, rate of growth, search of online video viewing, share of cloud services (where Google's principal competition came from Amazon, whose Jeff Bezos had been one of its original investors), and of course mindshare whenever search was mentioned. Microsoft tried promotions – offering 'Cashback' rebates to shoppers if they bought an item via Windows Live (and later Bing), which could earn them up to $2,500 per year. But the tracking system was flawed, as Samir Meghani, of the price comparison site Bountii.com, showed (you could easily spoof it to generate payments even without buying); and worse, merchants offering goods via Cashback were charging higher prices than elsewhere on the web – even after the rebate. 'Negative cashback?' Meghani wondered. Microsoft shut it down in June 2010: 'we did not see the broad adoption that we had hoped for', admitted Mehdi, posting on the Bing community blog.[38]

The shadow of antitrust

Shivaun Raff doesn't look like someone who would overthrow a multibillion-dollar company, nor have ambitions in that direction. Bespectacled, earnest and quickfire, she and her husband Adam created a site called Foundem that searched comparison sites and offered the best deals from them. But, when she noticed that Google seemed to be downrating the site they had set up, she first gathered as much data as she could and then complained to the European Commission (EC). At the core of the Raffs' complaint was that their site was repeatedly downgraded by Google, which meanwhile gave its own properties – Maps, News – prime billing on the first page in what it called 'Universal Search'.

That Google has a monopoly of search in Europe is undoubted: it gets about 95 per cent of desktop search traffic. The Raffs' argument was that first, it was intentionally downgrading their site, which did 'vertical search' (type in 'iPod' and it would find different prices to buy it at other sites) while putting its own 'shopping' results in a prominent box on the first page of results.

With Foundem's results relegated to the seventh or eighth page of results – a distant part of the jungle – which would people click on if they actually were looking to shop? Google's.

The key question, though, was whether such 'vertical search' was the same as 'organic search'. Is a price comparison site the same as one which indexes the web? Or is vertical search just a facet of the wider challenge of indexing the web and reading peoples' intentions from a word or two typed into a search bar?

Google argued the latter; that such results were part of 'Universal Search'. Yet it fenced off its vertical search results in a thinly bordered box labelled 'Sponsored' – implying they were somehow different from the 'organic' search results, rather than being part of them. That raised the separate question: if vertical search was so different from organic search that it needed to be separated, was it a different product? If so, why did Google's new 'vertical search' product always rank highest, ahead of all other vertical search offerings (such as Foundem's)? Was there objective proof that it was better? It looked as though Google was using its monopoly in organic search to annex a separate field – the classic maneouvre of a monopoly, and the one which had had such consequences for Microsoft.

The EC began collecting the data for an antitrust investigation early in 2010, sending out three long and detailed questionnaires to companies involved in advertising and search. In March 2011, Microsoft weighed in formally – though within Google the mutterings were that it had been helping the Raffs for months. (Shivaun Raff says that isn't true.) In July 2011, the US Federal Trade Commission began a separate investigation into the same questions. Sources inside the FTC indicated to me that the staff thought there were grounds to go after Google on antitrust grounds – as the Department of Justice had with Microsoft – and recommended as much to its five commissioners. But the five commissioners were unanimous in dismissing the accusation[39]. 'The introduction of Universal Search [and] changes to Google's search algorithms – even those that may have had the effect of harming individual competitors – could be plausibly justified as innovations that improved Google's product,' they wrote. They didn't seek a consent decree to enforce the behaviour. Microsoft's deputy counsel Dave Heiner called the resolution 'weak and – frankly – unusual'. Google was quietly triumphant: 'The conclusion is clear: Google's services are good for users and good for competition,' wrote head lawyer David Drummond.

The EC investigation, meanwhile, dragged on. The only expectation was that Foundem might see its wish – that Google's algorithms, which are hand-tweaked (for which Raff has the evidence, and Google has admitted in public many times), would stop discriminating against sites that appear to be perfectly optimized to show up high in Google searches. In October 2013, the EC's antitrust commissioner announced that a new set of proposals from Google to settle the dispute looked promising: rivals in fields such as shopping would be able to bid for position on the results page. Foundem, and other complainants, awaited publication; they had already rejected one proposal in April 2013 (which highlighted that the products were Google's; given its power as a brand, this would only worsen matters, they argued).

In November 2013, the new proposals leaked: Google was proposing that rival price comparison sites could bid to appear at the bottom of its own fenced-off 'vertical search' results – the shopping ones where product companies already bid to appear (thus destroying Google's promise of long before that it would not let payment determine where a site or link appeared in results).

The problem with this proposal was that it didn't deal with the issue of where vertical search engines should appear in 'organic' results (they were still suppressed); and it let Google effectively act as gatekeeper to them all, extracting a toll on their traffic (because they would have to pay for every customer who arrived via the fenced-off box, just as if they had bid via AdWords). The proposals were thus neither a solution to the complaints about vertical search – where Google's unproven assumption that it offered the best (for why else should it appear top?) was unchallenged – and organic search, which would otherwise provide unpaid traffic to those rival sites.

The hubbub about the antitrust investigation didn't stop Google rolling out further additions to its search product: Instant, which would generate a list of results as you typed and change them in reaction to each letter that was typed; and Plus One, which was portrayed as a 'glimpse of social search'. But, on the same day in March 2010 that Plus One was announced, Google made a shamefaced concession to the FTC over its Buzz 'social' product (which tried to create an ad hoc social network from people's e-mail contacts) that it would allow independent review of the privacy controls on Gmail and Street View every two years for the next 20 years. *Twenty years*. Google could be flattered that the FTC thought that it would survive that long. But it couldn't think that the FTC loved it. The criticisms – using 'deceptive tactics [that] violated its own privacy promises to consumers' – were meant to sting. Alma Whitten, the company's director of privacy in product and engineering wrote on the company's official blog that the launch 'fell short of our usual standards for transparency and user control' and that it had '[let] our users and Google down'.[40]

Yet Google still wanted more information. Having failed to persuade Facebook to cooperate, in June 2011 it launched 'Google+', seen by others as a Facebook competitor, but within the company as a sort of glue to hold each user's information together. It followed that in January 2012 by announcing that it would amalgamate all the data about users across its products under a single account. There was no opting out; if you signed into Gmail with one e-mail address, and then YouTube with the same one, the data about what you viewed would be shared within Google across both, and used to inform it about what ads to show you – and also to collect data about your behaviour and preferences.

At the same time, Google tweaked its search in the United States so that Google+ posts or identities ranked higher than those from much larger networks including Twitter. That provoked ire from rivals including Twitter and Facebook. But Google effectively ignored them. It had power enough to do so.

Microsoft is still fabulously profitable. But those profits come from its monopoly rents on Windows and Office; together they typically constitute more than 100 per cent of its profits, because those are offset by huge losses in Online Services. In 2009, Ballmer admitted his errors over Overture and LinkExchange. 'The biggest mistakes I claim I've been involved with is where I was impatient – because we didn't have a business yet in something, we should have stayed patient,' he said. 'If we'd kept consistent with some of the ideas' that Microsoft had in-house in 1999, 'we might have been in paid search.'[41]

Inside Google, Microsoft is still, just as in those early days, seen as the threat, and now even more as the enemy. But the weapons that the rival uses now are not just its size. 'The one area where Microsoft is really innovative these days is in litigation and [using] regulation', sniffed one Google employee I spoke to, whose job involves continual contact with the rival. 'Add sort of sales-related FUD [fear, uncertainty and doubt, injected into would-be defecting customers' minds to make them stick with their existing supplier].'

What really irks those working at Google is the idea that Microsoft is somehow playing dirty: that instead of letting the best algorithm, indexing software, hand-tweaked operating system and distributed hardware win in the battle for people's and advertisers' attention, it is calling for help from the authorities.

'Frankly, in any enterprise space, [Ballmer's approach is] probably right, like sales culture is – particularly in enterprise – very personal, very much about kind of the relationships that you have,' the Google employee admits. But, the employee added, Google hasn't worked that way because it never grew up in a direct person-to-person selling environment. 'Google's advertising model basically was started as largely self-serve for advertisers, so we obviously do have teams that work with our larger advertisers. But a lot of our advertising is self-serve.' Google isn't just born on the web; its ambition is to scale with the web. But person-to-person relationships don't scale; the company could never have grown to any size curating the web – or dealing with all its advertisers – by hand. Ballmer's mano-a-mano tactics might seem to date from a previous epoch to some inside Google. But they're sometimes very effective.

Contrast that to the view inside Google of another key rival:

> If you look at Apple versus Microsoft, Apple rarely engages in sort of fights with competitors in the regulatory arena or the legal arena. OK, sometimes they do, but very rarely. And I think philosophically their view is 'OK, we might face challenges but let's build a better product.' Microsoft? My perception is as a company that they devote a huge amount of resources to protecting what they've got. It's much, much harder for them to create a cool new product than it is for them to slug it out against Google or Apple in Washington, DC or in Brussels or in the courts, or slug it out for contract deals.

Still underdog

In July 2011, Microsoft announced its results for the April–June quarter. The Online Services division that houses Bing was doing as badly as ever, losing $728 million on revenues of $662 million. Online Services thus cemented its position as the worst-performing division in the company: it has not made a profit since the three months ending December 2005, when it finally turned off its Overture-powered service and moved to the internally designed search and advertising system Gates and Ballmer had insisted on. In the five years since, quarterly revenues had barely improved, averaging $620 million, while Google's had grown fourfold from $1.9 billion in the fourth quarter of 2005 to $8.6 billion at the beginning of 2011. Bing's quarterly losses have averaged $360 million. Since the beginning of 2006, Online Services has lost $8.7 billion. In the same period, Google had made a profit of $31.2 billion – the same sum by which its cash pile has increased.

Henry Blodget was a financial analyst for Merrill Lynch during the 1990s dot-com boom, but now focuses his talent for analysing balance sheets and markets on his financial and technology news website, Business Insider (neatly thumbing his nose at his 'insider' past).

In a typically trenchant piece on the site after the woeful results in the first quarter of the year, Blodget suggested that Bing and Microsoft's search services simply have no chance of reaching a profitable future. 'Bing is not doing well. It's doing horribly,' Blodget wrote. The truth, he said, was that 'Microsoft's Bing search engine is indeed gaining some share of search queries in the US market (globally, Bing is nowhere). But it is gaining this share at an absolutely mind-boggling cost. Specifically, Microsoft is gaining share for Bing by doing spectacularly expensive distribution deals, deals that don't even come close to paying for themselves in additional revenue.'[42] He calculated that the company was paying three times as much for every 'incremental search query' – that is, outside traffic directed to its site – as it was generating in revenue from the query. And you can never make a profit if you're spending $3 to bring in every $1 of revenue.

The source of this problem, Blodget pointed out, was that deal Ballmer had trumpeted: the one to run Yahoo's search. Microsoft was paying Yahoo around 90 cents for every $1 it made from Yahoo-derived search queries.

Mehdi, still in charge of the Online Services business after all this time, had insisted to Blodget in an interview in March 2010 that all it needed to do was capture 40 to 50 per cent of the US search market and all the pieces would fall into place: the economies of scale would work and (the implication went) Bing and Online Services would become profitable again.[43] Except, as Blodget pointed out, that can't work if the share isn't *organic* share. If Microsoft was paying Yahoo 90 cents on the dollar for each search, then every 10 percentage points of search share Yahoo gained was the equivalent of Bing capturing just 1 per cent of organic share. In other words, even together, where their US share added up to around 35 per cent, it wasn't enough and it could never be enough. Only if Microsoft owned Yahoo, so that all its traffic was 'organic' to Bing, would it ever approach break-even – and even then it would have to push Google from its 65 per cent of the US market. And that's before you look at the world market. Given that Ballmer had been prepared to spend $44.6 billion to buy Yahoo (that is, the equivalent of five and a half years' losses by Online Services) you get a glimpse of how he truly is thinking of the long term.

But he never said during the bid for Yahoo that its organic search business was key to Microsoft's future, only that Google was too dominant, and that, he implied, was a bad thing. There's an obvious irony in the chief executive of a company that has not one but two monopolies (PC operating systems and office applications) complaining about someone else's monopoly.

So the stark truth was that, even with the Yahoo search business, Online Services could not turn into a profit centre, Blodget argued.

The combined share of the Bing and Yahoo platforms is now approaching 30 per cent of the US market. That means that Bing already has significant scale. And yet Bing's economics just continue to get worse... it is almost impossible to believe that, if Bing gains another 10 points of market share, the economics of its business are going to change so radically that it will double its revenue per query, which it will need to do to break even (even if it doesn't spend another dime acquiring and processing the next 10 points of share, which it obviously will). In fact, because there are no more big distribution deals to do, acquiring another 10 points of share will likely cost Microsoft a lot *more* than acquiring the last 5 points of share. Which means that doubling revenue-per-query won't be anywhere near enough to make this a viable business.

On the desktop, perhaps. But what about mobile phones? Does Bing have a future there? In April 2011, Nokia – the world's largest standalone mobile phone manufacturer (though, by that time, already eclipsed by Apple for both size and profit in the mobile business) – finally sealed a deal in which it agreed that it would use Microsoft's Windows Phone operating system for its top-end smartphones, starting in volume from 2012. Bing would become the default search engine for users of those phones. Surely this would be its saviour, with mobile search a multimillion-pound business?

Not necessarily: the small print noted that, 'In recognition of the unique nature of Nokia's agreement with Microsoft and the contributions that Nokia is providing, Nokia will receive payments measured in the billions of dollars.'[44] Even if the Nokia partnership could capture significant market share (a proposition that, at the time of writing, remains uncertain), Bing would be stuck with a new TAC drain. BlackBerry agreed that Bing would be the default search engine on its QNX-based range of mobile phones to be released in 2012. The terms of the deal weren't released, but Microsoft almost surely paid handsomely to be featured there. But both became bit players in the smartphone world. Google's Android, and the iPhone (on which Google was the default for web search) had about 90 per cent of the market.

The future of search, meanwhile, remains unknown. In early 2005, Gates thought that the focus and method of search would soon move on anyway: that you'd search from within Word or Excel, and that the idea of 'going to the internet' and typing disparate words into search boxes would fade into memory. The time since that was written – eight years – isn't enough distance to know whether he's right. But here's what he thought: 'The idea that you type in these words [in the search box] that aren't sentences and you don't get any answers – you just get back all these things you have to click on – that is so antiquated', he told *Fortune*. And later he added: 'We need to take search way beyond how people think of it today and just have it be naturally available, based on the task they want to do.'[45]

The signs though are that, as with so many of Gates's musings, the reality is some way from happening. Google is experimenting with Google Now, an app for mobiles which monitors the owner's movements, behaviour and location and tries to make suggestions

– working out that you regularly take the train at 8.10am and warning you that it's running late, or finding hotels in the area when you arrive at an unfamiliar location.

Microsoft meanwhile is trying another tack: weaving search into its products, such as Windows, Xbox, Windows Phone, and Office (as the team had wanted) to offer a facility that is baked in, rather than having to be added and summoned. Gates may turn out to have been right.

Yet the huge losses from Bing continued to mount. When in August 2013 Steve Ballmer announced that he would step down as chief executive within 12 months (hinting he had come under external pressure), it dawned on staff that someone new would be looking at the cost of Bing.

'What if the next CEO just said "Let's close Bing"?' one Microsoft employee mused to me. 'I'm not saying they would. Just wondering what if.'

Ironically, such a move might cause the biggest problem for Google, which would abruptly become the equivalent of a public utility in the United States and Europe – and come under even closer scrutiny. But the idea that Microsoft might come from behind and destroy the upstart is dead. Though it has managed it before – with word processors, spreadsheets and of course those fateful browsers – and challenged successfully to become a worthy contender in games consoles, in Google it is up against a rival fighting on its own turf: the internet. Spolsky's musings about the generational difference between those at the top of Microsoft and at Google finds its exposition here. Google has won in search engines; Microsoft has lost because it was fighting on unfamiliar territory, and made the wrong choices, especially about whether to buy Overture. Google is more than an annoyance; long-term, it has the power to be just the existential threat to many of Microsoft's businesses that Gates feared in 2005. It took him a little over 15 years to turn Microsoft into the world's biggest business by market capitalization. Ten years later, the kids in the garage had begun to undermine the foundations of the big house overshadowing them.

Berkowitz, speaking from his perspective in 2006 of having gone from the third-ranked search engine (Ask Jeeves) to the fourth-ranked, commented: 'You don't win in the first 90 per cent [of what you do]. What matters to people is emotional attachment. And I think that's the last 10 per cent.'[46]

All the signs are, though, that Google has all of those.

Chapter Four
Digital music: Apple versus Microsoft

On Friday 1 December 2000 I was ushered into a nondescript London hotel room to meet Koji Hase, then vice-president of strategic alliances at Japan's Toshiba Corporation. He had a suitcaseful of gadgets and gewgaws, new ideas that he wanted to show off to the press; the intention, as with all such presentations, was to boost Toshiba's profile by being mentioned in print, and perhaps register on some executive's radar somewhere.

Hase already had an impressive track record: he had worked on the CD ROM and the DVD disk; some years before he had shared a sushi dinner with John Sculley, then in charge of Apple, and they had come up with the name of 'personal digital assistant' for machines that you would carry around to take notes. (The 'PDA' moniker stuck down the years, even if Sculley's Newton didn't.) 'He said, it's a personal secretary that's digital,' said Hase. 'We almost called it the personal digital secretary.'

From his suitcase, Hase passed over a thumbnail-sized card. 'Flash memory,' he said. I had heard of it, of course: it could store data without requiring a current, yet a computer could read and write its data more quickly than a standard hard drive (which has spinning 'platters' coated in magnetizable material) because it consisted only of transistors, without moving parts. 'At present we can only make chips which store up to 64 Mb,' said Hase. 'They are used mostly in digital cameras and MP3 players. But by 2002 we will be able to produce commercial amounts of 1-gigabyte flash chips.' Certainly the Rio MP3 player, which I'd tried, showed promise: its flash storage meant it didn't skip. The problem was it was expensive. Hase forecast that flash storage would mean we could download video and sound clips from the internet, more likely via a phone line or even satellite link.

He thought the ideal application would be in a watch 'One gigabyte sounds a lot but it's not enough for very much data,' he explained. 'You need five gigabytes to squeeze a film on to a DVD. But we think that one gigabyte will be enough for news clips. After all, you don't need to see much detail in news.'

So: the TV on my watch. I forbore to mention that I didn't see this as likely, since people could – and at the time did – already carry palm-sized portable TV sets around. Not to mention newspapers.

Hase moved on to the next part of his presentation, revealing that Toshiba was working with other companies to develop tiny hard drives that would be about 4.5 centimetres (1.8 inches) in width, rather than the 8.9 centimetres (3.5 inches) of those used in laptops. 'We have already started selling a 2GB version of this disk in the US,' said Hase. 'We think that by February next year we will get it up to 5GB, which is enough to hold a film.'

His thinking was that, by making the disk read-only, you could sell pre-packaged films for PC viewing, though he did recognize that consumers would probably be able to buy DVD players able to read and write DVDs within the year – and that they would take over the world, perhaps pushing out the internet on your watch or the tiny drives for watching pre-bought films.

In that hotel room, I turned over the prototype disk in my hands and wondered what you'd really want to do with that much storage on its own. Somehow, I couldn't see the attraction of putting the internet on your watch.

The beginning of iTunes

Five days later Apple announced that it would fall into loss for the quarter, walloped by a decline in its computer sales: while PC sales had grown by about 10 per cent (a slowdown compared to previous years, but still growth), Apple's sales had dropped by a third compared to the year before. A key part of the failure was the lack of 'CD-burning' drives in its systems: the digital music revolution was taking off, and people were using Napster to swap files (illicitly) over university and business networks, which were much faster than the painfully slow dial-up connections of the time. People also wanted to be able to burn their MP3 files into audio CDs. Jobs, who was warning analysts of the forthcoming shortfall, admitted that the company had 'completely missed the boat' there. 'We just blew this one,' he said, adding 'It will be fixed soon' and that there was 'amazing new hardware under development that will reassert Apple's leadership in several key product categories'.[1]

In retrospect, this might look as though Jobs knew that the iPod was going to come around and be Apple's salvation. But that's hindsight, and not even 20/20; as a product, the iPod project hadn't even been considered. Jobs was talking about new laptops, and updates to the existing product lines that added CD burning.

The CD-burning miss was an example of Apple's internal culture at the time completely failing to hear users. PCs with CD-burning capabilities were the hot sellers that year as computer makers rushed to satisfy the demand from consumers to create their own music CDs; businesses meanwhile liked being able to back up data cheaply on to a medium that would last effectively for ever.

Jobs, who had come in from the successes of Pixar, the film animation company of which he was also chief executive, had been sure that watching films would be what people really wanted – and so every Apple machine came with a DVD-reading drive. It was a spectacular miss. Yet within the company there weren't signs of dissent over the direction of travel that had been laid down. One employee who was there at the time told me that 'I don't have any recollection of lacking CD burners being a weakness. If anything, my recollection is that the DVD drives were generally available also as CD burners – what we called combo drives.' It's telling that his recollection is wrong. Apple had missed the boat partly because Jobs had in 1998 rejected 'tray' CD/DVD drives for the new consumer iMacs in favour of sleek 'slot-loading' ones that swallowed the disk. He had been warned by Jon Rubinstein, head of the hardware products division, that this would put Macintosh systems behind PCs in the drive to get CD burners. Jobs had ignored him.[2]

Gayle Laakmann, who has worked at all three organizations (Microsoft, Apple and Google), says that, of the three, Apple is the most top-down in organization, even while the developers who write the code have the most influence over what will happen. 'The developers worked with a manager to work out which direction the software should develop, but we also had a pretty heavy influence from Steve Jobs as well as some user interface designers', she explains. There would be periodic meetings in which managers and developers would show their offerings and get Jobs's feedback. 'There'd be periodic meetings with him and generally what he said – you don't argue with because he's fantastically good at what he does, but there's definitely a sense of intimidation from him,' says Laakmann.[3]

So Jobs didn't see the importance of burning CDs, and Apple lost out badly. Of all the machines it released in 2000, only the Cube – released in July, which sold poorly and was put on ice a year later – offered CD burning. But that impelled the senior team to look at music afresh. In the autumn, they decided that they should focus on music as the field with the broadest popularity – greater than cameras or film – and greatest potential for growth. As a first step, Apple bought a product, SoundJam, which could play MP3s and burn CDs, and worked on its reinvention.

In January 2001, Jobs unveiled Apple's new strategy: the Mac would become the 'digital hub', the centre of people's use of content: they would put their digital music and video into it, and create DVDs with it too. (The emphasis on film was still there.) He unveiled 'iTunes', the reimagined SoundJam, as Apple's brand new digital music organizer: it would rip CDs into MP3s and name the songs automatically, let you organize and search the resulting library, and even let you burn CDs of MP3s, or audio disks for CD players. Apple had started listening.

Gizmo, Tokyo

Even as the digital hub strategy was being unveiled, Apple's leaders were keenly aware that they urgently needed to build something that would get more people buying Macs, Apple's only real source of revenue. Only 659,000 had been sold in the fourth quarter, the lowest figure since 1998 and a dramatic dip compared to a couple of years of strong growth. They needed a new battlefield.

Apart from the chief designer Jonathan Ive and finance chief Fred Anderson, all of Apple's senior team at the time had either come from NeXT Computer with Jobs or been hired by him on his return. They were a tight-knit group who understood what it took to work with Jobs. (Remarkably, the members would not change for around a decade.) At the start of 2001 they sat down and tried to tease out the answer to the question: what do we need? The answer: a new gizmo that would hook up to their digital hub – the Mac (and only the Mac) – and offer some service that everyone would covet. Get them to buy the gadget and they'd buy a Mac as well. Also, they'd be tied to the platform because the gadget wouldn't work on Windows. The gadget would become part of a Mac ecosystem.

Now all they needed to do was invent the gadget. But what?

In February 2001, the Macworld show headed to Tokyo, and Rubinstein met the Toshiba engineers. Rubinstein, a New Yorker born the year after Jobs, who had run the hardware division at NeXT, is an engineer by training who weighs his words and the person he's speaking to carefully. A former Hewlett-Packard employee, he has a very deep understanding of the technologies used in consumer devices, from chip design upwards.

Toshiba showed him the same tiny drive that had been shown off in that London hotel room, and made the same suggestions. Pre-packaged video? Watches? Rubinstein saw at once that it could be used to build a music player – the device that could hook up to the Mac and make the most of the digital hub. That evening he met Jobs and told him that all he needed was the budget sign-off and he could build Apple's first big consumer electronics gadget.

When the company looked at potential rivals in the MP3 player market, there was no sign of Sony, the company which had created portable music with the Walkman, and that Jobs most revered – and feared. And there was one other thing: 'The [rival] products stank', as Greg Joswiak (later the head of iPod product marketing) put it. Existing products were either big and unwieldy, or small and limited, storing 32 MB or 64 MB of data – enough for just 30 or 60 minutes' music – in pricey flash memory. Changing the stored songs was tedious, because the USB 1.1 transfer speed took a minute at least to transfer 20 MB of data – equivalent to four or five songs. Larger players needed refreshing less often, but the slow transfer speed meant you wouldn't want to: transferring a gigabyte of files (equivalent to 200 songs) could take an hour or more. Once running, their big hard drives could suck the battery dry in an hour or less. Anyone who had fed a few of their CDs into a program like Windows Media Player or iTunes (which could convert a CD to MP3 five or more times faster than it took to play) would either find the small players too limited or find the big ones too slow for transferring data.

Apple however had a way around the transfer speed problem: a technology called FireWire that it had developed to transfer video from professional digital movie cameras. FireWire shifted data 30 times faster than USB 1.1.

Rubinstein headed a crash programme to build the iPod, bringing in outside help in the form of an engineer called Tony Fadell who had been hawking the idea of a handheld music player around Silicon Valley, without success, and acquiring software from outside companies. Apple signed a contract with Toshiba giving it exclusive access to those tiny hard drives for a limited period after a new product launch; nobody else would be able to mimic it. The clause was a little bit of inspiration, built on the realization that what would make the iPod special wasn't its capacity, or its technical features, but its physical dimensions.

iPod design

The design process for the iPod was remarkably collaborative. One example stands out from it: the scroll wheel, which became famous. It was an idea pushed by Phil Schiller, the affable, bear-like head of marketing, who had pondered the problem of how to navigate through the huge number of songs the disk would be able to store. He and his team came up with the 'scroll wheel' – which not only let you keep moving through a list as long as you liked (because the thumb can inscribe circles continuously), but also used software to accelerate the scrolling as you moved through a list. He brought a prototype along to one of the design meetings, where he said plainly: 'The wheel is the right user interface for this product.' The idea of a scroll wheel for a controller wasn't unique to Apple; the Danish hi-fi designer Bang & Olufsen had used it, as had Hewlett-Packard (HP). But Apple refined the interface – and the acceleration of scrolling stands out for its usefulness.

Schiller's role in the user interface design of the iPod highlights how different Apple is from other companies. It's hard to imagine there are many, or perhaps any, other companies where the international head of marketing would have thought of and then mocked up such an effective piece of interface design – or where he could have got it considered.

A lot of the rest of the design, as Jonathan Ive, Apple's chief designer, recalls, was about 'not trying to do too much with the device – which would have been its complication and, therefore, its demise... the key was getting rid of stuff'. Thus the iPod would not include an FM tuner, Bluetooth, Wi-Fi, a replaceable battery, cross-fading, playlist creation on the move, or many other things that 'experts' might think were 'necessary' in a specification list. The iPod wouldn't win a battle of tick boxes. Ive's design team was focused on making it win somewhere else: usability. The real specification was how it felt in users' hands. And he knew he had only one chance to get it right. The year after the iPod, I asked him what sort of designers he admired. His answer: those who build satellites.

'When you look at how a satellite is made – the formal solution that has to answer a bunch of imperatives, what goes in, what doesn't, how you fit it together – there's so much stuff that people don't think is consciously designed.' The iPod, too, would be launched into an unwelcoming void, with perhaps only one chance to succeed.

Once the feature set was determined, the next element was getting it made. Ive's team doesn't work in an ivory tower; a design that can't be mass-produced has no value to a consumer electronics company. 'Apple's designers spend 10 per cent of their time doing traditional industrial design: coming up with ideas, drawing, making models, brainstorming,' says Robert Brunner, a former head of Apple's design group. 'They spend 90 per cent of their time working with manufacturing, figuring out how to implement their ideas.' One thing Ive was firm about: there should be no gaps in the bodywork – no panels for replacing batteries, no spaces. Ive wanted to have a device as close to seamless as possible, so it would feel almost fluid. (Ordinary users wouldn't be able to replace the batteries when, as with any rechargeable, they no longer held their charge. But the team calculated that, by the time that was a problem, there would be a new product to attract a fresh purchase.) The only concession he allowed was a flip-up piece of plastic over the FireWire connector on the top, to keep the metal contacts clean. He demanded white headphones and earbuds, to match the front of the device, even though it would push up costs; it would be far cheaper to source generic black leads and earbuds. Such demands often brought Ive into conflict with Rubinstein, a far more cost-driven and pragmatic thinker, who was ultimately responsible for implementing Ive's designs. Jobs, however, saw Ive almost as a soulmate, and would back his vision, no matter how frustrating for the hardware team.

Marketing the new product

On 15 October 2001 Apple sent out an invitation to journalists to attend an event at its Cupertino headquarters. 'This coming

Tuesday [23 October], Apple invites you to the unveiling of a breakthrough digital device', the invite told recipients, adding: '(Hint: it's not a Mac).'

The invitation leaked, of course, and sent the Mac faithful – a small but eager band of loyal buyers – into a state of agitation. Not a Mac? Then what was it going to be? Guesses ranged from a wireless controller for your living room (extending the digital hub idea) to something including handwriting recognition (rescued, fans hoped, from the long-dead Newton organizer) and high-speed networking. *Wired* wrote a story with the name – discovered through an Apple trademark filing on 2 October – but guessed wrongly that it would have wireless connectivity.[4]

A few years earlier, the old Apple might have let some details leak out. But Jobs had spread his insistence that 'loose lips sink ships' throughout the company; people knew that to leak details of forthcoming products invited dismissal. For a consumer product company, secrecy mattered more than ever, Jobs said: the magician's 'reveal' would have more impact than carefully trailed explanations of what you were going to do months before. Microsoft, by contrast, had to keep its corporate customers aware of what it would be offering months ahead: the customers needed this to plan.

The iPod's collaborative design included Jobs's fingerprints all over it, such as an insistence that it take only three clicks to reach any song. Given that Apple's entire future rested on getting this product right, he pushed and pushed his engineers to make it better and better. Mike Evangelist, who worked at Apple on the DVD-burning software iDVD, recalls being in the room the day before the launch and hearing Jobs complaining that he didn't like the way the headphones clicked when he plugged them into the socket on a prototype model. 'These headphone jacks all have to be replaced by tomorrow,' Jobs told an engineer. 'Find a way to fix it.' (The engineer solved the problem, Evangelist guessed, by individually polishing every one of the headphone plugs in the samples that would be provided to the press to get the right feel.) Jobs then returned to sweating over the tiny details of the presentation he would give 24 hours later, such as how to prevent the white body of the iPod from fooling the exposure meter on the camera, which would focus on the iPod's darker screen. The rehearsals went on all day, and again for a final rehearsal on the day of the event – a typical rehearsal schedule, as all his presentations were minutely choreographed and practised.

On the day of 23 October, as the intrigued journalists watched from a few feet away, Jobs prowled the stage at the front of the small room.[5] He began by looking at the four areas of the 'digital hub' concept (photos, film, DVDs and then music), saying that Apple had looked at all four in deciding what device to build. 'The field that we decided to do it in, the choice we made, was music,' he said. 'Now, why music? Well, we love music, and it's always good to do something you love.'

More importantly, he explained, the burgeoning digital music business had no market leader: 'There are small companies like Creative and Sonic Blue, and then there's some large companies like Sony that haven't had a hit yet. They haven't found the recipe. No one has really found the recipe yet for digital music.' Apple, he said, had: 'We think the Apple brand is going to be fantastic, because people trust the Apple brand to get their great digital electronics from.'

It was at the time an entirely unsupported statement. Apple was a tiny player in the field, hauling itself out of the intensive care unit; but Jobs said it as though it had been accepted wisdom for years.

The logic of the iPod was explained in a slide comparing a $75 portable CD player (cost $75, able to hold one 10- to 15-song CD: 'That's about $5 a song'), a flash-based player ($150, 10–15 songs: about $10 per song), an MP3-capable CD player ($150, 150 songs, $1 per song) and, finally, a hard-drive-based 'jukebox' ($300, 1,000 songs, 30 cents per song).

'So we studied all these and that's where we want to be,' he said, pointing to the jukebox part of the table. 'And we're introducing a product today that takes us exactly there. And that product is called iPod.'

As with all Apple products, he didn't give it a definite article. You'll never hear an Apple employee – or at least a well-grooved one – talk about 'the' iMac or 'the' iPad. The products aren't named like objects – the door, the window – but like children: Bob, Steve, iPod, iMac.

Jobs paused. 'iMac, iBook, iPod', he said, Some of the journalists guffawed. iPod? What sort of name was that?

'The biggest thing about iPod is it holds a thousand songs. Now this is a quantum leap because for most people it's their entire music library,' Jobs said. 'This is huge.'

He went on to emphasize its 'ultraportable' nature, how FireWire would fill that up in less than 10 minutes (compared to five hours via USB 1.1), and battery life. In passing he mentioned that you could use it to store data, a nod to the arguments that had raged inside the company as to whether a music player alone stood any chance of success. Rather like Toshiba's Hase, some of the team felt sure that people would rather use the disk as a portable data storage device. The price: $399 (or 40c per song). iTunes also got an update: it would recognize when an iPod was connected, and synchronize songs, calendars and contacts automatically.

The iPod's smooth finish and neat design suddenly made other players such as the Archos 6GB player or Creative Labs Nomad look bulky and amateurish. The software – then Mac-only – was slick, and the auto-updating smooth. Yet, if Jobs had been expecting a rapturous reception from the technical press for the iPod's design, he may have been disappointed. Hard-core technologists weren't positive. The response by CmdrTaco – real name Rob Malda – head of the 'news for nerds' site Slashdot, then one of the most influential technology discussion sites, was typical: 'No wireless. Less space than a Nomad. Lame.'[6] Yet Slashdot denizens liked the idea of an ultraportable hard drive that could boot a Mac. Some began seeing iPods as a futuristic personal computer that would store your personal data in your pocket and plug in to any computer you liked and work with it – as long as the computer was a Mac, of course, though some geeks were considering whether they could reformat the disk to a Windows version. Other commentators, more prosaically, pointed out that the potential user base – FireWire installed, iTunes – already included millions of potential buyers. All Apple had to do was persuade them to hand over their money.

Analyst reaction was mixed:[7] Bryan Ma of IDC thought that in time, if successful, it could have the desired effect of getting more people to buy Macs. And, he added, its lack of space compared to a Nomad wasn't lame: 'They've totally polished the product. If I were an engineer at Creative Labs, I'd be scrambling.' Tim Deal of Technology Business Research saw that Apple was chasing Sony, but remarked that the iPod looked too expensive: 'Apple lacks the richness of Sony's product offering. And introducing new consumer products right now' – the world was still reeling from the 11 September attacks on New York and Washington – 'is risky, especially if they cannot be priced attractively.'

Meanwhile Paul Griffin could scent a new opportunity. Griffin Technology, his own business, which made connectors for Apple devices, had survived Apple's darkest days and been thriving since the launch of the first iMac (because people had to buy new mice, or buy connectors to hook up old ones). He thought music players offered a big opportunity, if he could think of stuff his company could build to go with the iPod:

> I knew that was the next big thing, because I had been using or trying to use MP3s and playing them, and there weren't a lot of good options. I had a Diamond Rio, and if you had one you know what the problems were: the storage was tiny, about 10 songs, and it took ages to transfer them – 10 songs in 30 minutes. I mean, the serial communication was bizarrely slow. And then Apple was positioned so perfectly: they had FireWire, which seemed almost silly to have at the time [because it was faster than seemed necessary], but that gave them the fast transfer of music onto the iPod. The day that came out, I knew it was going to be a success. There was no market there, and we were making product for something

that there was no market at all for, but you knew it was going to work – because if you'd ever played with a Rio, you knew [MP3 music] was going to be the technology. The iPod was clearly going to be a winner when it came out.[8]

It wasn't an obvious winner at first. In its quarterly results in January 2002, Apple didn't even break out iPods as separate items, nor say how many were sold.[9] (That was only revealed in the comparative figures a year later: roughly 125,000.) Apple didn't begin breaking out specific numbers for iPods sold in its results until after the summer quarter of 2003: on its face, a classic example of not attracting embarrassing questions about comparatively low sales. But there was method too: iPod sales were growing so quickly that Apple, like Google, was doing its best not to 'moon the giant' – that is, attract Microsoft's attention by touting how well it was doing in the potentially big market it was in. Among sharks, swim quietly.

Meanwhile, in Redmond: Microsoft

Microsoft was already acutely aware of the importance of reaching consumers with its new products. Showing the journalist Jay Greene around Microsoft's campus in January 2002, Robbie Bach, then in charge of the Xbox group, remarked: 'The technology revolution has changed the way people do business. The next five to ten years will be the digital entertainment revolution.'

It seemed futuristic. Digital downloads were a rounding error on any music company's business, where CD sales annually generated about $15 billion (though, worryingly for the record labels, the value of year-on-year sales had fallen off in 2000, for the first time ever). Besides cinemas and TV, the only effective way of watching a film was via VHS videotapes and DVDs; barely anyone had broadband at home.

Microsoft's staff were running a 'skunkworks' – a laboratory of unofficial experimental projects – in the then brand new Building

50 where the new eHome division had 200 engineers trying to turn Microsoft into, as Greene put it, 'the Sony of the 21st century'.

J Allard, whose 1994 memo had sold Bill Gates on the idea of the internet, was now lead technologist on the Xbox. He explained: 'This is the way to build a whole new Microsoft.' Bach and Allard's shared vision was of the 'digital home', a place where everything knitted together, via Microsoft software: the TV talking to the games console talking to the computer talking to everything else digital around the home. It was like Jobs's 'digital hub' idea, but on a much larger scale; and the Xbox, more than the PC, was the focus of the vision.

Greene observed that Microsoft 'has been missing the consumer gene for years', pointing to its stalled interactive TV efforts with WebTV (stuck at a million subscribers despite millions of dollars poured into its development and years of marketing effort) and its abandonment of voice-over-internet phones in 1999, just a year after launching them. In the consumer field, observed Minoru Arakawa, then the just-retired president of Nintendo America, 'Microsoft is spending a lot of money, but they are beginners.'

The roots of Microsoft's desire to reach consumers went much further back, though. In March 1999 Microsoft held one of its regular retreats; there Gates, Ballmer and Bach had talked about the idea of reaching consumers through devices based on PC technologies. The logic is simple enough: there are more consumers than businesses, and you can sell multiple devices to a single consumer. Therefore the consumer market is potentially far, far bigger than the business market. Nail that and make it profitable, and your future is assured. So Microsoft's engineers laboured away in Building 50, trying to ensure Microsoft's future via the digital home. The Xbox was part of that; though it ran counter to Microsoft's usual strategy – build a software platform, not hardware – Allard had prevailed in persuading Gates and Ballmer that they should pursue it. To succeed, he had had to persuade them first that the 'horizontal' model (Microsoft writes the software, other people build the hardware) wouldn't work in games consoles, which are sold at a loss, which is then recouped from publishers' fees on games.

The horizontal model could never unseat console incumbents. Then Gates and Ballmer suggested that buying Nintendo would be simpler. Allard prevailed again; the Xbox project had been born. So far it had cost billions without showing any prospect of profit. But games consoles were always loss-leaders on hardware; the profit was in the software.

Even though the iPod was only months old, by 2002 Griffin Technology had begun showing off add-on products. Griffin tasked his team with looking at the product and thinking of what had been left off it. 'We were thinking about "What would I want to do? I've got this new music player and I want to be able to... play it in my car." So that was our first thought: do an FM transmitter.' The transmitter took the output from the headphone socket and piped it through a mini-FM transmitter powered from the cigarette lighter socket; the signal could then be picked up by the in-car radio. Griffin is proud of the invention, which they called iTrip: 'Nobody had ever done that before with a personal device like that, so that was a novel idea. I was proud of that, and I was proud of the design. I was proud of *everything* we did on that. I think we named it the night before the [Macworld] show. It was great.' He shrugs. 'You do what you have to do, you hustle and you do the best you can, so we designed that product just in time for that show, shipped it a few months later and it was a big success.'

iPods and Windows

But the iPod couldn't really be a hit if it was limited to the Mac platform. What Apple needed was a way to get iPods to work with Windows. However, porting iTunes to Windows would be tricky, and wouldn't bring people to the Mac platform – which was the idea of building it in the first place. What Apple needed was some sort of intermediary.

MusicMatch opened its doors – if that's the right phrase for an online company – in 1997. Bob Ohlweiler joined it in 1999, with the dot-com bubble under way, when venture capital funding was plentiful. MusicMatch on Windows let people 'rip' the music from their CDs on to their computer, and transfer it on to the new MP3 players that had started to appear. Its MP3 encoder was allied to a music library management system, and functioned better than many of the hobbyist-style MP3 encoder/library systems that had begun to appear for Windows.

But in March 2000 the bubble burst. MusicMatch survived by marshalling its resources very carefully. 'Everyone had thought that as long as you had eyeballs [coming to your site] that was everything', Ohlweiler says.[10] MusicMatch's chief executive, Dennis Mudd, knew differently: cash in the bank spoke more loudly. People would still pay for good software for CD ripping on Windows. They husbanded their cash and hunkered down.

The iPod's launch intrigued the team, who were soon talking to Apple about tweaking the MusicMatch software so millions of Windows users – a huge, untapped market for the iPod – could use it with their machines.

Apple resisted at first: the iPod was meant to sell more Macs. But internally executives were already debating: why give it over to Windows? Would people buy an iPod if they didn't have a Mac? Would they buy a Mac eventually if first they used an iPod on Windows? Jobs resisted: Windows users would get it 'over my dead body'. Fadell insisted that 'this needs to get to the PC'. In the end, the prospect of expanding the iPod market 20-fold was too persuasive. There was a recession on. Anything that got more people buying Apple products was good.

In July 2002, Apple introduced its second-generation iPod, with up to 20GB of storage – and also 'iPod for Windows', using MusicMatch's software to connect to Windows PCs. Ohlweiler knew though that the relationship with Apple was on borrowed time: 'We could see that if it took off then they would write iTunes for Windows and steamroller us,' The concern was that an iTunes for Windows might hurt MusicMatch's ability to sell software upgrades before it could turn users on to music subscriptions and sales. He had a number of meetings at Apple, where the details of forthcoming products would be discussed, generally at the engineer or manager level.

Ohlweiler could see a clash coming between Apple's ambitions and those of the Windows-based MP3 players, and computer manufacturers like Dell, which saw this as a market that could bolster its otherwise lacklustre consumer business. What the PC makers needed was some software that would save them the expense of having to devise their own on the computer – because writing software that could work with Windows Media Player would be reinventing the wheel if Microsoft was already doing it.

Microsoft, it turned out, was already doing it. All the PC companies would need then was to offer a physical player. The horizontal model was ready to be reapplied to the MP3 player market. Clearly Apple and the third-party software companies like MusicMatch faced a death sentence: Microsoft and the PC makers were about to come in and take it over, using the same economies of scale to crush the opposition.

The record companies were keen for this too, especially if Microsoft could write software that would protect their property – the songs being ripped off CDs. Although they had crushed the file-sharing incarnation of Napster in the courts, a more dangerous form of file sharing had replaced it, using true peer-to-peer systems such as LimeWire and Grokster, which simply didn't have a central company running them. In future the record labels would have to go after individual users pirating their material – not a situation they relished, though they felt that making an example of a few people would quickly solve the problem, and leave the market wide open for legal download services where they could control the pricing.

Microsoft was listening to the record companies' calls. Its strategy was to rip songs into its Windows Media Audio (WMA) format, which independent tests said sounded better than MP3, even while creating smaller files. Files ripped on PCs using Windows Media Player, the default system, would be transferred with digital rights management (DRM) – a sort of digital padlock – on to music players, preventing the songs being copied on to another PC, and tying the player to its owner's computer. WMA files protected in that way and uploaded to file-sharing networks wouldn't work on the PCs of anyone else who downloaded them.

It was a brilliant strategy – except for two things. First, on Windows, CD ripping was still a minority sport limited to people who understood how to do it and what its purpose was; that made them specialists wise to Microsoft's machinations, especially over DRM. (The high profile of Microsoft's conviction in the antitrust case had eroded user trust that the company was really acting in users' best interests, rather than its partners'.) So they instead used other programs – such as MusicMatch – that could play WMA files but could also rip songs into MP3 format.

The second problem was that Microsoft 'overcooked' the software, says Ohlweiler: 'It was just too hefty for the hardware. It didn't quite work right. There would be glitches, and the drivers didn't quite work right. And the transfer was really slow.' That was because they relied on USB 1.1 connections; the faster USB 2.0 standard – comparable in speed to FireWire – wouldn't arrive in volume until late 2003, and take some time to become widespread in consumer electronics devices, particularly digital music players.

There was another problem: industrial design. Ohlweiler recalls seeing the prototype for the third-generation iPod during a discussion with Apple executives. The MusicMatch team learnt about Jobs's habit: the Apple engineers explained that he would drift in, say the product was rubbish and walk out. 'Or he would say "This is far too big. It's too bulky." Then he'd walk out.' (The picture that emerges is of Jobs prowling the corridors of Apple, moving between meetings in which he offered minimal but essential advice and then moved on.) The relentless focus inside Apple on product quality and user experience – and the constant goading of engineers to do better – couldn't be clearer.

A month or so later Ohlweiler was at the headquarters of Dell Computer in Austin, Texas. Dell was eager to get into this burgeoning market, reasoning that it could use Microsoft's software, design its own hardware (as it did with PCs) and use its buying heft to drive down costs to undercut Apple. Dell's revenues at the time were six times larger than Apple's. It was going to be easy. The market was there for the taking.

Or perhaps not. Ohlweiler recalls being handed a prototype for the Dell DJ player, which like the iPod used a 1.8-inch hard drive. 'This thing is *huge!*' he thought. His spoken words were more moderate: 'I'm a bit surprised by the size', he remarked. 'Does it have to be so large?'

It was noticeably deeper than Apple's existing iPod, and substantially more so than the forthcoming iPod. The MusicMatch team had of course been sworn to secrecy about the forthcoming iPod design, on pain of extremely costly legal action, and probably of being dumped. (Apple had been known to drop suppliers who leaked details about Apple designs even a day ahead of the official release.) Dell had done its part of the horizontal model: it had driven down costs by dual-sourcing components from Hitachi and Toshiba. The result, though, was a bulkier machine: 'One of the Dell designers explained that that was because the Toshiba version of the hard drive had its connector on the side, and the Hitachi one had it on the bottom, but because they were dual-sourcing they could get the price down by 40 cents,' Ohlweiler recalls. 'That was the difference in a nutshell. Apple was all about the industrial design and getting it to work. Dell was driven by procurement.'

Music, stored

In April 2003, Apple introduced its third-generation iPod, supplanting the one that Dell's engineers had been comparing their design with. This one was notable for a particular feature: a proprietary 30-pin dock connector on the bottom of the device. That allowed it to connect to a FireWire or USB 2.0 port via a cable. Buyers had to specify which cable they wanted.

That dock connector turned out to be the start of a billion-dollar industry that Apple could control and profit from, though at the time it just looked like a convenience to let people choose between connection cables. In fact the purpose was much more carefully planned: it would be the gateway to the iPod. And Apple would extract a toll from anyone who wanted to get anything in or out.

The far bigger announcement in terms of its wider impact – on the record business, Apple, Microsoft, and how everyone would in future think about music – was the iTunes Music Store. This was Jobs's dream for the iPod made real: frictionless buying via the internet. He had enunciated it publicly as long ago as 1995, while still working at Pixar and NeXT, and told Gary Wolf of *Wired* that in the future the internet would be the way to sell things, or not-things: 'stuff' that had only a digital existence. 'People are going to stop going to a lot of [physical] stores. And they're going to buy stuff over the web!' he said, later adding: 'The best way to think of the web is as a direct-to-customer distribution channel, whether it's for information or commerce. It bypasses all middlemen.' The elimination of middlemen, he added, would be 'profound'. He loved the web's ability to democratize between the very large and small: 'It's a very profound thing, and a very good thing.'[11]

While the record companies had been fretting in 2002 about Grokster and LimeWire, Jobs had been persuading them to go with his plan of selling music directly via downloads from Apple.

The labels initially weren't convinced. In January 2002 they had launched their own music subscription services, called PressPlay and MusicNet. Together they had the copyrights (and so sales and licensing permission) for 80 per cent of recorded music. PressPlay was a joint venture between Sony and Universal/Vivendi; MusicNet had the backing of EMI, BMG, Time Warner and Real Networks. Some record labels, notably Sony, also introduced DRM on music CDs, which made ripping their content impossible.

PressPlay and MusicNet were nightmarish to use. PressPlay required a $15 per month subscription – equivalent to buying one or two CDs every month – to get low-quality music streaming, at a time when only half the US population was online, and four-fifths of those were using dial-up, not broadband connections. MusicNet demanded a $10 per month payment for streaming and downloads. Not every PressPlay song could be downloaded; not every download could be burnt to a CD; you couldn't burn more than two tracks from a single artist each month. On MusicNet, you could play downloaded songs only on the PC that bought them; and you couldn't burn to a CD. They used different DRM: MusicNet's came from Real Networks, headed by Rob Glazer, an ex-Microsoft employee who had struck out on his own. PressPlay used Microsoft DRM.

Reviewers hated them. The services clearly weren't a good deal – for the price, you were left with nothing better than you would get from listening to the radio – and infinitely worse than simply going on to one of the file-sharing networks and illicitly downloading whatever you wanted for free.

Yet analysts were optimistic. Jupiter Research reckoned that, by 2006, the US music industry could see $5.5 billion in online sales, equivalent to about 30 per cent of the entire recorded music market. At the time, it was impossible to see how they could get to there from here.

In his negotiations with the record labels, Jobs set expectations low. 'Apple's target, believe it or not, was to sell one million songs in the first year. That was the expectation Apple set with record company executives. Can you believe it?' Cringely told me. Even then it was a very modest target, representing only seven songs per iPod sold per year (and even less per copy of iTunes in use). But Jobs had been negotiating since before the iPod, when iTunes was the entire musical part of the digital hub, with millions of copies already installed. You didn't need an iPod to use the iTunes Music Store.

Jobs lowballed the record companies, playing on Apple's minnow status – suggesting that, even if things went terribly wrong and the Store turned out to be a gateway to piracy, 'only 5 per cent of computers will be affected'.

The crucial contract was with Universal, the big beast of the record labels. Jobs talked to Doug Morris, its chief executive, who talked to Jimmy Iovine, head of the Universal label Interscope. Iovine could see the threats to the business, but also believed in its online potential. Iovine met Jobs and the pair clicked. Iovine persuaded Morris, who signed. Then things began rolling.

The labels acquiesced – but demanded that Apple also put in DRM. Ohlweiler adds his own context to the labels' drive to get

DRM installed everywhere: 'In the record business, everyone feels that they got screwed in their last deal. So in the next deal they're always looking to get to where they thought the last one should have ended. The record labels and the publishers don't see eye to eye. It's a recipe for disagreement, and you need both ingredients.' It's also a recipe for stalemate. The DRM was partly there to prevent file sharing, but also to prevent music being transmitted and distributed in regions where licensing wasn't in place for its sale or reproduction. The movie studios had done this to great effect with DVDs' 'regional coding', which prevented DVDs pressed in the United States from playing in Europe. Record labels looked on that foresight with envy.

File-sharing networks of course didn't know or care about national borders or regional licensing. Still, some progress had been made from the CD's global format: 'Sony had had success in Japan with the MiniDisc format, which prevented you from copying songs back and forth,' said Ohlweiler. 'Together with Sony Music, they seemed to have the formula. And Sony Electronics was huge in those days.' So the labels pressed for similar copy-prevention technology to be included in music players and ripping software.

Apple agreed – but crucially didn't go with Microsoft's widely available (and freely licensed) Windows Media product. Instead Jobs got his engineers to implement an entirely new system, which they called FairPlay: it tied each iPod to a particular Mac, so songs on each couldn't be transferred to another Mac (though third-party software quickly appeared to implement it), and which allowed purchased (and so DRM-protected) songs to be played only on three 'authorized' computers; the authorization was done simply by the user giving the username and password used to buy the song on the iTunes Music Store. Crucially, the songs could also be burnt on to a CD – effectively tearing off the DRM wrapper and allowing people to create MP3s of the songs and so, if they wanted, to upload them to file-sharing networks. (One study suggested that this happened within minutes of new songs appearing on the Music Store.) Microsoft's software didn't allow that. The technology that had blindsided Jobs and his team – CD burning – turned out to be a benefit, because for those who disliked DRM, which was pretty much everyone, the answer was simple: turn it into a CD and then re-encode it.

Ohlweiler points out that the 'Heavy DRM' approach Microsoft used also meant the retailer had to manage the DRM protection for each piece of content – for ever. 'At 99 cents a song, there's only about 10 cents of margin left, after costs. Imagine needing to provide a lifetime of technical support for 10 cents. Apple's "authorized computer" model is much simpler,' he explains. 'It was only when the industry finally went to MP3s and no DRM that the business finally became feasible for the long term for digital retailers.'

The Music Store also took another diversion from Microsoft's model. The record labels wouldn't countenance the use of MP3 (which couldn't be protected). Apple – more particularly Jobs – wouldn't countenance the use of Microsoft's WMA format. Even though the chipset inside the iPod could in theory decode WMA files, the functionality was never enabled. Instead iTunes on the Mac compressed songs in MP3 format or Advanced Audio Codec (AAC).

AAC was a strange beast in the PC audio jungle. At the time of the iPod launch, it was the only player to use AAC; literally everyone else was using WMA (which the iPod didn't play) and MP3 (which it did).

After all the machinations, negotiations and hassles, the iTunes Music Store opened on 29 April 2003 to sell music online – but only to Apple computers. Its success astounded the record labels: the 1 million target for purchases and (legally) free downloads was hit within the first week, making Apple at once the biggest legally sanctioned music download site in the United States and the world. Within a month, 3 million songs had been downloaded.

Celebrity marketing

One thing made music significantly different to Steve Jobs than any other element of human enterprise: he looked up to the people who did it. Bob Dylan was a hero. Joan Baez had once been a girlfriend. He delighted in the music of The Beatles and Johnny Cash. Music had that amazing cachet: the people who did it were celebrities. His repeated insistence about loving music wasn't faked; his heart probably wouldn't have been in cameras or video if somehow the analysis by Rubinstein's team in 2001 had pointed towards those as the best way to exploit Toshiba's tiny new hard drive.

But if musicians were celebrities whom Jobs admired, perhaps they could get some of their glitter to rub off on the device. It turned out to be the winning strategy at precisely the time Apple needed it.

First, though, Apple needed the iPod to get a dose of visibility. The issue was becoming urgent. In 2002, Apple's computer sales had begun slipping; in the first three months of 2003, they began heading towards the near-death levels last seen in 1998, while the 78,000 iPods sold had hardly set the world on fire (despite being a 37 per cent improvement on the same quarter of the previous year).

And then something remarkable – and remarkably fortuitous – happened. In May 2003, Oprah Winfrey, then one of the biggest names on US TV, introduced one of her seasonal 'Favorite Things' shows, in which she would shower her studio audience with gifts that she said she personally liked.[12] With its audience of millions, presented by one of the United States' most-loved icons, having a product on the show was a shortcut to enormous popularity. If Oprah liked it, then *of course* you would too.

In May 2003, not long after that disastrous quarter, amidst a list that included a Hewlett-Packard digital camera-printer-dock combination, Roomba automated floor vacuum, Le Mystere Tisha Bra, and Weber Q Grill and Cart, there was the 15GB iPod.

An Apple set-up? Officially there was no way to get on to the list of Oprah's 'Favorite Things' except by being one of her, well, favourite things (although the companies featured had to pay for the items that were given to the studio audience – a tolerable marketing cost). Apple sources from the period denied to me that the company ever paid for placement on TV or in movies.

In that April–June period, Apple sold 304,000 iPods – a quintupling of sales compared to the same quarter of the previous year. That wasn't bad – but they were still less than 10 per cent of revenues, which were running at $1.5 billion per quarter. For a company that made almost all its money selling computers, the iPod still looked like a sideline. It needed something more. Jobs had diverted $75 million from advertising Apple's Macintosh computers to the iPod – even though, as he acknowledged later, its sales didn't yet justify it.

Marketers know that if you want to get noticed, you should get someone noticeable to use your product. So the company took a leaf from Sony's book in marketing the iPod, explains Don Norman, who worked there before Jobs's return.

Norman is famous as a usability expert who has examined how we interact with all sorts of objects, and takes a particular interest in our how emotional response dictates our choice, purchase and use of products and services: any choice we make is determined partly by rational reflection, but also by an emotional element that we may not be aware of – and yet that can be teased out by querying our reactions.

'When Sony brought out the Walkman, the marketing campaign they did, that's a classic – it's studied in business schools,' Norman says.

Instead of doing the normal technology release, they gave out Walkmans to movie stars, people in the pop business, actors, musicians, a lot of non-technical people that the public really respected. And those people really loved it, and [Sony] showed lots of photos of them saying 'Wow, this has changed my life, I can have it with me at all times', and so on.

He pauses. 'It's what Apple did too.'[13]

Apple did indeed have a concentrated programme to get celebrities using the iPod. It was cheap (important for a company then operating on a tiny marketing budget compared to rivals), but could have a huge impact. Apple's marketing team began using their contacts to connect to more widely known names. More and more celebrities began appearing in photos with white headphone leads attached to their ears. You didn't even need to see the device; the unique white headphones told you they were using an iPod. Apple had caught a wave: in the United States and the UK, celebrities were news, creating globe-spanning stories, while magazines that hung on their every prearranged outing and pre-publication-agreed photos and remarks were blossoming. Celebrities using iPods were grist to the news mill. David and Victoria Beckham (known in the UK by their tabloid moniker, Posh 'n' Becks) were pictured clutching them. 'Beckham was a key one. That went around the world,' one Apple employee from the time remembers. Musicians such as Craig David, Fatboy Slim, Robbie Williams and P Diddy also had them. It seemed that everyone famous was using an iPod.

Well, not quite everyone. In August 2003 the *Sun*, Britain's best-selling daily tabloid, ran a taunting headline, 'iCan't believe Geri hasn't got an iPod'. In its favoured combination of lower and upper case, the Showbiz column asked rhetorically: 'IS GERI HALLIWELL the only celebrity NOT to have caught on to the iPod craze yet?' It added: 'My picture shows the former Spice Girl preparing to jet off from Heathrow to the South of France with her CD Walkman.'[14]

Her CD Walkman? Oh, the irony.

The iPod began to be noticed. Commentators, meanwhile, awaited the charge of the Dell DJ and other players. It didn't seem to be coming. In July the Oprah 'Favorite Things' show was repeated, after which some viewers commented that Oprah didn't appear familiar with the device: she 'seemed to be totally clueless about how it worked', said one commenter on a discussion board.

She didn't know how to start it playing. When her tech guy pointed to the button and she got it started, she danced for a few seconds, then turned to him and asked in an incredulous voice 'That music is coming out of this?' She didn't know how to get music into it. She really didn't seem to know anything about it, which I found disappointing.

(In 2005 Winfrey also featured an iPod – this time with video – among her 'Favorite Things'.)

In that July–September quarter, Apple sold 336,000 iPods, more than double from the year before. In September, Apple upgraded the iPod again, expanding its storage. Later that month I met Jobs in Paris, where he was typically bullish about the achievements of the iTunes Music Store. 'It isn't easy to do the Store, you know. It looks easy – but isn't,' he said.

We have to write software for the users' machines, because a web browser isn't enough. And it has to be able to do a lot of transactions. We already have an online store [selling Apple computers] that does between $1 billion and $2 billion annually. We also need to be able to pump a lot of bits over the net. And we have iPod, which is the number one player in terms of both volume and value sales. We are the only company that does all this. No other company does the player and [software] jukebox. Does it? We are the only company that has all this under one roof. The others are trying, and finding it's harder than they thought.

The iTunes Music Store's simple front end hid a complex back end. Apple's experience in running an online store meant it knew about handling demand. Selling songs meant validating credit cards, running transactions securely and then transmitting sizeable volumes of data. Once sold, songs had to be encoded so that only iTunes could unwrap the DRM around them. And it had to happen seamlessly and easily.

Apple was offering a cloud service. It just didn't call it that. But it was gaining expertise at exactly the sort of cloud computing that Google and Microsoft (and, separately, Amazon) were also getting good at. There was one other thing: it was acquiring hundreds of thousands, and soon millions, of credit card numbers, building a customer relationship song by song.

iTunes on Windows

Just over a month later, on 27 October 2003, the Dell DJ was launched. Dell made much of the idea that it would offer an online music store; but even though it had one of the biggest web stores (for its computers) observers were sceptical, given its non-existent track record writing consumer software. All of the Windows-based online music stores were a pain to use. A key problem was being sure your player would be able to play any DRM-encoded music: users could find themselves caught in the 'dance of drivers', being told that their player didn't have the right version of software to play or transfer a song.

And the Dell DJ was late to the game. Eleven days earlier, Jobs had stood on a stage and said there was 'one more feature' being added to iTunes. 'A lot of people thought we would never add until this happened,' he said, and put up a slide saying 'Hell froze over'. 'So, I'm here to report to you today that this has happened', he said, gesturing at the slide. 'Today we are announcing that the second-generation iTunes doesn't just run on the Mac; it runs on Windows as well... this is not some baby version. It's the whole thing.' Jobs dismissed MusicMatch, accusing it of crippling encoding and restricting burning because it wanted to get users to buy a $20 upgrade. 'This is the game that's being played, and we're not playing it,' said Jobs. 'It's all built in; it's all free.' However, as Ohlweihler points out, Apple carried on for some years giving its basic QuickTime video viewing system away, and charging an upgrade fee for premium features – just like MusicMatch.

Apple could do this because it owned the entire system. It could decide where it wanted to make money: hardware, software or songs. Rivals that didn't make hardware, or didn't make software, or didn't sell the songs, had to rely on someone else helping them out.

What Jobs didn't reveal was that he had been opposed to the idea of iTunes for Windows; it spoilt his idea of the Mac as a class of computer above and separate from Windows. But Schiller and Rubinstein had pressured Jobs continually: it didn't make sense to insist that a $300 device could only work with a specific make of $1,500 computer which made up – at best – 5 per cent of those in use. The upside was far too great. As recounted in 'Design Crazy', by Max Chafkin, which interviewed Rubinstein and others, a key meeting on the topic ended when Jobs eventually told them 'do whatever you want. You're responsible,' and walked out of the conference room.

Within three days, a million copies of iTunes for Windows had been downloaded. It was just as the team at MusicMatch had feared. They warned their users not to allow iTunes to take over the control of their iPod on Windows, because it would be a one-way step. Unfortunately, MusicMatch couldn't offer US users anything comparable to the iTunes Music Store, which was gaining traction.

Jobs forecast then that the iTunes Music Store for Windows would expand the market so much that by the store's first anniversary, in April, it would have sold 100 million songs. There was a promotion with Pepsi: people would get free downloads via bottles and cans.

By October Apple had 70 per cent of the market for digital music players. By the end of the year it had sold more than 25 million songs, up from 10 million at the end of September. Jobs's quote to *Fortune* magazine ahead of the launch – 'This will go down in history as a turning point for the music industry... This is landmark stuff. I can't overestimate it'[15] – began to look prescient rather than pompous. It seemed that the music industry might be saved not by the might of Microsoft but by a little company with a minuscule share of the computer market and, until two years previously, an insignificant presence in the consumer electronics industry.

It was time for Microsoft to go on the attack, and Dave Fester, general manager of its Digital Media division, duly did so.[16] At the end of October 2003 the company website added a staged questions-and-answers session with him. He was asked: would a Windows-based iTunes affect the now-legal Napster or other Windows-based services?

Fester's reply: 'iTunes captured some early media interest with their store on the Mac, but I think the Windows platform will be a significant challenge for them. Unless Apple decides to make radical changes to their service model, a Windows-based version of iTunes will still remain a closed system, where iPod owners cannot access content from other services.'

Why would this be a problem for iPod owners? Because, he explained, 'Windows users... expect choice in music services, choice in devices, and choice in music from a wide variety of music services to burn to a CD or put on a portable device.' His argument: if you bought music on iTunes, you wouldn't be able to play it on any of the 40 other digital music players out there that used Windows DRM.

Except, of course, that you could, by burning the music to a CD and then ripping it back. But Fester was portraying the market as one where people carefully pick and choose the optimum element at each step of the value chain – computer, operating system, music library software, player – rather as audiophiles pick hi-fi components. But most people accept the package – they buy an integrated hi-fi system because it's simpler; they buy a player and use the software that comes with it; they buy a computer and accept the operating system it comes with. Microsoft used the faux interview with Fester to try to frame the situation in terms of breadth of 'choice' and 'services', the same ones as had driven the PC market. Except it wasn't, and never had been.

Still, in financial terms, 25 million downloads amounted to around $25 million: for Microsoft, not much more than a rounding error on its balance sheet, a few big corporate or government contracts. The download business was young. Microsoft could afford to let the horizontal model take over.

But it had its little bit of revenge. The version of Windows Media Player released for the Mac in 2003 couldn't play the songs encoded with version 9 of Microsoft's WMA DRM. And it didn't release another until 2006. The few per cent of Mac users in the market were locked out of Napster and other services using WMA DRM.

As Fester's question-and-answer session was being prepared, the aggressive head of Hewlett-Packard, Carly Fiorina, was considering the results of focus group testing of the company's own music player design. HP was a corporate behemoth, the world's biggest maker of PCs, inventor of the laser printer, the original 'company in a garage'. But the player wasn't a hit with the focus groups; they preferred the iPod. So Fiorina contacted Jobs. A deal was struck: HP would announce at the Consumer Electronics Show in January 2004 that it would resell the iPod, under its own badging. When the announcement was made, some commentators expected that HP's iPods would – unlike Apple's – support WMA and Windows DRM, because of HP's close links with Microsoft. When HP's iPod appeared in mid-2004, it was just the iPod, with blue styling.

Fester wasn't impressed: 'Windows is about choice. You can mix and match all of this [encoding software and music player] stuff,' he said after HP's announcement. 'We believe you should have the same choice when it comes to music services.' This was the same Fester who in April 2001 defended Microsoft's decision to make WMA, not MP3, the default encoding in Windows XP: 'We think, at the end of the day, consumers don't really care what format they [record] in.' Now that people's lack of interest meant they were using Apple's format, he seemed more concerned.

Something deeper was happening too. After the launch of iTunes for Windows, I met more and more businesspeople running competitions offering iPods as prizes – and who told me it was remarkably effective at attracting interest. The devices combination of portability, style and ease of use was irresistible. The iTunes Music Store fascinated people because it offered the idea of the internet as jukebox; the music business was starting to see it as another potential saviour, just like ringtones on mobile phones (then a promising business).

People running news websites dependent on getting hits from readers (so they could serve them advertisements) noticed that, if you wrote a story with 'Apple' or 'iPod' in the headline, it attracted huge numbers of viewers. It couldn't just be hard-core Apple diehards. Something was going on: the iPod was gaining cachet and that essential element – cool. In December 2003 the *Observer* newspaper in the UK commented that: 'The iPod may be just a hard-disk storage device, but it has become a cult consumer gift that has achieved a unique festive status over the past few days: it is the fastest-selling item being snapped up by internet shoppers.'[17] Some stores couldn't fulfil Christmas orders. The iPod had gone from 'what?' to hot.

On 2 January 2004, the *Guardian* newspaper's G2 feature section devoted its front page and main feature to an examination of the iPod's appeal, calling it 'the coolest thing to come out of California since the Beach Boys'. The article quoted a woman called Hannah who went to a meal as one of six; three had iPods. 'I was sitting opposite someone who had a [Sony] MiniDisc – I felt really sorry for them,' she said. If anyone in the music industry had hoped that the MiniDisc, with its ferocious DRM system, would be its saviour, quotes like that should have disabused them. The iPod was cool. The MiniDisc was not. It was a choice of Coke or Pepsi, between neckties, and the iPod was preferable to wear. For the first time since Microsoft had utterly eclipsed it in August 1995 with the global launch of Windows 95, Apple was getting noticed for its products rather than its problems.

iPod mini

Having signed Fiorina, Jobs caught her unawares. Two days before she announced the iPod reselling deal at the Consumer Electronics Show, he unveiled a completely new form of iPod – the iPod mini.[18] It had a 4GB hard drive, less than the original iPod, but was much smaller, and lighter, than anything on sale. And it used that 30-pin dock, because it was too thin for a standard USB or FireWire connector. Jobs cited the statistic that Apple now had 70 per cent of the music player market in the United States: 'It feels good to be above that 5 per cent share, doesn't it?' Jobs joked with the adoring audience at Macworld.

On sale from February 2004, the iPod mini took off. Many liked its elegant size and multiple colours – a style trick that had worked to some extent with the iMac, but was much more popular with the iPod. Rivals remained dismissive. 'They're a one-trick pony,' Hideki Komiyama, president of Sony Electronics, told *BusinessWeek*.[19] Jobs responded: 'There's no company in the world that's better [than us] at making complex technology simple. That's Apple's primary skill, and it's a skill that has never been more valuable.'

Accessories quickly followed; Apple was fostering a hardware ecosystem, but unlike Microsoft, which had explicitly courted PC makers to build PCs to run Windows, was doing it without really trying. The 30-pin dock on the bottom and a 9-pin remote controller on the top gave hardware companies something to aim at. You could build devices like Griffin's FM tuner, or play songs through an attached device.

The third-party hardware designers felt uneasy, though. Microsoft continued software support for ageing hardware (such as IBM's PS/2 or serial mouse connectors) because consumers or corporations might always put a new version of Windows on an old machine; in business terms, it made good sense. The code was written, and unlike hardware it wouldn't fall in value.

Apple, however, treated consumer electronics more like a fashion business. The first iMac, in 1998, had made a complete break with Apple's hardware past, dumping its proprietary connectors for the broader USB standard. (That had been the first big boost to Griffin's business.) In 2001 it had cut one of its software ecosystems adrift by shifting its computers over to Mac OS X, the NeXT-created Unix-based operating system.

So, the accessory makers wondered, would the iPod docks really last, or were they just a design tweak that Apple was trying out? Griffin himself repeatedly asked Apple mid-level executives to explain their long-term intentions with the dock and remote connector, since if one or the other were abandoned he would be left with stock that would be hard to sell – because Apple ran down its supplies ahead of every new iPod launch, but didn't tell the ecosystem what was coming. 'It's been a problem,' Griffin says simply. 'I mean, they will communicate with you, help you any way they can, but that's where they can't [tell you] because they're just not going to talk about what their upcoming plans are.' Even if you suggest something to them? 'They're probably listening, but they're not going to just do it because you ask them to', Griffin says.

He never got a definitive answer, only 'guidance'. A veteran of dozens of tiny tweaks to iPod, iPhone and iPad models down the years, Griffin thinks a willingness to abandon old things works in Apple's favour. 'I think that, if you get caught up trying to make legacy things work, you limit yourself in a lot of ways,' he says. 'Remember the original connector on the top of the iPod' (introduced in April 2003, but abandoned with the iPod nano in September 2005). 'They'd be limited by that now; instead they have so many more options.'

In his view:

I think they're right not to get too caught up in trying to support legacy [connectors], and if they had told us they were going to stick with something or not stick with something then they would have been forced to; it would have curtailed their future development plans. So I think they were smart to just say we're listening but we're not going to promise anything.

The growth of iTunes Music Store

Meanwhile, the iTunes Music Store kept growing. In March 2004 it passed another milestone, of 50 million songs downloaded.

More than half of iPods were connected to Windows machines, and more than half of iTunes installations were on Windows. Apple was using the Windows platform that had crushed it in the 1990s to build its own. In April the Store hit its first anniversary with 70 million songs downloaded – and a small profit, no small feat given that the majority of the 99 cents received went to the credit card companies and music labels. Announcing the milestone, Jobs once again reiterated the idea that there wasn't any interest in subscription services: people would rather own music than rent it.

Apple was demonstrating, brutally, the value of scale to internet success. Smaller companies that now wanted to get into the music distribution business – such as the now-reconstituted Napster, offering a legal download and subscription service, or eMusic, which offered a similar service with MP3-encoded music – couldn't get public attention in the way that a 30-year-old company with a charismatic leader, its own music player line, billions of dollars in revenues, a web audience that microscopically followed its every move, and a growing advertising budget could. Apple turned digital downloads into big news because it had a name and the products.

But appearances can be deceptive. Despite the huge numbers that Apple was touting – a million songs sold in five days, 25 million in seven months, 70 million in a year – it wasn't really the salvation of the recorded music industry. Nor was the method of selling necessarily good news for the record labels.

The iPod wasn't actually the amazing channel through which the digital music download world exploded. Although Jobs did announce at the January 2004 Macworld Expo that one (unnamed) person had bought $29,500 worth of music from the store, that person was very much an outlier. By the time the Music Store was a year old in April 2004 (and still available only in the United States), and 70 million songs had been downloaded, about 2.8 million iPods had been sold – 2 million of them in the year the store had been open. As the United States is about half of Apple's business, and the iPod was available there first, it's a reasonable guess that

Two million of those 2.8 million iPods were connected to the Music Store in its first year.

In other words, there was an average of 35 songs downloaded per year per iPod – equivalent to buying 3.5 CDs in that period. That's only slightly ahead of the average purchase per person in the United States. (If you assume some people were just downloading to iTunes, the per-iPod average falls further.)

'That's only 1 per cent of all legal music sales [in the United States],' Rob Schoeben, Apple's head of product marketing, said later. 'But it also represents a technological disruption, to gain 1 per cent in just one year. And, you know, there's a lot of headroom for us to grow into.'[20]

But were they additive purchases that people wouldn't otherwise have made, in which case Apple was helping the music business to grow? Or were people shunning 10-track CDs for cherry-picked individual tracks? Record labels increasingly suspected the latter. The CD, formerly the staple of the music business, was being atomized by the ability to choose individual tracks. Meanwhile piracy and buyer indifference meant that, in 2003, the worldwide music business slumped again, by nearly 8 per cent year on year, to a total value of $32 billion. It was the trend, as much as the value, that was worrying. And, if every iTunes track sold for 99 cents meant a $10 CD forgone, that was very bad news.

In 2004 iPod sales really took off. In the first three months, sales were 10 times greater than in the previous year. The next quarter was only three times greater (but of course a year ago had seen the Oprah boost). Apple's revenues grew 17 per cent from $2 billion to $2.35 billion, but its profits rose 74 per cent from $61 million to $106 million. Something had happened. The iPod was handily profitable. The iTunes Music Store had enough scale that it was turning a profit on each song sold. Apple also got money from licences from companies hooking into its 30-pin dock to make tuners and 'docks' to play music.

In June, Jobs launched the iTunes Music Store in Europe – the UK, France and Germany. In the first week, 800,000 songs were downloaded, 450,000 of them in the UK. British companies I spoke to such as OD2, which had been plugging away at the digital download market for years – based on Windows Media files with DRM – and had seen Apple reduce it from market leader to also-ran in the matter of seven days, were resigned: they could see that they didn't have the brand to compete. Still, they were sure the iTunes launch would raise their profile.

Physical retailers had cause to worry too. Before then, about 500,000 to 700,000 CD singles were sold in UK shops each week. The iTunes Music Store UK had almost equalled them while still in its infancy. Music on the move, and over the internet, was being transformed.

Apple and the mobile phone

At the end of July 2004, Jobs announced in an e-mail to Apple staff that he had been treated for a rare form of pancreatic cancer. Most pancreatic cancers kill within six months. But Jobs had neuroendocrine cancer, a rare, treatable (and survivable) form, given the right treatment. (What Jobs didn't reveal was that he hadn't taken the right treatment; the cancer had been diagnosed the previous October, but he'd declined surgery until June.) Jobs worked from home after his treatment, and returned to the office occasionally later that summer before returning full time in October.

In that period he instituted a programme to build a mobile phone entirely designed by Apple, even though a parallel project to develop a phone with Motorola using flash memory to store songs was nearing completion. Jobs had let news of the work with Motorola leak out earlier in July, when he had told the audience at a Motorola event that Apple would let people 'transfer iTunes music' to the next-generation handsets; Apple would create an iTunes mobile music player that would be 'standard' on Motorola's mass-market music phones. It seemed like an obvious acknowledgement of the power of the mobile phone, whose sales had hit 520 million worldwide. Compared to those, the iPod – with not quite 6 million sold in its lifetime – was a drop in the ocean. But it was still growing: between July and September 2004, 2 million were sold, more than twice the number in the previous year. The iPod had arrived.

Microsoft and the horizontal model still hadn't, though. Where was the PC business model on music players? Where was the 'iPod killer' – a phrase that had begun to be used every week about each new music player (having first appeared in October 2002, attached to a review of a Creative Technologies MP3 player)? Commentators were sure there would inevitably be one. Yet Microsoft, through people like Fester, was suggesting that there wouldn't be just one, but many – just as in the computing field there isn't a single 'leading' computer, but many contenders.

As 2004 wore on, there were many competing devices. But Apple continued to lead the field, with a majority of the market.

Stolen!

On Sunday 3 October 2004, Steve Ballmer blew through London as part of a European tour. He was lined up with various meetings, including a couple of media events – a one-to-one meeting with the *Financial Times* and the other with a round table of technology journalists from newspapers and prominent online sites.

He had plenty on his mind. Oracle was making a $9.4 billion bid for PeopleSoft, which provided human resource management and customer relationship management systems, just the sort of field Microsoft might want to compete in. Ballmer indicated to the *Financial Times* that Microsoft would not be entering the bidding. If Microsoft was going to buy anything, he implied, it would be Germany's SAP – a leading maker of CRM software – for which, Oracle had revealed in June, Microsoft had privately begun bidding in June 2003.

With the discussion about billion-dollar business deals done, Ballmer went on to the round table meeting. He was a veteran of such encounters; it was unlikely that he would encounter anyone who would know more about almost any subject than him, and certainly nothing regarding industry information. He could feel confident.

Ballmer began by declaring that he had a 'fundamental optimism' about the future of information technology and Microsoft's role in it, and especially 'integrated devices': 'the number of smartphones [presently] sold is relatively small,' he said. 'That number will grow.'

The questions moved through the European Commission antitrust case (which was grinding on over the tying of Windows Media Player to Windows, and access to Windows systems), the problems of security with Windows ('There are bad people out there in cyberspace and they are not going to go away'), browser rivalries, and spam.

Then came the question. 'Despite digital rights management, isn't piracy still rampant?'

The transcript by Jack Schofield of the *Guardian*, one of the attendees, records Ballmer's reply:

Ballmer:	Let me first talk about DRM. Now we've had DRM in Windows for quite some number of years, there's nothing new about that...
Journalist:	[interrupting] Having said that, that hasn't stopped, you know, pirates from running rampant...
Ballmer:	Of course not: nothing does! I mean, what's the most common format of music listened to on an iPod?
Journalist:	On an iPod...
Ballmer:	Stolen! Stolen!
Journalist:	[confused] On an iPod?
Ballmer:	Yes. Most people still steal music. [laughing] The fact that you can buy it and it's protected doesn't affect the fact that most people still steal [music]. I'd *love* to say all problems have been solved, whether it's iPod/iTunes – where Apple has done some nice work, no doubt about it – but the truth of the matter is we can build these technologies, but as long as there's alternate forms of music acquisition, there still will be ways for people to steal music.[21]

What Ballmer, then 48, meant was that it was inconceivable that someone under 25, as most iPod owners probably were, could possibly own the 8,000 songs you'd need to fill the largest 40GB iPod released that July; iPods at the time couldn't display photos directly. Logically, the majority must have been 'stolen' – downloaded from file-sharing systems.

On its face, this was true. But the chief executive of a truly consumer-facing organization would have recognized two elephant traps to avoid. First, telling iPod owners that they're knowing thieves (which the news organizations did with delight, using headlines such as 'iPod users are music thieves says Ballmer') is hardly good marketing, especially if you want those people to use your forthcoming products.

Second, the majority of iPod owners used Windows PCs. (Jobs had confirmed this at the European iTunes launch.) In that case those being insulted by Ballmer for their alleged thieving were using software from his company – and could feel doubly aggrieved. Jobs's words at the April launch of the European store make an interesting contrast: 'Piracy is the biggest market for downloads – we have to understand it and offer a better product,' he said. Conciliatory rather than confrontational.

Ballmer's real error, though, was failing to realize the loyalty that iPod owners felt. The woman in the *Guardian*'s feature section pitying her friend with the MiniDisc was subconsciously preening about owning an iPod. Ballmer hadn't grasped the emotional attachment and how, when you attack something people feel emotional about, they will react emotionally.

His attitude was entirely natural for someone more used to dealing with the corporate customers who would be expressing outrage at the wholesale theft of their content via file sharing. Had the room been filled with music executives, they would have been hanging on every word, waiting to hear what silver bullet Microsoft's coders had created to solve the piracy problem. To a bunch of journalists writing for a consumer audience, though, he came across as gauche.

'Part of the reason people steal music is money, but some of it is that the DRM stuff out there has not been that easy to use,' Ballmer said. 'We are going to continue to improve our DRM, to make it harder to crack, and easier, easier, easier, easier, to use.' He agreed that it wasn't going to be simple, and pointed to his own child as an example: 'My 12-year-old at home doesn't want to hear that he can't put all the music that he wants in all of the places that he would like it.'

Lapping it up, another journalist asked: were they close to a tipping point with digital media devices and home entertainment?

'I think we are close to the tipping point, to where we may get a device that can take on critical mass,' Ballmer agreed. 'There will be an explosion in demand. People weren't really sure where these new devices fitted in. At 200 bucks, maybe, but at 300 or 400 bucks it was too hard to bootstrap the device type.' He paused:

> You mention Apple, and with great respect for Apple I don't think you'll get... there's no way anything gets to critical mass with Apple, because Apple just doesn't have the volumes. They don't have the volumes anywhere in the world; they don't have the volumes particularly in some countries... The critical mass is going to have to come from the PC, or the next-generation video device.

He made another comment that is interesting in hindsight. One journalist asked: 'Microsoft's smartphone has been a slow seller [its Pocket PC-based phones sold such small numbers Microsoft didn't announce sales figures until 2005, when they hit nearly 6 million], while Apple and other companies have stolen a lead in portable music player markets. How will Microsoft tackle that?' Ballmer's reply:

> Over time most people will carry a phone that has a little hard disk in it that carries lots of music. Mobile phones are about 600 million units a year. Now, how many devices do we want to carry? We have to have a more compelling value proposition. [Research In Motion's] BlackBerry has a niche market position

[at the time, around 2 million users worldwide] but it's not a very sticky device. It allows you to make bad phone calls but it's a good Exchange client. We will see an explosion of larger keyboard devices.

What's interesting about that comment – apart from how well it illustrates Ballmer's gadfly salesperson's mind flitting about the subject in search of a compelling way to persuade people to buy an integrated device that could make phone calls and play music – is its lack of technological foresight. First was that most people would carry a phone with a 'little hard disk'. Apple had already bought up supplies of solid-state flash memory for an iPod with no moving parts, and when meeting me four years earlier Hase had introduced the idea of a 1-gigabyte flash chip – enough to hold about 250 music tracks. The Motorola phone being co-developed with Apple would store its songs in flash memory; and any technologist knew that prices for flash storage were, like those for hard drive storage, halving every year.

Second, the idea of the explosion of larger keyboard devices is classically short-term thinking that also ignores the relentless march of processing power. Although touch computing was still mainly in the laboratory, it was already conceivable: Nokia had that year built a prototype touchscreen phone, and a small company called FingerWorks had been working between 2001 and 2005 on 'multi-touch' systems for screens, and making presentations at conferences. A technologist – an engineer – keyed into the industry's future would have known of it and seen its direction.

But it was Ballmer's remarks about the iPod and piracy that captured the moment. The internet was soon aflame as the comments were spread from news site to news site; the story itself barely mattered. People didn't like being called pirates by extremely rich people.

Ballmer acknowledged that he might have put a foot wrong in subsequent interviews that week. 'I don't [recall] what I said, but it was *bad*', he told some European journalists. But soon there was to be a growing gap between what the iPod offered – a simple system for getting music from your computer to a music player – and Microsoft's efforts to build a DRM system called 'Janus' that aimed to be the Windows of the digital music player world.

Two-faced

Within the Microsoft campus in Redmond, there was a growing recognition that something needed to be done about Apple's tightening grip on the digital player market. That concern had been amplified by delegations from the United States' biggest retailer, Wal-Mart, and its biggest electronics retailer, Best Buy: they desperately needed Microsoft to offer something that would compete. Apple wouldn't let them sell the iPod, so they needed to offer something that would be, if not an iPod killer, then at least an iPod peer. Microsoft wasn't about to let an invitation like that go to waste.

Apple's decision not to sell through those two giant chains was, on the face of it, suicidal: wouldn't going through such huge, powerful channels multiply sales enormously? But Jobs and Schiller had thought it through. What looked like madness was a smart mixture of careful branding and retail strategy. First, as always with Apple, was the branding. The iPod was positioned as a premium device, not the electronics equivalent of fast food. In designing it, Ive had wanted people to have a personal, emotional reaction, to feel that the iPod was individually theirs. (Once they owned it, the addition of their own songs would individualize it further.)

But Apple's executives knew the fate of consumer electronics items sold through Wal-Mart, which was synonymous with cheap and quick. The iPod would be arrayed in some misbegotten part of the store, untended by staff, where passing shoppers would paw at the models on display, which would probably look worn and tired. The choice between an iPod and another make would come down to a split-second comparison of price, or a tick box list of specifications on a card. The iPod would be at risk of losing out because it had too few green ticks, or too many red crosses, or cost $10 more than a rival Apple saw as clearly inferior. The same argument applied for Best Buy. Apple's staff believed that seeing the device sitting on a display was insufficient; tick boxes wouldn't show you how easy it was to synchronize songs or buy music.

So rather than buying display space in those big retail chains, 'in the US, Apple aggressively advertised iTunes and iPod, particularly on TV, while its competitors did no TV advertising', observes Joe Wilcox, then working for Jupiter Research. 'Based on Apple's clever advertising, which consumers would see several times during prime-time TV, iPod appeared to be the only choice.'[22]

Staying out of the big chains where the rival MP3 players were sold had another advantage: by refusing to let the iPod be compared with its rivals, Apple made the competition look second-rate. Everyone interested in such a player had heard of the iPod; celebrities used it; it was one of Oprah's 'Favorite Things'. A shopper who scanned a display of music players and didn't see an iPod would conclude that none was as good as the iPod. Subtle; but Apple excels at discerning such subtle messages and branding.

It also had a retail strategy: besides selling through its website and some favoured retailers, it had since 2001 been opening its own range of retail stores, where iPods were displayed beside Apple Macs in a setting that emphasized hands-on experience over the hard sell. You could wander in and around an Apple Store for as long as you liked. There weren't big star stickers about price cuts. It was more like a high-class car showroom, if the cars were all white and none bigger than a computer. Giving people the chance to play with an iPod raised the chance of their actually buying it – and giving them no alternative meant that price and feature comparisons didn't enter the sales equation. When Apple first announced the stores, retail analysts said it was a foolish act of misplaced faith; but Jobs trusted that Ron Johnson, whom he hired in 2000 from the giant Target chain, would make it work. (Johnson worked under an assumed name before the stores launched so rivals wouldn't be tipped off: a typical Apple cloak-and-dagger approach.)

Apple's stores helped build buzz too. The staff didn't work on commission. 'It's not the boring, laborious, I've-got-to-move-merchandise and take care of customer problems,' Johnson explained in 2005. 'It's "I'm suddenly enriching people's lives." And that's how we select, that's how we motivate, that's how we train our people.'[23] Jobs held an executive meeting every weekday between 9 am and noon; store figures, including visitors, were fed to headquarters every 15 minutes. In a sense, the Apple Stores are the ultimate expression of Apple's philosophy: build stuff, and then get it directly into the hands of consumers, with no intermediaries. The footfalls through the door were heard in the boardroom.

Finally, Wal-Mart and Best Buy hadn't supported Apple when it had been in trouble; as a company, it knows how to hold a grudge. Yet all that could have been forgotten if either chain had been a good fit with the branding. But they were not. HP was allowed to sell its branded iPod through Wal-Mart in mid-2004; but it would not be until January 2005 that Wal-Mart was allowed to start selling the iPod mini.

At Microsoft, the urgency of those retailers' pleading led to the creation of the first plan to achieve dominance: leapfrog Apple by offering not just music, but also video. First came Portable Media Center (PMC) – which, despite its hardware-like name, was software to let companies build a handheld device able to store films and other video, as well as music and photos. In September 2004 PMC products from Creative, Samsung and iRiver (barely known in the United States, but the second-biggest seller of MP3 music players through its Far Eastern success) began appearing.

Brian King, a co-developer of the system at Microsoft, suggested that it was 'a great opportunity, and we jumped at it'. Microsoft's press release heralded a 'new era of digital devices enabling consumers to take entertainment throughout the home and on the go', using a new brand: PlaysForSure. The imagined market was commuters and people making long journeys, who would want PMC for those long, boring car, bus, plane and train rides. The players cost about $500, though of course the horizontal market would surely drive those prices down, just as they had for PCs, as soon as they gained traction and scale. So that was the software and the hardware. Now, where was the content?

Microsoft's answer: there, on your Windows XP computer. This turned out to be the wrong answer. Not many people had much in the way of video content on their PCs, and those who did might not want to transfer it to a handheld device, or wouldn't get much viewing from it: videos shot on the family camcorder don't make great viewing for long car journeys. Microsoft made deals with Major League Baseball and CinemaNow, an online film rental service that at the time offered a total of 200 films and TV programmes encoded in the right format for the devices. The figure equated to just four months' output from a typical year in Hollywood. Even Bruce Eisen, CinemaNow's executive vice-president, had to admit to the *New York Times* that 'in the beginning this is going to be a little niche'.[24] Todd Warren, then corporate vice-president of the Windows Mobile division, told the paper that 'It is not sure to us entirely how [the category of use] is going to evolve.'

It didn't. Instead, PMC went extinct. King, Warren and their team had ignored the fact that people could already get video-playing devices to play long-form video legally and cheaply: handheld DVD players cost about $100, and DVDs were getting cheaper by the month. And, whereas the PMC software prevented you copying a video file from a computer and then uploading it to a different one, a DVD can be played on any compatible machine. The DVDs offered all the benefits – long-form, cheap, broad selection, no direct restrictions on playback – that the PMC didn't. It was a classic case of pushing a technology instead of its use. People did want to watch video on the move (and Apple would eventually release a video iPod), but ease of use and broad choice of content were what mattered; a single sport and 200 films would never be compelling. In addition, people wanted using them to be easy. A DVD was easy to put into a portable DVD player. Transferring a film to a PMC was a drag.

That left music as the other battleground. Microsoft had developed software called Janus (after the two-faced Roman god who guarded gates), which it released to music player and software companies in mid-2004, around the same time as Ballmer's embarrassing interviews.

Janus ran on Windows and let people join 'subscription' services just like PressPlay and MusicNet from a couple of years earlier. (Those had quietly disappeared as the iTunes Music Store had taken off.) While you paid your monthly fee, the songs would play; if you unsubscribed, the songs would stop. The player companies and the subscription services both had to adopt Janus; you couldn't play it back without having the right software on the site, your player and the PC. Systems using Janus also bore the PlaysForSure brand.

Stephen Wildstrom, then the technology writer for *BusinessWeek*, suggested in November 2004 that the 'maze of incompatible standards' between the iTunes Music Store and all the other services posed a threat to the future of all of them. Apple's FairPlay, RealNetworks' Helix and now Microsoft's Janus: none could play the others' DRM-protected songs. But he felt confident that Microsoft would, in time, dominate the market. 'When [the] Windows Media 10 [format] and Janus were released in early October, Microsoft took a self-serving step that simplifies things for consumers', he wrote. 'It created a "PlaysForSure" logo for sites that sell Windows Media music and devices that play it.' He listed the sites and players selling such products – Napster, MusicMatch, Wal-Mart, Dell, Creative, iRiver, Gateway and (new to the business) Virgin Electronics.

'None of these players is as easy to use as an iPod, these web sites aren't as easy to use as the iTunes online store, and no rival can match Apple's brilliant marketing,' Wildstrom wrote. 'But the gap is narrowing... in the end, what consumers care about is getting the music – and in the not-too-distant future, the movies and video – they want and having it play without hassles on the device of their choice. Microsoft's big-tent approach offers a way out of this morass for everyone,' he added, before concluding dangerously 'except perhaps Apple.'[25]

But there were problems with the tent: people didn't like the show. PlaysForSure quickly turned into a marketing car crash. Players didn't work. Transferring music could lead to freezes. Influential technology analysts such as Michael Gartenberg, then at Jupiter Research, and others blogged about their dislike of the experience. One such was Jason Dunn, a writer and consultant garlanded by Microsoft itself as an 'MVP' – a 'most valued professional' for 'exceptional contributions to technical communities worldwide'; with an MVP, the company says, you 'can be confident that the information shared by the MVP will be of the highest caliber and will help every user make the most of the technology'.

Here's the information Dunn shared: PlaysForSure frustrated him in the extreme. He described how the music on his system – Napster using PlaysForSure on his PC running Windows Media Player 10 – would stop playing and demand re-authentication 'eight to ten times a week, despite the fact that I always had the box checked off for "remember my password"'. In addition, 'it was so incredibly sluggish and crash prone it made me weep. Napster customer service was next to useless helping me with the issues I contacted them about.'[26] He managed to get music on to a Creative Zen player after 'some issues' – but eventually went back to just ripping CDs. With Dunn's experience not unusual, the subscription services didn't thrive (as was evident from their reluctance to boast about their numbers of subscribers, even privately). Napster, despite having the best-known name in digital music after Apple, stumbled.

Microsoft however continued attacking Apple on the topic of 'choice'. Giving the keynote speech to the Consumer Electronics Show in Las Vegas in January 2005 (with a warm-up by the comedian Conan O'Brien), Gates announced that there were now more than 50 digital media players carrying the PlaysForSure logo.[27] Amidst the joshing, O'Brien challenged him: 'There is a perception out there sometimes that Microsoft doesn't get it when it comes to the consumer. Do you think that's fair?' Gates pointed to Windows, and to Halo, the hit video game. The Creative Zen Micro and Rio Carbon had sold out over Christmas, he said. Enabling subscriptions via a monthly fee was an area where 'we'll see if that catches on in a very big way'.

It was a constant irony, never remarked on, that Gates represented a company whose only consumer electronics offering before the Xbox was rebranded computer mice and keyboards, and whose income derived almost entirely from corporations; yet for years he would pop up at CES to tell consumer electronics manufacturers how he expected their future to look. Often, it didn't pan out. In his time Gates showed off a SPOT watch (essentially a wrist-worn computer that would let you know the weather), and integrated 'homes of the future' where the living room, bedroom and kitchen all spoke to each other. (The irony didn't end with Gates's retirement from the company in 2008; Steve Ballmer took over the gig until 2012, when Microsoft made its last appearance at the show.)

Watching Gates's speech, Gartenberg, then at Jupiter Research, observed: 'Unfortunately, none of those [50] players have the name iPod, so I'm not certain that this matters all that much for now.' He pointed to the complexity of PlaysForSure: some players could play only downloaded content; some could play only subscriptions. Some music was subscription only. To find out which was which, you had to do a lot of squinting at boxes.

'The fact that they need a coding system to figure out what content, from what source, using what DRM, will play on what player is *not* a good thing IMHO [in my humble opinion],' Gartenberg noted. Soon after, he began testing iPod rivals, and wrote:

> During one test I started using the rather excellent SanDisk Sansa e100. The problem was that even though it had the PlaysForSure logo, it wouldn't work with subscription content. It only took me a few minutes to figure out why. A closer look at the PlaysForSure logo indicated this device would work with downloaded content but not subscription content. Oops...

'I'm actually in good company,' he mused. 'Last summer when I was at Microsoft, one of the senior executives made the same mistake in front of a whole room of snickering analysts and reporters.' But, he added, the problem was that 'this is likely to happen to consumers as well who might not be as careful at parsing language between subscription and download content. After all, didn't I just download that file? And now it doesn't work with the device I just bought. Especially when the logo for both looks exactly the same.'

As an example of unwarranted complexity, it couldn't be equalled. Apple's offering, by contrast – buy it from us and you can play it on your computer or iPod, no questions asked – was the model of simplicity.

I asked Wildstrom in 2010 why he thought now that his prediction about Microsoft's domination of the music player did not come to pass:

> Microsoft and I made one mistake in common. We both
> believed that subscription music would turn out to be
> a lot more popular than it has (so far, anyway). Part of the
> problem was the music industry forcing the pricing to be
> way too high – $15 a month for mobile devices. I – and I
> suspect Microsoft – also underestimated the pace of Apple's
> innovation in exploiting its early advantage with iTunes/iPod
> and the advantages of delivering an excellent end-to-end user
> experience through control of the player (iPod), the interface
> software (iTunes), and the retailer (then, the iTunes Music Store).

'But Microsoft also let me down,' he observed.

> PlaysForSure was a good idea destroyed by terrible
> execution. It never quite delivered on the promise of cross-
> device compatibility, a problem that has generally plagued
> multi-device digital rights management systems. Many of
> the players introduced by Microsoft partners weren't very
> good, or at least were perceived as being inferior to iPods.
> Dell and Gateway weren't very committed to the business,
> and Virgin Electronics never really got out of the gate.

Why though was the execution of Janus terrible? Microsoft, after all, is a company staffed by extremely capable programmers who could (and did) create the software to perform the task. But Windows users couldn't download Janus, as they could iTunes; it was embedded in the music players, software media players and music they bought. If it didn't suit them, their only recourse was to abandon the whole ecosystem around Janus, which included Windows Media Player and the digital player manufacturer and the subscription service. If any one of those three got their execution wrong – bad firmware in the player, a version or two behind in the media player, a newer version of Janus encoding the subscription site's music – it wouldn't work. Nobody controlled the whole stack; nobody was ultimately responsible.

If Microsoft got Janus wrong, both users and digital player manufacturers suffered, but Microsoft's only penalty would be to lose some inconsequential sales of its Windows Server product to sites selling Janus-encoded songs. It was highly unlikely that any end users would abandon Windows because their music player didn't work. They'd just download iTunes instead. The effect on Microsoft's bottom line was microscopic. The effect on the other partners, though, was dramatic.

Apple, by contrast, had every reason to be highly attuned to problems with the iPod or iTunes or the iTunes Music Store: if any of them fell short, users would let it know quickly, by not purchasing or downloading the product, and that would show up on Apple's bottom line at once – and probably be picked up in the Monday meeting of the divisional heads. And of course there were those quarter-hourly updates from the stores about footfall and sales.

By contrast, any failings in Janus took months to filter through the system, from player manufacturers (which would of course test it, but couldn't check it against the enormous hardware and software ecosystem of Windows machines and operating systems), which would ship them to shops, where they would be bought by end users, who would then try them out. Any faults would have to be reconciled: did they lie in the version of Windows, the version of Windows Media Player, the PC and its software, the firmware or software on the digital player or – finally – in Janus? Tracking down faults in that supply chain involved two different divisions of Microsoft (Client, for Windows, and the Devices division for Janus), the music provider, the PC manufacturer, the player manufacturer and the music provider. If you were lucky, the latter two might be the same, but there were at least three companies involved, each of which might end up blaming another.

In short, the Janus system lacked the tight feedback loop needed for a successful consumer electronics product. And, for a consumer, what was the proposition that companies offering Janus-powered products, such as Napster, were offering? Even the companies themselves couldn't quite decide. A former Napster employee told me that to begin with they believed that the winning line was simple enough: 'All the world's music library in your pocket – for 10 dollars a month.'

Yet it didn't seem to sway people. 'Looking back on it, I don't think people *want* to listen to all the world's music,' the employee said. 'Apart from a few unusual listeners, people tend to have quite limited musical interests. That means that subscription music is quite a difficult proposition to sell them. Whereas à la carte [the iTunes model] is much simpler: you buy it and you listen to it as much as you like.' And, of course, people could rip their existing CD library and listen to that, or get huge amounts of music through file-sharing services (which were still thriving).

Subscription content on a music player also carried the prospect – or threat – of expiration. Digital subscriptions say: 'Pay up or the bits get it.' Unless you're the Mafia, it's difficult to build your business on threats. In the absence of ubiquitous streaming from the mobile internet, subscription services never gained any momentum. That caused Napster other problems: in order to build its revenue, it needed to attract more customers, but if they weren't interested in the 'world in your pocket' idea then what *were* they interested in? The company used to hold meetings in which its best minds would struggle to come up with new encapsulations of Napster's USP – or a new USP – while advertising agencies waited impatiently for instructions.

Gartenberg's opinion turned out to be correct. PlaysForSure turned into a sure-fire flop. The reason went back to Jobs's observation that he had used to persuade the record industries to license the iTunes Music Store: people don't like subscriptions for their music.

There was another element. Retailers liked selling iPods, because of accessories such as the Griffin iTrip, or cases, or speaker docks. Typically, retailers got about 15 per cent margin on the sale price of an iPod, but 25 per cent on add-on electronics, and 50 per cent on the cases. Sell a $100 iPod with a $60 speaker dock and $30 case, and you'd triple your profit on the original item. Even better, you didn't even have to sell iPods to benefit: some other shop might bear the upfront cost of buying and stocking them, and you could catch passing customers and make a handsome margin while bearing the far lower stock costs of obtaining speaker docks, chargers, FM tuners and cases.

That drove a virtuous circle in the hardware ecosystem, which by the end of 2005 was big enough in its own right to attract analysts' attention. NPD Group's Steve Baker estimated that by then, for every $3 spent on an iPod, $1 was spent on an accessory, and that in-store sales of items like cases, car chargers and tuners (like Griffin's original, now copied hundreds of times over) totalled $850 million. But, he added, he didn't know how big the internet business might be. Reasonably, it could have been at least half as large again. Over a quarter of sales were simple cases, costing between $10 and $30. And Baker calculated that the amount spent doubled from 2005 to 2006. Apple knew it was on to a good thing. 'For us it's great, because the decision to buy an iPod is reinforced when consumers see all the accessories', said Greg Joswiak, Apple's vice-president for worldwide iPod marketing at the time.[28]

By contrast there was no supporting ecosystem for the minor players: they never got enough market share to make it worthwhile for manufacturers to make them or retailers to stock them. 'Choice' destroyed brand loyalty. If all the players were interchangeable, why would you stick with any of them? You'd just go for the cheapest that did what you wanted. The manufacturers' margins would be destroyed (just as happens in the PC market, where people generally buy on price alone).

In digital music players, the horizontal market structure worked against, rather than in favour of, the hardware companies. Microsoft, which got licence fees from the manufacturers and those running servers to serve PlaysForSure music, hardly saw the effect; it certainly didn't hurt its bottom line, because people still needed PCs to synchronize their iPods, so Windows kept selling (in 2004 the PC market grew 17 per cent), and corporations were still buying Office. Compared to the billions in profit from those monopolies, what did or didn't happen in the tiny division of Entertainment and Devices was just the sugar dusting on the icing on top of the cake.

iPod in the ascendant

By August 2005 the digital music story for Microsoft and its partners still wasn't improving. In the three months to June 2005, Apple had sold 6.1 million iPods, more than a sevenfold increase on the same period in 2004, generating $1.1 billion of revenue. Sales were growing by more than a million every quarter. The iTunes Store had passed 500 million songs sold, and was selling about 50 million per month. Adding in the money from the iTunes Store, and other products, computers were now less than half of Apple's revenues. The iPod was in the ascendant.

Gartenberg noted that, 'The problem is that Microsoft continues to focus on a complex message of "functions" and Apple keeps it focused on music.' Microsoft's smartphones, which as he pointed out already existed, could play MP3s, use Napster, Real or Yahoo subscriptions, play videos and even stream live TV, as well as 'RSS web readers, e-mail, the web, games, GPS [location] and mapping and a whole slew of other functions'. Enough? No: too much, and too confusing, he suggested: 'In the meantime the real story is on music and the emphasis that all you need to know is iPod, iTunes and now perhaps a new iTunes-capable cell phone.'

He thought the problem was what Gates and Fester and the rest of the Microsoft team thought was the solution: the horizontal model. 'There are too many parts of the ecosystem, from hardware players to the device software and from the music stores and services and the carriers and no one leading the charge. Once again, it looks like Apple will seize the high ground and leave Microsoft and her partners in reactive [as opposed to] proactive mode.'[29]

Apple wasn't standing still either. It decided to start selling games on the iPod. It was the dawn of what would later, on the iPhone, become a fully fledged business model.

Ecosystem: hardware and apps

In November 2004 I asked Danika Cleary, then grandly titled Apple's worldwide head of iPod marketing, whether the company would let third-party developers write software to run on the devices. (Technically, this is called 'exposing the API' – where 'API' stands for 'application programming interface'. An API is like a short-order cook working off a set menu: send us these ingredients, it says, and this is what you'll get back. So an address book API might accept as the query something like 'First name begins DA'; it would return a list of the matching contacts, which the third-party software could then use in some way.)

From the beginning, the iPod could clearly do more than just decode MP3s; there was a clock, alarm calendar and contacts organizer. And it could also, people discovered, run games – if Apple included them. The original one contained, carefully hidden but quickly uncovered, a version of the game Breakout, also known as 'Brick', though on the iPod it was just called 'Game'. The 'bat', which hits the ball against the wall, to break the bricks, was controlled by moving the scroll wheel. The third-generation iPod in mid-2003 added Solitaire and a game called 'Parachute': the player had to shoot down parachuting soldiers.

'Games' meant an operating system underneath – and hence new frontiers where developers could write (and perhaps even sell?)

programs. After all, there was an international iTunes Store; why not offer iPod games through it too?

So had Apple considered exposing the API? Cleary indicated that the idea had been the subject of 'some discussion' inside the company (a phrase that I took to mean 'argument'). 'But our stance is that right now [the iPod is] very simple, and it works the same for everyone. We have decided to keep it closed. And basic', she told me. Why? 'Essentially, it's a music player,' she said. 'We don't want to spoil the experience. The success of the iPod is due to its simplicity and ease of use.'

Apple could have stolen a march on everyone else: at the time no other handheld device had an online store where you could directly download games and apps. But nothing happened until September 2006, when it began offering nine purchasable, downloadable games for the classic iPods, starting at $4.99, from the outside publishers Electronic Arts, Namco and Fresh Games. (Eventually by 2009 the portfolio reached 50 games, from 18 different publishers, including Apple.)

So why did Apple turn down the chance to build a software ecosystem around the iPod? Matt Drance, who at the time had the job title of 'developer evangelist', putting him in charge of enthusing the people who would write the apps, tells me it was quite simple. 'Apple doesn't do things until they know it's the best possible experience,' he explains. 'Obviously they had interests in third-party software because they [included it] in the first place.' But, he says, opening up the APIs through a developers' software development kit (SDK) complicates things.

> They kept it kind of close to their chest, because I think they were probably making very rapid changes to the [iPod] SDK. If you have a small number of partners, then you can control that without creating problems. You can call those five developers, like [games developers] Electronic Arts or whatever, and say 'Hey, guys, we need to shake things up a little bit. Can you come in and we will help you get things ready for the next release?'

That's not possible, he explains, with a much bigger group of developers. 'If you've got an ecosystem of 100,000 developers, it's a lot harder to move quickly. So that's probably one angle.'

The other, he says, is the question of what the App Store experience would have been like in 2004 or 2005. Even in April 2005, broadband was used for only just over half of all internet connections in the United States and the UK. YouTube had set up in February 2005, but before then most people simply didn't have fast enough connections to the web for a streaming video service. Drance says:

> If you look at what the App Store now has – not just talking about the library [of apps] but the actual experience, the wireless installation, the delivery, the ease of use – that just wasn't there in 2004. We didn't have high-speed wireless technology everywhere. I think that's also part of it too, where [the people at Apple] say: 'What's the user experience going to be here if we open up this marketplace? What's that going to look like?'

Of course, the installation would have been over wired broadband. But he adds meaningfully: 'This whole App Store thing is something that they've been thinking about for a long, long time.' How long? 'I don't think it's unreasonable to look at what happened with the iPod – we could call that a pilot programme for third-party software.'

Scratched!

The invitation for Apple's 'special event' in September 2005 had a peculiar motif: it focused on a pair of blue jeans, and specifically on the change pocket on the right hand. It was puzzling, and online forums lost no opportunity to puzzle over it. During the presentation, Jobs was his usual ebullient self – although while unveiling a Motorola phone called the ROKR that could also store and play songs, iPod-style, he lost his usual equilibrium: the demonstration went badly as he struggled to find the correct button to press. Journalists at the event wondered whether this was all – but expected it wasn't; after all, Jobs had by this time become famous for 'one more thing', the rabbit pulled from the hat. Certainly, iTunes had an 82 per cent share of the download market. Certainly, more than 20 million iPods had been sold, a 74 per cent market share in the United States. But come on. What was the big news?

Or, in this case, tiny news. 'Did you ever wonder what this pocket is for?' Jobs said abruptly. 'I've always wondered that. Well, now we know.' He pulled the iPod nano out, apparently from his change pocket. Watching via a satellite link in London, I could hear the crowd in the United States go wild. Jobs looked pleased. It may have been his most audacious unveiling ever. The nano was remarkable: a tiny device with 2GB or 4GB of flash storage, enough for 400 or 800 songs. Simultaneously the hard-drive-based iPod mini, launched only 21 months earlier, and Apple's most successful product ever, was killed so it could be supplanted.

Apple lent me a nano to test. I was impressed by how small and light it was, and the legibility of the screen despite its tiny size. Except... I noticed that the screen quickly became scuffed – with marks that couldn't be wiped off. The difference between the nano and the older classic iPod I had been using was surprising, though: the screen on the latter still looked clear. The nano, despite – or perhaps because of – its bright colour screen, showed off every mark.

A week or so later, Jobs gave the keynote speech at the Macworld Paris Expo, and then held court to a group of journalists, including myself. He was utterly in his element, delighted at the reception for the nano. And he revealed how ruthless Apple now was about its products. The new iPod minis released in February had already been earmarked for death even before Jobs had enthused about them:

We put a programme in place about a year ago – we started working on [the nano] even before that, but we put a plan in place to have [the nano] replace the mini. That was a giant step, given iPod mini's world success. We called it a heart transplant – right before holiday [season], which is the biggest season of the year for a product like this. And everyone would think we were crazy because we had to decide six months before to stop making parts for minis, and make sure this was ready in time – because the manufacturing ramp is very steep. And we succeeded and were ready to go.

His pleasure at the coup shone through. Why hadn't he waited the week or so until this Paris keynote speech to announce the device? 'Every single week before holiday counts, and we didn't want to wait weeks, when every week counts with very high volumes.'

His face filled with delight as he described how one site – Ars Technica – had tortured a nano, including dropping it on to solid surfaces, sitting on a chair on it, throwing it out of a speeding car and eventually, in desperation as the device kept playing, driving over it with a car (survived) and throwing it 40 feet into the air to land on concrete. That finally stopped it.[30]

Some didn't quite get it. 'Why did you kill the iPod mini?' asked one. Patiently Jobs replied, 'Because we have the nano.'

It was pointed out that, 'Quite a lot of people think the ROKR doesn't rock': why have a phone that could hold only 190 songs? 'We did the iTunes client and we think that's something we're going to learn from, that will help iTunes,' Jobs replied elliptically. 'Motorola did the phone and I can imagine other products in the future. It's a way for us to put a toe in the water and learn something.' In retrospect, he was alluding to the iPhone, then under development, but avoiding letting on that it was little more than a year away.

He even took on the challenge of creating an 'elevator pitch' – the 30-second encapsulation of the company – for Apple. 'Who's it for, an analyst?' he queried. The reply: 'No, someone from Mars.'

'At its core, Apple,' he began at once, 'has great engineering, just superb engineering, but –' He paused briefly, seeking the words:

The distinctive competence it has, that I think propels it above other companies in the world, is that Apple has always had the ability to take really complex technology and make it easy to understand and use by the end user. We did that with computers, several times, and we've done that now with music players and the music ecosystem.

And that need becomes, is becoming, greater than ever as technology becomes more and more sophisticated, and more and more and more complicated, and the need for a company to be able to engineer that complex technology but make it simple is greater than ever. I think Apple does that better than any other company in the world. And I think there's growing demand for that.

Given that at the time the iPhone and iPad hadn't been unveiled – though both were in different stages of development – it's interesting to look back at what he said: 'engineer complex technology but make it simple'. It's a dogma within Apple, but at the time its only real visibility was the computers – which only a tiny proportion of people used – and iPods, which didn't seem like particularly complex technology, until, that is, you compared them against Janus-based systems.

Not long after the interview had finished I met Rubinstein and Schiller. As I walked into the room, I mentioned that I'd been trying out the nano. 'How are you liking that?' Rubinstein asked.

'Scratches easily,' I replied.

'Nah,' said Rubinstein. 'You don't really think that? They make it out of the hardest polycarbonate plastic and steel.'

'I managed to get the screen scratched up in a couple of days', I replied.

'You carry it in your pockets with keys?' asked Rubinstein, a detective hunting a clue.

'Maybe,' I answered, 'though other people have said the same.'

Rubinstein shrugged and we moved on to other topics, specifically how Apple chose what to include in or leave out of the iPod, and what its success meant for the Mac business.

'What happens when iPod revenue outstrips that of the Mac, and the tail begins to wag the dog?' I asked.

'Ouch!' said Schiller. He and Rubinstein replied by emphasizing the work that was going on to develop the Mac line and its software, that the company wasn't going to abandon its origins.

Then Schiller, like Jobs, enunciated the thinking at the heart of Apple's product philosophy – something, he said, that remained the same whether it was on computers or iPods. 'We are very careful about the technologies we put into products,' he said. 'We should put new features in because it makes sense for customers, and because a significant percentage will want it. A lot of rivals suffer from feature-itis: it's easier to sell a checklist than to sell a better product. But if we think some features aren't great then we shouldn't do it.'

Rubinstein pitched in laconically: 'The interesting thing is that press and analysts have different perspectives from customers [about what's important]. You guys [in the press] see it differently; customers see the world differently from you.' Schiller added that there was a 'very vocal' customer base that kept Apple executives connected to their customers: 'People tell us stuff. Probably the best way is e-mail – we get tons every day.' ('Yeah,' agreed Rubinstein.)

In designing products, Schiller said, 'It's organic, it's iterative. Apple is a very product-driven company. We love making the world's best products, and we have a very creative culture.'

Silence from Apple

But my experience turned out to be a harbinger that would give Apple its first real taste of the Faustian pact of having a runaway product hit: visibility.

The screen on some iPod nanos, it transpired, really was easily scratched. Within a day of meeting Rubinstein and Schiller, I was contacted by a nano owner who complained that the screen scratched 'insanely easily' and pointed me to a thread on an Apple support forum that already had 188 posts on it. People weren't happy. Another owner, Matthew Peterson (later described by the BBC as a 'loyal Apple fan'), had discovered that the screen on his nano broke dramatically easily after just four days of 'gentle use'.[31] On 15 September – just a week after the product's release – he set up ipodnanoflaw.com (which was quickly renamed, for trademark reasons, flawedmusicplayer.com), whose headline was 'iPod Nano = Flawed Product'. Some, including me, wrote about the scratching, while others wrote about Peterson's site. The theme was rapidly picked up on websites and quickly percolated up to national news organizations, including the BBC, which featured the issue on its influential *Today* morning talk programme. The *Washington Post* asked semi-rhetorically: 'Is screen glitch the iPod nano's fatal flaw?'[32]

Apple declined to comment. In a world where every other organization seemed ready to put up a spokesperson to feed the 24-hour news cycle the minute a problem arose, it seemed peculiar. Some thought it a tacit admission of guilt, or arrogant – a word often attached to Apple.

It was the first time that the company had really been thrust into the broader media spotlight against its will, a situation where it couldn't apply its usual meticulous product launch and media control. The silence while it worked out its strategy, and especially its message, became its template for handling such furores, which were to become more frequent as first the iPhone and then the iPad propelled it further into the public eye. For five days after the story had surfaced it said nothing, not even 'We're investigating this, so stand by.'

Inside, though, a crisis management team called the 'Quality Council', which pre-dated Jobs, had convened. A sort of Star Chamber of problems, it met to decide, first, how significant the problem was. Having determined that it was limited to a small number of early products, the team plotted a response. Schiller and other spokespeople began popping up offering quotes to news outlets. Schiller admitted to a problem with one manufacturing batch, affecting less than 0.1 per cent of the units shipped, in which the screen would break too easily. As for scratches, he said that, 'We have received very few calls from customers reporting this problem – we do not think this is a widespread issue.' He suggested that customers 'concerned about' (note, not 'suffering from') scratched screens should buy 'one of the many iPod nano cases to protect their iPod'.

That would of course please retailers, and help establish the brand – and the new device – even more effectively. He insisted, as had Rubinstein, that the screen was a tough polycarbonate, the same one that had been used for the fourth-generation iPod (the colour-screen devices launched in June, which were also discontinued the next month with the release of video-capable iPods).

The message – problem in one batch, not many calls, same material, concerned users should buy a case – became the only one that Apple would put out. There was no off-the-record nudge and wink, no backroom briefing. Apple had its message and stuck to it. Later in October, during Apple's quarterly results, chief operating officer Tim Cook was asked about the scratching issue. He sang from exactly the same hymn sheet: 'We've had very, very few calls from customers,' he said. 'We don't believe it's a widespread issue. It's made of the same material as the fourth-generation iPods. For customers who have concerns we suggest they use cases now on the market.' There it was: batch, not many calls, material, case. Cook noted that, a month after its release, supply of nanos was 'still far short of demand'.

The reaction to the media storm – whether teacup-sized or not – is interesting. Apple wasn't paralysed by size (a problem that sometimes afflicts Microsoft when trying to respond to questions). Yet its deliberate approach is in stark contrast to that of Google, where – even while Larry Page has no love of the media's demands on his time – the company's PR staff are quick to call journalists if they sense a story about Google or search is beginning to spin unfavourably against it. Their calls are also always made on 'background' – the same no-fingerprints approach used by political spin doctors to get their point across without having to take a platform.

Apple has a different approach to journalists. To the extent that Apple reflected Jobs's thinking, as we know it did, the approach is a monolithic one: everything is great, and the new product is the best Apple has ever made. Uncomfortable questions are evaded or stonewalled with 'no comments'. Over the years, as its value and income have risen, Apple's staff have become increasingly secretive: the potential cost of a leak has risen exponentially. (The price of leaking is dismissal, a discipline Jobs brought back in 1997.) Background briefings for the press don't happen. Information is kept tightly to those who are known to be trustworthy. Outside partners are kept in the dark too until the last possible moment – often only finding out about products at the same time as the rest of the world. Jobs never saw his role as keeping the media happy; his interaction with it suggests that he saw it as a necessary evil, and certainly never to be feared or requiring ingratiation. To some, that's arrogant. To Apple, it's business.

Apple's best results

Those financial results in October 2005 brought some good news for Apple. Its fiscal year to the end of September was its biggest ever, with revenues of $13.9 billion and profits of $1.3 billion, in which the fourth-quarter revenues were $3.7 billion – also a record. The company had finally emerged from the shadow of 1995, its previous biggest year, when Michael Spindler was in charge but $11 billion in revenues had earned just $424 million of profit. Having almost slipped over the edge and been ignored as an irrelevance, Apple was back, and bigger than ever.

Moreover, the difference was almost entirely due to one part of its product line-up. Computer revenues were just under half of the total, and iPod revenues about a third. The rest, around $3 billion, came from software and 'services' – such as the iTunes Music Store, the smallest but fastest growing, which had generated almost $1 billion on its own.

Zune

Billion-dollar digital businesses tend to attract Steve Ballmer's attention – especially if Microsoft isn't getting a thick slice of them. Inside Microsoft at the beginning of 2006, the rising tide of iPods, and more importantly the continuing failure of PlaysForSure and subscription services based around it to attract customers away from Apple's little boxes, had people concerned. 'There was this big debate about whether we should build [music features] into phones, or go full frontal into battle with the iPod', recalls Pieter Knook, who was at Microsoft for nearly 20 years and ran the Windows Mobile team from 2001 until spring 2008. 'Steve [Ballmer] and Robbie [Bach, head of the Entertainment and Devices division, which included the Xbox and Windows Mobile businesses] really favoured that. Bill [Gates] didn't. But by that stage Bill really was already checking out of the company.' Gates avoided getting involved in the decision, Knook says.

Microsoft hadn't been able to satisfy Wal-Mart and Best Buy; the horizontal approach had failed. Ballmer called a war conference with the heads of Entertainment and Devices. The trajectory of the current strategy was clear: the iPod was murdering rivals, and PlaysForSure wasn't working. 'We need something to compete with these guys!' said Ballmer, his voice rising in frustration. 'We need a player, our own player!' he said, snapping his fingers.

He was determined that Microsoft needed, in the short term, an iPod competitor with its own, powerful brand name on it. Longer-term, a phone that played music, just as he had spoken about in 2004, made sense too. Microsoft was rich enough to do both.

The message was passed down, and responsibility came to rest with someone who had already proved his ability to see what was coming and how to deal with it. In March 2006 'Project Argo', as it was named, was handed to Allard.

He reckoned that, with $500 million of investment, Microsoft could build its own player and beat Apple, using the quality of Microsoft's software and its branding and distribution power. As a pitch, it's remarkably like the one that Chris Payne had made for search a couple of years earlier – though with a higher price tag for a market that was arguably significantly smaller, and with a more limited life than internet search. After all, hadn't Ballmer himself told those journalists back in October 2004 that, 'Over time most people will carry a phone that has a little hard disk in it that carries lots of music'?

During the debates inside the Entertainment and Devices division, Knook said a Microsoft music player would be a huge and costly mistake. 'All of us in the [Windows Mobile] business said: "Look, you've underestimated the cost of entering into every other hardware business"' – he pointed to the Xbox, which had cost $21 billion and had yet to turn a profit.

> When you say you can beat Apple in this space for
> $500 million, you're smoking [mind-altering substances].
> There's no way you can do that. You're not factoring in
> the cost of market and, because you're going to have to get
> this new brand known, you're going to have to tell people
> about it. And you can't depend on anybody else, because
> it's not as though the ODM [original device manufacturer,
> which would actually build the player and put Microsoft's
> logo on it] is going to invest in promoting it. So you're going
> to have to do it.

Knook says he pointed out that the Microsoft player might achieve some gross margin initially. 'But guess what – when Apple comes after you, and you don't have a complete product range like they do, which of their product prices are they going to drop? The ones that you're in.'

But more powerful people at Microsoft were insistent on a 'full-frontal' battle. The idea had become a meme within the company, which had coincidentally just relaunched its efforts in search with what was intended to be a full-frontal attack on Google, which dominated that market much as Apple did music players. 'It was a typical example of Microsoft looking back on its history and saying "Well, we beat Lotus in a full-frontal battle, and we beat WordPerfect in a full-frontal battle; we beat Novell in a full-frontal battle; why don't we just take out that playbook?' Knook shakes his head. 'That wasn't going to work with Apple.'

Tying the Zune to the Xbox

Allard and his team focused on the challenge of how to get Microsoft back into the digital music race, and to beat the iPod, the iTunes Store and Apple. One key decision: their player, named Zune, would not use PlaysForSure. This meant anyone who had bought PlaysForSure music wouldn't be able to play it on a Zune. So much for choice. But Allard's intention was to tie it to Microsoft's other big consumer success: the second-generation Xbox 360, which had launched in November 2005 to a rapturous welcome, getting the whole next-generation games field to itself; the key rivals, Sony and Nintendo, hadn't shown up yet.

The team decided to add features the iPod lacked. Wi-Fi connectivity would let you share songs and photos (though not video) with other Zune users. Get enough people, and a song would go viral – though of course you couldn't just let someone *copy* your songs; the record labels would have a fit. So DRM was built in: a song (even your own composition) shared to another handset would delete itself after three plays. Now it needed to license music to sell through its own store.

The record labels saw Microsoft's weakness and pounced. Executives from Sony's Howard Stringer to Warner Music's Edgar Bronfman to Universal's chief Doug Morris had grumbled more or less loudly that Apple's machine was used to store music they'd licensed (to CDs, from which it had been ripped), and yet they weren't getting anything from it. So, when Allard came seeking the rights to sell music for the Zune, Universal demanded – and got – a royalty of $1 per player sold. Finally, they were getting some payback. (Having succeeded there, Universal later tried brinkmanship on Jobs, threatening in mid-2007 to withdraw the licence to sell its songs from the iTunes Music Store unless Apple offered it a better deal on pricing. Jobs called Universal's bluff: completely withdrawing its songs would cost the record label around $200 million annually. Universal didn't re-sign the contract – but the songs remained available on an 'as is' basis.)

Word about the project started leaking out in June. Because it included Wi-Fi, an application for compliance testing had to be filed in August 2006 with the US Federal Communications Commission (FCC), where reporters immediately picked up on it. On Slashdot, news of the device's capabilities earned the ironic comment: 'Wireless. More space than a Nomad. Lame.'[33]

Technology reviewers liked some of the ideas of the Zune, but were dubious about its colour – brown – and limitations. The sharing limits in particular struck many as peculiar. Despite the undercurrents of unease – and the fact that Apple had sold more than 8 million iPods in each of the first three quarters of 2006 – Allard sought to rally the troops. In October 2006 he sent an e-mail to the team – now 230-strong – working on the Zune, with a link to a YouTube video of Steve Jobs discussing, in a 1980s documentary, Microsoft's inability to create desirable products. 'The only problem with Microsoft is they just have no taste... They have absolutely no taste, and I don't mean that in a small way; I mean it in a big way, in the sense that –' Jobs pauses for seconds, reflective. 'They don't think of original ideas, and they don't bring much culture into their product... I'm saddened... not by Microsoft's success; I have no problem with their success; they've earned their success. For the most part.' (A subtle putdown.) 'I have a problem with the fact that they make really third-rate products.'[34] (Later, Jobs called Gates to say: 'I'm sorry. I shouldn't have said that in public. I feel bad about it.' Gates thanked him for the apology, at which Jobs blurted out, 'But, you know, it's true!')

Allard said he wanted to see Jobs 'eat his words', because 'Those are fighting words. He is speaking to every one of us and saying we don't get it.'

A month later the Zune arrived in stores, after a gestation of just eight months – a short time for any hardware product, about the same as the original iPod, and amazingly short for a Microsoft product. But if the timescale was commendable, the outcome wasn't. Analysts expected it to sell perhaps 3 million units in its first year. They also expected – as Knook had warned from the start – that it would lose money for the foreseeable future.

In an interview whose message was easily overlooked, Allard played down the immediate ambitions for the device, describing the Zune as an 'intermediate step': it would do for now until you could store all of your music in the cloud and access it any time you liked, through any device you liked. The Zune was just the necessary incarnation for now of something far more comprehensive to follow. Ballmer meanwhile joked that he had loosened up over the device branding, resisting the urge to name it the 'Xbox Music Machine'.

Together, their comments point to the future they really saw for the Zune: integration with the Xbox, which has always been the company's play for the living room, and connection to the cloud online.

For Microsoft's PlaysForSure licensees, knifed by the company's decision, the Zune was galling. Jonathan Sasse, chief executive of iRiver, tried to suggest that having to compete with his own software provider wouldn't necessarily be bad – although, he conceded, '[Zune] is liable to compete directly with an existing device.' But the combination of the iTunes Music Store steamroller – by then selling more than $600 million of music per quarter – and Zune's lack of support for PlaysForSure pulled the rug from sites using the software. Neither the market leader nor the software provider believed in it. One by one, they began closing. The last service to use it, Napster, abandoned it in mid-2010.

White Christmas

Christmas 2006 marked the Zune's first 'holiday' season. Superficially, the signs looked good: in its first week, it came second in the United States in retail sales – excluding Apple stores and online retailers such as Amazon.[35] But even without those caveats the Zune wasn't a smash. NPD calculated that it took 9 per cent of the retail sales and 13 per cent of value of digital music players sold. In the same stores, the iPod managed 63 per cent unit share and 72.5 per cent dollar share. The Zunes were thus more valuable per device than the iPods – but Apple's range spread across devices all the way down to the cheap 'shuffle' devices. Meanwhile, half of all iPods were being sold outside the United States, where nobody saw the Zune.

By the start of December, Microsoft was projecting 1 million sales for the fiscal year (which ran for seven more months, to the end of June 2007). Jason Reindorp, the Zune marketing director, added: 'We feel pretty good about that number.' Other forecasts suggested that those 1 million would give the Zune about 10–15 per cent of the 30GB-and-over hard drive MP3 player market and that, together with Apple, the duo would have 98 per cent of that market. It was reminiscent of Jobs visiting Gates in 1997 and convincing him that *together* they controlled the desktop.

Allard's suggestion that the Zune was an intermediate to a cloud-connected service didn't resonate, because there wasn't any such service to connect to yet. Most couldn't follow the long-term strategy behind the Zune. As hardware, it simply didn't cut it. John Sculley, who had schooled Jobs in the importance and method of making people want one apparently indistinguishable product over another, was unimpressed. 'I remember going to the Consumer Electronics Show [in January 2007] when Microsoft launched Zune, and it was literally so boring that people didn't even go over to look at it,' he later said. 'The Zunes were just dead. It was like someone had just put ageing vegetables into a supermarket. Nobody wanted to go near it.' Then he considered why:

> I'm sure they were very bright people [in the Zune division], but it's just built from a different philosophy. The legendary statement about Microsoft, which is mostly true, is that they get it right the third time. Microsoft's philosophy is to get it out there and fix it later. Steve [Jobs] would never do that. He doesn't get anything out there until it is perfected.[36]

Ballmer didn't see it that way. Interviewed by *CNBC Business News* in January 2007, just after Steve Jobs had completely shaken up the smartphone business by announcing the iPhone, Steve Ballmer was asked about the Zune's sales performance. Having suggested 'synergy with things we're doing', he added that 'we took, I don't know, but I think most estimates would say we took about 20–25 per cent of the high end of the market. We weren't down at some of the lower price points, but for devices $249 and over we took, you know, let's say about 20 per cent of the market.' (The downgrade of the share in the space of two sentences is acute.) 'So, I feel like we're in the game, we're driving our innovation hard, uh, and, uh, okay, we're not the incumbent, he's the incumbent in this game, but, uh, at the end of the day, he's going to have to keep up, uh, an agenda that we're gonna drive as well.'[37]

Knook had predicted that Apple could come after the Zune any time it liked by dropping prices. Yet Apple simply ignored it. Partly, there was nothing to worry about: NPD's numbers showed that the Zune was getting about 2 per cent of the US market, barely anything in the world market. Nor was the Zune Music Store doing anything noteworthy, while in 2006 Apple's iTunes Music Store sold 1.15 billion songs and generated $2 billion of revenue.

Perhaps more surprising is that Microsoft, the company that best exploited the killer combination of the software and hardware ecosystem to cement its monopolies, never got to grips with building a hardware ecosystem around the Zune. Griffin recalls that, 'We did a little bit with Zune. They wanted to build the same kind of ecosystem, and have the same sort of accessory opportunities. Nobody's going to say no to that. It sounds OK. I didn't really like the player as much, but we thought "It's Microsoft. They're going to win some share."'

But Griffin recalls that, instead of nurturing the ecosystem, Microsoft trod all over it. 'They would tell us: *you* do this particular accessory.' Griffin thought it was an exclusive arrangement. 'But then they would just let everybody do it. They never really shot straight with us, and a lot of people took chances based on what was told, what was relayed to them verbally – and they got burned. And I think [Microsoft] really hurt their future ecosystem on that product.'

Was that worse than Apple's approach where it keeps accessory makers in the dark until – or even after – the very last minute of a product change? 'I respect that approach!' says Griffin. 'I would do [that] if I was them.'

He didn't like the Zune: 'Very splashy, very Microsoft. A lot of stuff moving around and everything, but Apple's was much more refined, and much simpler to use, really. Apple's worked on that ease of use, and it was an important thing, particularly when you're working with very small screens.'[38]

Twilight

In July 2009, Apple announced its financial results covering the period from April to June. They were better than ever, but for one thing: after 26 quarters when iPod sales had grown year on year as much as tenfold, in spring 2009 they fell. Peter Oppenheimer, the chief financial officer, brushed it off: 'We expect our traditional MP3 players to decline over time as we cannibalize ourselves with the iPod Touch [in effect, an iPhone without the phone call capability, introduced in September 2007] and the iPhone.' He added: 'we have a great business that we believe will last for many, many years, and which we will continue to manage well.'[39]

The decline happened again the next quarter, and the next. The age of the iPod was over; though the iPod retained the same dominant share, the whole market was drying up. As Steve Ballmer had predicted five years before, people now were listening to music stored on their phones.

The sales figures show that the iPod's real sales growth happened in the first months of 2004, and continued for two years, subsiding in 2006 when the multiplier (between each quarter's sales and its previous-year comparator) dwindled to 1. All that time, Microsoft had skewered itself on its devotion to the horizontally segmented business model; by the time Allard rose to the challenge, the sector's burst of adolescent growth was already over. Allard was trying to inject brand buzz into a market that had already seen its explosive growth. Like a surfer trying to ride a wave that had already passed, Microsoft had had to paddle as hard as it could to gain even the most minimal benefit.

By the time the wave had passed, Apple had sold 208 million iPods. And sales kept ticking over: by June 2013, a total of 378 million had been sold. As a business, it shifts about 40 million per year, declining by 10 per cent annually. If Apple wanted to be bloody-minded, it could string the line out for another decade, to the iPod's 20th birthday in 2021, before finally killing it. Instead, its marketing concentrated on the internet-enabled iPod Touch – by mid-2011 constituting half of sales – and the nano. The 'classic', now with 160GB storage, and 'shuffle', with 2GB, were ignored (though still sold).

Meanwhile iTunes had become a platform to sell music, films, TV shows and series, and to offer podcasts, university lectures, games for the original iPods, and eventually apps for the iPhone, iPod Touch and iPad. Over its lifetime, the iPod also made millions of pounds for retailers and manufacturers of add-ons. But it also saw two other dramatic effects.

The first was on the record labels, which had swaggered through the 1990s, fattened on the proceeds of CDs that were often re-pressings of the albums that customers had bought on vinyl years earlier. They discovered that their old model couldn't work online; the internet tends to atomize everything into its individual parts. The album, a format invented for the long-playing vinyl record, with 20-odd minutes on each side, and then re-imagined for the CD, with its monstrous 74-minute playback time, couldn't survive the net's onslaught: it exploded into individual tracks, and for many people 'iTunes' became synonymous with the record store. This was fortunate, because the second effect was on record stores, which were going out of business, unable to cope with the combination of online retailers' CD prices and Apple's tempting offer of listening to a 30-second sample and then immediately buying and downloading the two, perhaps three, tracks that you really liked off the album any time, day or night. Yet perhaps the record companies could count themselves lucky. What if Apple hadn't come along and made buying music really simple? When Jobs was negotiating with them nobody (to a near enough approximation) used the existing online services such as PressPlay. Many just bought CDs, or used file-sharing networks, where they got what they wanted free. Imagine then that the iPod had never happened. That would have left the record labels looking to Microsoft, and to digital music players and tracks loaded with DRM, to achieve their ends. Yet, even by 2004, with the incentive of a competitor that had proven the market, Microsoft couldn't make DRM work smoothly on multiple players.

So although the record labels lost from the atomization of the album, they won through being kept relevant and visible online. In fact, they even managed to achieve an amnesty of sorts. In June 2011, Steve Jobs announced a new paid service as part of Apple's free 'iCloud' service, which would synchronize documents and data across devices. For $25 per year, iTunes Match would search through your iTunes library and let you share any song that also existed on the iTunes Music Store (by then up to 14 million) on any other device you owned. If it didn't stock the song, it would be uploaded to iCloud. Rumours – unconfirmed, but from multiple sources – suggested that Apple had paid the record labels around $100 million to seal this deal, which was a sweet victory for both sides. The record labels would, finally, get a cut from all those songs that had been, as Ballmer said, stolen, and also see a subscription-based service. And Apple stole a march out of both Google and Amazon, which had tried to announce their own 'music locker' services in the cloud, but which didn't have the simplicity of use – or the cooperation of the labels – that Apple had.

A confidential presentation within Google in 2010, released as part of a patent dispute trial with Oracle, revealed that by 2013 it expected to have around 10–15 per cent of Android devices using a pay-to-download service generating $300m per year. (Google has never broken out revenues from music sales.)

However the rise of faster internet connections, both for home and mobile, brought a new perspective on the subscription services which had flopped so badly a decade earlier. By 2013, there was a profusion of music services such as Pandora and Spotify offering paid or ad-supported streaming services: you didn't own the music you listened to, simply consumed it and then moved on. The stream was a river of music; the iTunes model was like owning bottled water. In May 2013, Google moved into the streaming business with its own 'Google Play Music All Access' streaming service. Unusually, for a company which usually tries to offer free services to maximize takeup, it was paid-for. Apple soon followed in the United States with iTunes Radio, a streaming service on the iPhone and desktop. Subscriptions – in the form of streaming, the most evanescent form – seemed to be back.

There was one catch, though: streaming wasn't profitable. Pandora, Napster, Spotify – all lost money. Google had to charge for All Access. Apple's negotiations over iTunes Radio were hugely protracted, running for at least a year; and those only brought the service to the United States in the first instance. Yet within a week it had around 50 million users, through its giant installed base in the country – somewhat short of Pandora's 200 million at the same time, but an abrupt incursion into another rival's space all the time.

Rout or strategy?

Outside Microsoft, rebranding is recognized by observers as the sign that a product has passed its zenith; from there on only diminution and darkness can follow. (The exception is Bing, which survived its long dark night of the soul as 'Windows Live Search' and returned with a snappier, consumer-oriented name and focus.) In December 2007, Microsoft rebranded the PlaysForSure programme to cover more broadly all sorts of media, as 'Certified for Windows Vista'. Observers set their watches. In April 2008 Microsoft announced that from the end of August it would turn off the PlaysForSure validation servers for songs bought from the MSN Music Store. PlaysForSure was being killed.

By the beginning of 2011 the Zune had still not been released outside North America. Then observers began to notice that, while its rhombus-like logo kept appearing in Microsoft slides, its name didn't. They realized that the Zune was being downplayed – the prelude to being 'rebranded', and so doomed. The Xbox brand became more prominent near the rhombus logo. Ballmer's joke that he had nearly called it the 'Xbox Music Machine' began to look less funny and more like reality. The Zune Store, where you'd once bought your music, was rebranded as the 'Xbox Live Music Marketplace' on the Xbox and Windows Phone. Zunes? The whole concept was being replaced by Allard's idea of music in the cloud.

Cringely commented to me in mid-2011:

> Microsoft is like General Electric, in that it has to be first or second in market share, or not even bother. By that definition the Zune might even be considered a success. But Microsoft isn't good at playing catch-up. Apple was simply too far ahead. I've never heard an Apple person speak of the Zune with any sense that it was competition at all. They always worried more about Sony, because Steve loves Sony, not realizing that Sony ceased being Sony long ago.[40]

Microsoft had to face some uncomfortable truths: it had been bested in software development by Apple, which might have had a smaller and more tightly controlled set of hardware to work against, but also had much smaller teams, less money and tighter deadlines. Microsoft had been first to develop DRM that satisfied the record companies; but Apple was first with DRM that satisfied users too. It wasn't the best DRM in the world, but it didn't need to be. All it had to do was stay out of people's way – something that for the most part it did. The reward for that was the sweetest Steve Jobs could ask for: a victory over his old foe Bill Gates, plus the bonus of a multibillion-dollar business selling music, and a refreshed position on the world stage.

Microsoft finally killed the Zune in June 2012. There was no physical replacement; instead it too moved into purchased and streaming music under the title of 'Xbox Music', available on the Windows Phone mobile platform, Xbox console and Windows devices. Apple had won the iPod battle. But now the war moved on.

Chapter Five
Smartphones

Mobiles and Microsoft

Pieter Knook started working at Microsoft in October 1990. Previously he had been running a small business in the UK offering local area networking to let PCs (running MS-DOS; Windows 3.0 had only just been introduced, and wasn't yet widely used) connect to each other. The business grew, and was sold: 'I then had the choice of staying but I was attracted to Microsoft because of its crazily audacious goal at the time to put a PC on every desk and in every home,' he says. 'The "on every desk" seemed vaguely sensible, the "in every home" seemed completely stupid because at the time they were so expensive and it was completely unrealistic. PCs cost five thousand pounds; they were geeky tools.' In addition, none of his friends had heard of Microsoft; they'd heard of Lotus, or WordPerfect, or the word processing program WordStar. 'So I joined Microsoft, because I thought we could change the world.'[1]

In 1997 he went to run Microsoft's Asia business, and lived in Tokyo for four years, where he was astonished by the impact mobile phones were having. Japan was embracing i-mode, which allowed rapid data transfer; for some Japanese, life revolved around constant internet updates on their i-mode phones.

Knook was an enthusiastic convert, and when he returned to Microsoft's headquarters in 2001 Steve Ballmer gave him the task of creating a sales force to sell Microsoft's mobile offerings, generically called Windows Mobile. The opportunity was clear: mobile 'had the same attributes potentially as [the PC as] a platform – we'd sell a piece of software to run on a range of different pieces of hardware, upon which you would then layer other pieces of software, like Office for Mobile, or Database or whatever.'

Microsoft might have stumbled originally in getting on to the internet with PCs, but it was ready for the mobile internet.

The sales model for mobile phones is crucially different from that for PCs, because the infrastructure required for making mobile calls – the grids of cell towers, the authentication systems, the billing – have to be handled by a mobile operator. They are the gatekeepers of what gets on to their network: if your mobile operator blocks your mobile phone's unique IMEI number, you'll never be able to make a call. Similarly, for phone manufacturers, if mobile networks don't take their products, they'll never have a customer base. By contrast the PC model, where direct selling, retail sales and corporate accounts sit side by side, offers multiple ways to reach customers.

By January 2007, the company that was best at pleasing the mobile operators was Finland's Nokia (pronounced, Finns insist, NO-kee-ya). It was the world's biggest mobile handset maker, measured by revenue and volume: in the last three months of 2006 its mobile phone revenues were €7.1 billion, 60 per cent of the group's total revenue, from selling 106 million handsets worldwide. For the year, it had sold 347 million handsets.[2]

It had also pioneered the idea of the 'smartphone' – a mobile phone that could do more than just make phone calls, because it could act like a handheld computer, running its own programs natively, browsing the web and handling e-mail. The Nokia Communicator was its first attempt in 1996, and by the start of 2007 it owned the category, having sold 39 million of the 80 million smartphones sold that year, in a category roughly doubling in size annually.

There were rivals: a key one was Palm, which had started out simply as a handheld computer maker and then added phone functionality – coming at the problem from the opposite end of the spectrum from Nokia. By 2005, Palm had survived splitting into two companies (Palm and Handspring), then merging, then splitting into a hardware and software company and then reuniting. The Treo smartphone was popular in the United States, although Palm's struggles with an outdated operating system (OS) – which had worked fine for unconnected handheld personal digital assistants (PDAs), such as the Palm Pilot – meant that, by January 2004, Ed Colligan, Palm's chief, had decided that the company could not develop its way forward; Palm's mobile OS was, effectively, put on the shelf. The market for PDAs without phone connectivity was shrinking; standard mobile phones were beginning to absorb their functions, such as calendars and even e-mail. PDAs didn't have a future. Smartphones did.

In a series of secret meetings and e-mails, Colligan opened up negotiations with Microsoft to begin licensing Windows Mobile (in which, perhaps betraying the age of the deal's architects, Microsoft was codenamed 'Woodstock', Palm 'Purple Haze' and the Treo running Windows Mobile 'Hendrix'). But Colligan insisted that Palm should be able to tweak the operating system in a way that other licensees could not.

That tie-up was announced in September 2005. For Microsoft, getting Palm on board was a great conquest, and was seen as 'a significant win in its decade-long quest to crack the mobile market', in the words of Ina Fried, then reporting on the market for CNET.[3] As part of the deal, Palm was allowed to tweak the Windows Mobile interface and some of its features – to ignore calls rather than sending a text to the caller, and to navigate voicemails more easily. Because in the United States the devices would use the EV-DO 3G data networking system – an add-on for CDMA networks – they would have to cost more than the existing range of Treo 650 smartphones, which then retailed for around $500.

Colligan also said that Windows Mobile would become Palm's focus; there was no interest for the company in using the open source Symbian (as Nokia and others including Sony Ericsson were doing) nor any flavour of the free open source operating system Linux (which was viewed as an immature system for mobiles, with no coherent champion). Speaking at the unveiling of the deal, he said: 'We are going to focus on what we have on the table. This is for customers who want that familiar Windows user experience. Certainly for Palm, we will reach into many more companies with these devices.'[4]

Analysts agreed: in February 2006, Nick Jones, an analyst at the industry research company Gartner, declared that Windows Mobile had more than 10,000 developers working on applications, 'far more than any rival mobile operating system', ahead of Symbian (and Nokia) and that of Research In Motion (RIM), the Canadian maker of the BlackBerry.[5]

Android

The September 2005 announcement of the Microsoft–Palm tie-up grabbed the interest of one particular Google employee: Andy Rubin, a former Apple employee, whose second mobile start-up, called Android, had been purchased by Google the month before. (He had left his first mobile start-up, Danger, which produced the Hiptop phone and would later be sold to Microsoft.) Larry Page in particular saw mobile as the future; Eric Schmidt was less convinced. So Page, with co-founder Sergey Brin, bought Android without consulting Schmidt.

Like Knook, they could see that phones with computer power were going to become more plentiful than PCs. The computing capacity of mobile devices was also increasing roughly in line with Moore's law – a doubling every 18 months – and more and more people were buying them. There had been 680 million mobile phones (not smartphones) sold in 2004, growing by about 15 per cent annually, and forecast by the researchers Gartner to hit a billion by 2009.[6] Fold in the expectation that wireless connectivity would fall in price and become pervasive, and you had the next area that Google had to conquer: the mobile market.

Page, Brin and Rubin knew you could extrapolate the lines on the graph and see a point where not only would more search queries come from smartphones than PCs, but also people would use them more often, in more places. And because they wouldn't be in a fixed place – unlike people using desktops or even laptops – you'd get more data about their location as they searched and browsed. More data meant better targeting of search results and advertisements, reinforcing Google's search leadership.

So both Google and Microsoft in 2005 saw the future of the internet as being mobile. But they saw that future slightly differently: Microsoft wanted to use it as an adjunct to its profitable back-end software such as Exchange. Google, however, couldn't rely on a mobile user doing a search being offered its page: handset makers would demand huge sums from rivals (Microsoft was the obvious one) to set theirs as the default. And the majority of users don't change their default settings (which Google was already exploiting by paying millions per year to be the default on Mozilla's Firefox and Apple's Safari desktop browsers).

It would be a nightmare. And given Microsoft's very visible ambitions, and collaborations like that with Palm, Microsoft's search engine (then called Windows Live) could become the default on millions of mobiles. While Google could always complain to antitrust regulators if Microsoft were to use its billions in cash to buy its way to the top of mobile search, it would be a catch-up strategy; if or when Microsoft was slapped down by the courts, Google could have been defeated on the newest and most important computing platform, the one that would matter in the foreseeable future all over the world. And what use were antitrust settlements anyway?

The only way to secure Google's future was to offer handset makers something they'd love: free software that would run their phones. The fact that it would have Google search baked into it was just incidental.

ROKR and a hard place

In January 2004, Steve Jobs called Ed Zander, Motorola's newly installed chief executive; the two had met when Zander was at

Sun Microsystems. Jobs suggested a tie-up: Motorola would build the handset and deal with Cingular, the biggest mobile carrier; Apple would develop the music software.[7]

It was the only time that Apple would ever let device design go outside its control. But it was forced; despite its growing success with the iPod, Apple was then still a relative minnow in the consumer space, and the mobile phone business was enormous and complex. Apple wasn't in it, and didn't have the heft to push into it.

Zander had been brought in to turn the company around. He knew that there were potential hits in the design pipeline, such as the super-thin RAZR design that had been started in July 2003 under the former chief executive Chris Galvin. Zander thought that getting Apple involved, with its reputation for design prowess, would be a definite plus.

Instead the ROKR development turned into a classic multi-company design car crash. Sources inside Motorola told me that the company's bureaucracy simply got in the way of the design process; it wasn't prepared to focus unreservedly on the user experience in the way that Apple does reflexively. It became a committee product, and the ROKR – a dreadful, compromised device that was like a bad iPod with a telephone keypad – was the result. For a device ostensibly designed for consumers, it wasn't. For example, how many songs should the phone hold? The answer: up to 100 – because Apple's team didn't want to cannibalize iPod sales. How should they be transferred to the phone? Via a USB cable to a computer running iTunes, because Jobs wanted to keep the revenues and slim profits from selling iTunes songs, rather than letting the mobile networks sell songs via wireless for $3, to profit on their data provision. Jonathan Ive's design team at Apple didn't get to design the handset, only the interface to iTunes.

Despite the compromises, the phone was ready to launch by March 2005. Then Cingular's data division found out about the USB connection, and threatened to dump the phone: they wanted to sell songs over the air. Eventually Cingular was persuaded that the iTunes association might help. But the ROKR was left off the subsidized plans – meaning buyers would have to pay the full $250 price as well as taking out a monthly contract.

The delays, compromises and politicking frustrated Jobs, who could see a potential chance to cross over into the mobile market vanishing. Some of that annoyance vented in May 2005, when he declared at a conference that, 'As you know from our limited success at getting our computers into the Fortune 500, Apple's never been very good at going through corporate orifices in order to get at the end users. And if we can't do it with 500 companies, you can imagine it's even harder when there are only four.'[8] (There were four main carriers in the United States: Cingular, later AT&T, Verizon, T-Mobile and Sprint.)

That sentence more than anything sums up Apple's ethos: cut out the intermediaries and deal directly with the customer. It comes up again and again. Apple is happy to enable an aftermarket – software and hardware – but the purpose that all its staff understand is that the outcome is better for them if they can get the devices and the software directly into the hands of the people who will use them. It was one of the purposes of the retail stores: get the products directly from Apple into people's hands.

The ROKR design – finally unveiled early in September 2005 (along with the far more interesting iPod nano) – was unexceptional. Why would anyone want to buy a phone that looked rubbish and also combined the worst aspects of an iPod and a phone? On that, nobody knew the answer. Consumers saw there wasn't one – especially when Jobs himself didn't make the ROKR the highlight of his presentation. He demonstrated it – and soon hit a problem when the end of his staged phone call didn't automatically restart his music selection. 'Well... I'm supposed to be able to resume the music right back to where it was,' he said, and then added: 'Oops! I hit the wrong button!'

Buttons. Too many buttons. And not enough functionality. Within a month, returns of the ROKR were piling up at six times the average rate for a new phone. 'People were looking for an iPod and that's not what it is. We may have missed the marketing message there', Zander said in an interview. The question still lingered of exactly what the ROKR *was*. If not an iPod – which clearly it wasn't – then what? Just another mobile phone?

And it's not as if there wasn't competition. The Nokia N91 was expected in early 2006 – costing around $700 – with a 4GB (rotating) drive, enough for 1,000 songs, like the iPod mini. If only Nokia could have got on to iTunes-like terms with the music labels, it could have held sway with consumers who wanted to buy and listen to music on their phones.

But Nokia's interests weren't aligned with the people who would be using the phones; they were aligned with the people who would pay Nokia for the phones – the mobile networks. Despite its incredible heft in the mobile marketplace, Nokia couldn't drive the music business on to mobile handsets; US carriers simply wouldn't let Nokia have its way, and nobody at the Finnish company had Jobs's negotiating expertise. (And the record labels were ready for new entrants looking to license their music.)

So Apple's first foray into the mobile phone market ended in shameful failure, rejected by consumers and carriers, and marking the point where Motorola's mobile business began to slide downwards. Zander himself lashed out at how the ROKR had been downplayed by Jobs (who had focused on the iPod nano at the launch): 'Screw the nano. What the hell does the nano do? Who listens to 1,000 songs?' he said at a leadership forum a couple of weeks later.[9] Instead, he suggested, people would want devices able to do much more than just play music, and the evidence was clear from other countries with more advanced mobile networks. (Knook might have thought of Japan.) Motorola's PR tried to suggest that Zander was joking. Nobody believed it.

The ROKR was a painful learning process for Apple's team, who found out a lot more about what a future Apple phone would have to do than Motorola's team learnt (or needed to know) about music players. The key lesson was that handset makers – aided and abetted by the carriers – would make a botch of things. You could trust only yourself.

iPhone, that's what

Jobs knew well before the ROKR launched – even before Cingular threw its fit over the data transfer – that it was not how he wanted to enter the mobile business. In February 2005, according to Fred Vogelstein of *Wired*, Jobs had laid out his plans to build a phone to Stan Sigman, chief of Cingular, then the biggest mobile network in the United States.[10] Apple, he said, could build something completely revolutionary – and would do an exclusive deal to get into the business. Sigman said yes. Jobs went back to his team, which had already been working on a touchscreen tablet (inspired by Bill Gates showing one off at Comdex in November 2000), and told them to change direction.

By the end of 2006 the rumours had begun to swirl in earnest that Apple was about to produce a phone – and that this time it might not be as awful as the ROKR.

Colligan was unimpressed. Meeting journalists in November 2006, he laughed off the suggestion that Apple might do to the phone market what it had done with the iPod. 'We've learned and struggled for a few years here figuring out how to make a decent phone,' he replied. 'PC guys are not going to just figure this out. They're not going to just walk in.'[11] After the struggles Palm had gone through, he had reason to feel vindicated. And he could feel confident. In the financial quarter ending 2 December 2006, Palm's net profit was $13 million, its revenues were $393 million, and it had sold 617,000 smartphones – up 42 per cent year on year and up 8 per cent from the previous quarter. Colligan could feel the wind at his back for the first time in ages.

Another company with the wind in its sails was RIM, the Canadian company best known for its BlackBerry range. BlackBerrys were born out of pager systems; RIM worked out how to add the sending and receipt of e-mails from big companies (which had to install its expensive server system and proprietary handsets); in effect the e-mails back and forth were pager messages, with the added advantage of being heavily encrypted. E-mail, easy connectivity on the move and a QWERTY fixed keyboard made the BlackBerry the first truly useful smartphone; the Treo was as close as Palm could offer. The BlackBerry's encryption meant financial companies (its earliest adopters) were confident that highly valuable details of multimillion-dollar deals would not be 'sniffed' over the air, while handset password protection and remote wiping meant a lost handset wouldn't yield its secrets either. In the three months to December 2006, RIM's $835 million revenues were twice as big as Palm's, and its $176 million profits 10 times greater; it had shipped 1.8 million phones.

By the end of 2006, Microsoft had been in the mobile business for years – and hoped to corner it. As with Windows on PCs, manufacturers could buy Windows Mobile licences and install them on handsets (which would be sold to operators or retailers that would sell, rent or lease them to the people who made the calls). Microsoft would offer help such as development assistance, and even direct financial aid. Between July 2005 and June 2006 (its 2006 fiscal year), it sold 5.95 million licences. In the next year, from July 2006 to June 2007, it sold 11 million licences. Windows Mobile was on the up.

Of the mobile operating systems in contention, Windows Mobile had easily the most functionality, designed from the start to be able to handle Microsoft's e-mail formats, web browsing and internet connectivity. It could also be used to edit and upload documents in Office formats. Bill Gates had seen the potential of the mobile internet and wanted to control the gateway back to previous products such as Office.

Operators, though, were wary: they had seen what had happened to PC manufacturers, which scrapped among themselves for tiny slices of profit while Microsoft raked in its monopoly earnings. They didn't want to be caught in the same way.

At Google, Rubin had discovered that handset manufacturers who had laughed at him when he had been an independent business were much more interested now his business card had a Google logo. His plans to develop software for smartphones – handsets with keyboards like the Treo and BlackBerry – were under way.

Just walk in

Horace Dediu began working at Nokia in 2001 as a technology manager in its content distribution side: the plan was to sell content, such as e-books (a plan it abandoned) or music. Then his team was absorbed into the mobile software team for the Symbian S60 software, which Nokia hoped to license rather as Microsoft was doing with Windows Mobile. 'I was the Microsoft analyst', he says. 'My job was to understand how Microsoft was planning to disrupt the mobile industry.'

He recalls that 'everybody was afraid – even the operators were afraid – of Microsoft "doing a Windows" on the mobile space. I was on top of that in 2003 to 2005.'[12] Partly because of the operators' fears about Microsoft, and because of the relative lack of power in the phones and the operators' determination to wring every last cent from their existing networks, data-driven phones didn't take off in that period.

Having cut his teeth on Microsoft, Dediu was asked to do competitive analysis, looking at how the mobile landscape would evolve for the next 10 years: which mobile operating systems would there be, and what would demarcate them? 'We did anticipate that there would be Microsoft, and Linux, and [Nokia's open source, but closely held] Symbian.' (That turned out to be true – Google's Android is, at its heart, a version of Linux.) 'We did a curve of how adoption would change and how many phones would be sold.' He pauses. 'We were too optimistic in the short term, and too pessimistic in the long term', he recalls.

In 2004–05 he was shifted again, to the enterprise division, 'looking at disruption and operators – around VOIP [voice over internet, which encodes voice signals into data packets to be sent over the internet; on a mobile phone with a data plan it would be much cheaper than placing a standard end-to-end mobile call, which would disrupt operators' business plans]'.

By the end of 2006 the rumours that Apple was going to launch a mobile phone were impossible to ignore. In the absence of any official encouragement, Dediu made himself the Apple analyst –

looking at what the company might and could do in the market, and whether it could have any effect on Nokia's business.

Inside Apple, they were indeed working on a phone. It was going to be called iPhone, and it wasn't ready. A team of around 200 people had been working since mid-2005 on it, and they had big problems. The work was being done under enormous secrecy – one team built the software; another team built the hardware; barely anyone saw the two working together before the end.

The hardware effort forked in two directions: one trying to use an iPod-like scroll wheel to dial numbers, the other using a touchscreen. The software did the same: Fadell led one team trying to scale up the iPod's OS to run a phone, while another – of fewer than 15 people – was led by Scott Forstall, who had led the creation of the 'Leopard' version of Mac OSX. Forstall's software team won; according to *BusinessWeek*, he then adopted Jobs's secretive approach, to the annoyance of other executives and teams.[13] In hardware, the touchscreen won; the scroll wheel was desperately impractical even for dialling numbers.

Now all they had to do was build it. The challenge was that Apple, unlike all the other existing phone companies, unlike Microsoft, unlike Rubin at Google, didn't have any experience writing mobile phone software and handling the competing demands of something that is a radio and a transmitter – and they wanted it to be a self-contained handheld computer with an unusual interface as well. They knew that their deadline was January: Jobs wanted to reveal it on the stage of Macworld. Building a revolutionary device against the clock is not a pleasant experience. The four months leading up to the announcement at Macworld had taken work stress to new levels for those on the team. Fred Vogelstein of *Wired* reported that:

> Screaming matches broke out routinely in the hallways. Engineers, frazzled from all-night coding sessions, quit, only to rejoin days later after catching up on their sleep. A product manager slammed the door to her office so hard that the handle bent and locked her in; it took colleagues more than an hour and some well-placed whacks with an aluminum bat to free her.[14]

Jobs wanted the iPhone to be really different. He demanded that it have one – only one – button on the entire device. Apple's engineers had been trying to build a touchscreen tablet for a couple of years, but the price was too high to be reasonable. But a touchscreen phone – that could be affordable. And touch systems were finally coming out of the laboratory. Apple acquired a company called FingerWorks that was developing multi-touch systems, using capacitive screens (which consist of two films with a thin separation with a voltage between them; when a conductive item such as a finger comes near, it changes the electric field. The location of the item is determined by a matrix of wires arranged around the edge of the screen, which is why there is a black edge around touchscreens).

Altogether, the iPhone was a titanic engineering effort, for Apple's software engineers had not only to produce the touchscreen software – something they hadn't done before – but also to squeeze down the Mac OSX operating system used on Apple's PCs to fit into a phone's much more limited storage. Unlike with the iPod, Apple was going to do the whole thing itself. And this came just after the software team had completed the task of rewriting Mac OSX to run on Intel chips instead of the PowerPC RISC chips of previous Macs. The rewrite also had to be recompiled to run on chips using the ARM architecture used in all mobile phones and smartphones for its low power demands.

Somehow, it all came good. After more than 100 prototypes had been built and tested competitively against each other, on Tuesday 9 January 2007 Steve Jobs took to the stage in San Francisco. Anticipating the announcement (whose name now felt all but certain: iMac, iPod, iPhone), scores of journalists had abandoned the first day of the annual Consumer Electronics Show in Las Vegas to be there.

In an ironic twist, at the exact time that Jobs took the stage, his one-time would-be nemesis Michael Dell was on stage at the Consumer Electronics Show to show off a 'concept' laptop with a 20-inch screen and, with the help of Mike Myers (recapping his

Dr Evil role from the Austin Powers films), a cloud back-up service. As they took the stage, Dell was worth $30 billion, Apple $73 billion. (Apple had thoroughly passed Dell in value the previous July, after briefly capping it in January – prompting Jobs to send a company-wide e-mail suggesting: 'It turned out that Michael Dell wasn't perfect at predicting the future. Based on today's stock market close, Apple is worth more than Dell.') In Las Vegas, Dell's performance was excruciating. ('It might have been funny half a decade ago when that character meant something,' said one observer – probably about Myers.)[15]

In San Francisco, Jobs walked on and opened with the simple line: 'Thank you for coming. We're going to make some history together today.'[16] He then ran through some announcements: the iTunes Music Store had now sold 2 billion songs; the sales rate was accelerating, with 5 million songs being sold daily; Apple was now the fourth-largest music reseller in the United States, real or virtual (bigger than Amazon), and that it would also sell films from Paramount. He took a moment to laugh at the Zune's position – a 2 per cent US market share in November, against 62 per cent for iPods. He showed off the Apple TV, a device for streaming films to TVs.

And then after 26 minutes he paused. 'Every once in a while, a revolutionary product comes along that changes everything', he began. 'Apple has been – well, first of all, one's very fortunate if you get to work on just one of these in your career.'

Introducing the iPhone, Jobs said: 'Well, today we're introducing three revolutionary new products. The first one is a widescreen iPod with touch controls.' The crowd, as so often, went wild. 'The second is a revolutionary mobile phone.' The crowd almost came to its feet – partly in relief that finally the much-rumoured phone really was happening. 'And the third is a breakthrough internet communications device.' He paused. 'But... these are not three separate devices.' A showman's pause while the crowd whooped. 'Are you getting it? These are not three separate devices. This is one device. And we are calling it iPhone! Today, Apple is going to reinvent the phone.'

He then ran through the remarkable similarity of existing smartphones – all driven by buttons, fixed below the screen. 'Every application wants a slightly different user interface, a slightly optimized set of buttons. And what happens if you think of a great idea six months from now? You can't run around and add a button to these things. They're already shipped.' Another pause. 'Well, how do you solve this? It turns out we have solved it. *We* solved this problem – we solved it in computers 20 years ago. We solved it with a bitmap screen that can display anything we want – with a pointing device.'

It was classic Jobs: framing the argument as being about interaction, rather than any other element. Not about battery life, call quality, aerial sensitivity, storage, screen size. Apple's phone would be classed on its interaction.

'What we're going to do is get rid of all these buttons and just make a *giant* screen. A giant screen.'

And how to manipulate it? Not a separate stylus: 'You have to get them and put them away, and you lose them. Yuck. Nobody wants a stylus... We're going to use a pointing device we were all born with. We're going to use our fingers.'

He recapped again, emphasizing how this fitted into Apple's history. 'We have been very lucky to have brought a few revolutionary user interfaces to the market – the mouse, the click wheel [on the iPod] and now multi-touch,' he said. 'Each has made possible a revolutionary product – the Mac, the iPod, and now the iPhone. We're going to build on top of that with software. Software on mobile phones is like baby software. It's not so powerful. Today, we're going to show you a software breakthrough. Software that's at least five years ahead of what's on any other phone.'

He proceeded to show off the capabilities of the phone – particularly the browser, e-mail, Google Maps, pinch, double-tapping to zoom text. Liveblogging the event, Ryan Block of Engadget noted that, 'People are rapt, everyone is actually literally leaning forward and on the edge of their seat. We've never seen a presentation like this before.'[17]

Eric Schmidt then appeared for Google, beaming. 'We can take the enormous brains trust of the Apple team and the open protocols of companies like Google and put them in an environment for end users,' Schmidt said. 'From a Google perspective, we've pushed very hard to partner with Apple and working with many many different data services... This is the first of a whole new generation... Steve, my congratulations to you, this product is going to be *hot*.' He certainly hoped so; Google was its default search engine, maps provider and video source.

A few moments later, Jobs returned to the stage. 'So, an internet communicator, an iPod and a phone. Let's put them all together and see what you can do in a real-life scenario.' He began playing some music on the phone. 'Let's see what happens when a phone call comes while listening to music – music fades out and the call comes through.' Jobs and Schiller swapped a picture by e-mail during a call, and then ended it.

The music faded back up without Jobs having to press any physical buttons. It was the culmination of years of effort, and a final swipe at the failure of the unbearably compromised ROKR.

'After today,' Jobs remarked, 'I don't think anyone's going to look at phones the same way again.' He then introduced the prices for the phones on a two-year contract – $499 for a model with 4GB storage, or $599 for an 8GB version.

Cingular's then chief executive Stan Sigman told the audience he had signed the contract for the iPhone without ever seeing the phone: 'That's because of the confidence I have in Steve to deliver on his vision.'

While literally true, Sigman's words neatly glossed over the fact that Sigman and Cingular had negotiated hard with Apple for more than a year, continually concerned that they were giving up too much. Sigman understood from the popularity of the RAZR that a hot handset could bring millions of people to a network; and, in a market that was becoming saturated, he wanted something that would pull people over from the three rival US networks. He also wanted to shift towards a data-centric model. The trouble was that Jobs wanted unheard-of control. He wanted to decide when software updates would go out. He wouldn't let Cingular have its logo on the phone. He'd decide the price.

And even if Sigman had wanted to see the phone working before signing up, he couldn't have. In the audience, a group of Apple employees were watching on tenterhoooks – because they knew the software on the phone was shot through with bugs. Jobs had insisted on showing it off in January, six months before release, because before going on sale it would have to be submitted for testing to the US Federal Communications Commission (FCC) – from which details were sure to leak. Jobs wouldn't let the FCC steal his thunder.

So the team had figured out what they called a 'golden path' to avoid embarrassing crashes – say, open a picture, then make a phone call, then this web page, but not in a different order. The journalist Fred Vogelstein in his book *Dogfight* recounts the painstaking efforts, exhausting rehearsals and jury-rigged setups the team went through to get the demonstration to work flawlessy on the day. They were swigging from hip flasks as the demo proceeded. They ended up drunk, and delighted. It had all gone perfectly. Jobs had bet the company on a single demo of a phone with unfinished, buggy software – and it had worked.

The iPhone's launch marked the high point of Apple and Google's cooperation. Vogelstein reckons that it was a Nietschean life-or-death moment for Apple, rather as the Yahoo deal had been years earlier for Google; there was no 'other thing' for Jobs to show off if the iPhone's designers had missed their deadline.

It's interesting to speculate. Jobs would surely have found something to fill the time – perhaps a shorter presentation with a paean to the new Apple TV set top box, retail success, and so on. People would have been puzzled by its absence. But Apple could still have launched it a few months later – for Jobs and the executive team could see the iPod's inevitable decline ahead. The iPhone was necessary if Apple wasn't to fade into oblivion as 'the company that made those MP3 players'.

So how big did Apple think the iPhone might be? Jobs brought up a slide showing the sales in 2006 of various device categories:

games consoles, 26 million; digital cameras, 94 million; MP3 players, 135 million; personal computers, 209 million. And then mobile phones:

> Just about a billion, worldwide. So what does this tell you? That 1 per cent market share equals 10 million units. This is a *giant* market. If you get just 1 per cent market share, you're going to sell 10 million phones. And this is exactly what we're going to try to do in 2008, our first full year in the market, is grab 1 per cent market share and go from there.

But the smartphone market in 2006 had only comprised about 80 million units, so 10 million units would have been 12.5 per cent. Apple wasn't competing against every handset maker, only those making top-end smartphones, notably RIM, Nokia and Symbian licensees such as Sony Ericsson, and the Windows Mobile licensees. Even with the smartphone market roughly doubling annually, Apple would still be going after anything between 3 and 10 per cent of that part of the market in 2008. Jobs's aim was far bigger than he made it seem. Apple was actually making a huge bet. Jobs could see a giant market and wanted to get in on the ground floor. By October 2006 – just as the iPhone's development was reaching its most intense point – the research company Gartner was predicting that the smartphone market would hit 81 million for 2006, up 66 per cent. As with the iPod, Apple was aiming for a fast-growing market at the point where it had just begun to inflate. With Microsoft licensing around 11 million Windows Mobile devices per year, and growing, Jobs's proclamation actually meant he wanted to put Apple on a par with Microsoft in his company's newest market incursion.

Matt Drance, watching, was astonished:

> The minute he announced it, I was thinking 'I can't believe I didn't hear about this internally.' I wasn't angry, I was in awe, because Steve said on stage he'd been waiting two and a half years for this. Really? Two and a half years, and I never caught any window? It's a fairly large team to build something like that. So yes, Apple can keep a secret.[18]

What did the mobile leader Nokia think of its newest rival? Chief technology officer Tero Ojanpera said he'd reserve judgement on the iPhone until he had used one, but suggested it was nothing new: 'Things like internet browsing we introduced a couple of years ago,' he remarked dismissively.[19] 'The touchscreen is interesting, but a number of vendors already have touchscreen capabilities in their devices.' All Nokia's line-up of devices for 2007, shown off a couple of weeks later in Helsinki, had a built-in keyboard.[20]

Tomi Ahonen, formerly head of Nokia's 3G Business Consultancy and now an independent telecoms consultant, thought that the user interface looked 'intuitive and revolutionary', but said the phone was 'seriously flawed': the low-spec (2-megapixel) camera, no flash, no video recording, no 3G, no replaceable battery. Although, he added:

> I like the iPhone. And I'm not faulting Apple. They had to invent it in secret, without consulting operators, projecting the specification 18 months ago when the design started, trying to guess the right screen size, camera resolution, radio technology, processor speed, battery endurance, etc. A smartphone is by far the most complex design Apple has ever attempted. And it has to get it rather close to perfect at its first attempt. Apple cannot sustain a Newton-like failure, not now when it has changed its name from Apple Computer to Apple Inc.

But, he added, 'It is a landmark device, and will revitalize the industry.'[21]

Inside Nokia, having watched Jobs's presentation, Dediu decided that Apple very definitely could make a huge difference to Nokia's business – in a negative way, if the company didn't adjust.

'I was going around the canteen saying to people "You know, this is going to be big; this is going to make a difference",' he told me. But nobody took any notice of him. Irked, Dediu penned a forecast of how Nokia – the market leader, which had built a touchscreen phone the year before – would react to Apple's incursion into the mobile space. It now forms the first post on his blog at asymco. com, entitled 'Assessing Nokia's competitive response'.[22] For 2007, his forecast was: 'No response within the first year. No process change. No roadmap changes and no business review. Apple is not considered a competitor.'

Indeed, few thought Apple would be a serious player. On 10 January 2007, the day after Jobs's introduction, Steve Ballmer was interviewed by CNBC's Scott Wapner on its *Business News* segment. Wapner began by asking: 'Steve, let me ask you about the iPhone and the Zune, if I may. The Zune was getting some traction, and Steve Jobs goes to Macworld and he pulls out this iPhone. What was your first reaction when you saw that?'

Ballmer guffawed:

$500? Fully subsidized? With a plan? I said, 'That is the most expensive phone in the world!' And it doesn't appeal to business customers, because it doesn't have a keyboard, which makes it not a very good e-mail machine. Now, it may sell very well or not, you know. We have our strategy; we've got great Windows Mobile devices in the market today. You can get, uh, a Motorola Q phone today for $99. It's a very capable machine. It'll do music. It'll do, uh, internet. It'll do e-mail. It'll do instant messaging. So I kind of look at that and I say, well, I like our strategy; I like it a lot.

The scepticism wasn't limited to Ballmer. 'The iPhone is nothing more than a luxury bauble that will appeal to a few gadget freaks,' wrote Matthew Lynn, a columnist at Bloomberg, a week later.[23] He quoted Charles Golvin, an analyst at Forrester, who in a report that month wrote: 'The iPhone will not substantially alter the fundamental structure and challenges of the mobile industry.' Lynn argued that the iPhone was 'late to the party', and Apple was unfamiliar with working with carriers: 'The provider subsidizes the handset in the UK and hopes to recoup its money with ridiculously expensive charges for calls and data. Yet Apple has never been good at working with other companies. If it knew how to do that, it would be Microsoft Corp.' And finally, he argued, rivals such as

Nokia would 'attack' the iPhone with deals to encourage carriers not to sell the iPhone – which was anyway 'a defensive product... mainly designed to protect the iPod, which is coming under attack from mobile manufacturers adding music players to their handsets'. Yet, Lynn noted, the mobile industry needed some change: it was 'becoming a cozy cartel between the network operators and a limited range of manufacturers. It could certainly use a fresh blast of competition from an industry outsider.'

Apple was certainly an outsider. As Sigman had discovered, and other carriers were to discover, it simply didn't think like other companies. But an entire generation of phone users was about to re-imagine how you would interact with a screen.

As Don Norman explains, it was that element of touch that made all the difference. 'Touch is a very important sense,' he says.

A lot of human emotion is built around touching objects, other people, touching things. I think that we lost something really big when we went to the abstraction of a computer with a mouse and keyboard. It wasn't real. And mobile phones were the same: they had this bunch of menus, and people got lost in the menus and buttons to push. It felt like a piece of technology, where the iPhone felt like –

He pauses and struggles for the word. 'It was a piece of delight. And it really is neat to go from one page to another not by pushing a button, but by swiping your hand across the page. The correct word is "intimacy".' He adds: 'Think of it not as a swipe. Think of it as a caress.'[24]

The transformation was a tectonic shift, an earthquake on the way. The carriers were to discover that a company could become more important than them, and that their ability to pick and choose handsets to attract customers would be completely reversed. Instead, it would be the customers that would choose the network, based on the availability of a phone. That was what Sigman had hoped the iPhone would do. But he wasn't quite prepared for how it would work out.

Apple was about to do to the networks what it had done to the record labels: persuade them that its business model (commoditize the data, profit on the hardware) wasn't a threat, that it would only ever be a small player, that the upside was big but the downside of failure (again) would be carried by Apple. And then disrupt their businesses entirely.

When the iPhone finally appeared in the summer, reviewers compared it to their checklist of technical specifications and found it wanting. 'Apple provides next to no information about the features of the iPhone's camera – and for good reason,' wrote Shawn King at PC World, reviewing it in June 2007.[25] 'It's a 2-megapixel (2MP) camera phone with all the limitations of any other camera phone. There's no flash and no zoom, and... it does a poor job of capturing motion or images in low-light conditions.' At a time when many manufacturers were offering 5MP cameras with digital zoom and video recording, the iPhone was fixed focus and took only still pictures. In the *Australian*, Ian Grayson called the camera 'paltry', calling its 2MP 'well below many other phones'.[26] It lacked 3G or forwarding for text messages too.

Reviewers also noted that the phone was imbued with the same design sensibility that Ive had brought to the original iPod: invisible seams, a smooth metal back, no replaceable battery (because removing and replacing the back bends seams, and destroys the unitary idea of the product). Most other phones were built down to a price, with plastic painted to look like metal, and seams everywhere. The iPhone was expensive, but felt expensive too. The screen was responsive, and the e-mail set-up – a bugbear on so many other phones – simple. The virtual keyboard was a completely new experience, and its autocorrection ability (necessary, because typing on a virtual keyboard was inaccurate) was surprisingly, charmingly good. It's difficult, years later, to realize how different it was from what preceded it. Buyers loved having the internet in their hand, wherever they went, available at a touch or a swipe.

Disrupted

At Microsoft, Knook recalls that:

> Some of the operators freaked out and said: 'We need
> something we can go and compete with iPhone; give
> us something now.' They would come in and say: 'We need
> you to build a device with this, this and this spec.' Of course,
> that was a complete redo of the entire roadmap. We weren't
> really focused on the consumer – that was a major problem.
> We couldn't just sort of wheel that out and address that
> overnight.

Knook resisted those calls. Windows Mobile was for business, and the iPhone wasn't.

For RIM, the arrival of the iPhone was a complete surprise. Former employees say the company had fallen into a culture of complacency. Before the iPhone, one said:

> All these companies were fighting over what amounts to
> overgrown PDAs with phones and wireless stacks strapped
> on. Everyone assumed power density [the amount of energy
> stored in a battery of a given size] was nowhere even close
> to what was needed for general computing, that a fully
> featured browser and heavy-duty internet services were
> impossible due to [network] bandwidth and latency... even
> Danger [the company Andy Rubin had founded and then left]
> was just working on a better BlackBerry.

Another told me that the quarterly 'vision meetings' held by co-chief executive Mike Lazaridis 'were normally quite unremarkable... They were very much "We don't need to do anything special, because people love us and aspire to owning our devices."' Ahead of the release of the iPhone, Lazaridis showed off a new phone – yet another keyboard-based one. Then 'the iPhone came along and it was panic,' the ex-employee says. Although, he adds, the company had 'some of the cleverest people I know'.

The first ex-RIM employee says its engineers didn't believe the demonstration of the iPhone (understandably, because demos are easy to fake): they were sure it couldn't do what Jobs had demonstrated without using huge amounts of power and so having no battery life. 'Imagine their surprise when they disassembled an iPhone for the first time and found that the phone was a battery with a tiny logic board strapped to it,' the ex-employee comments.

It was ridiculous. It was brilliant. I really don't think [people are] giving Apple enough credit here. They did something amazing that many very prominent people in the industry thought was either impossible or at least a decade away. And they did it in a disgustingly short time frame. What stands out in my mind was how it proved that these assumptions [about power and processing] were flat out wrong, beyond any reasonable doubt. Apple pretty much gave everyone the finger and said, 'We can build your distant impossible future *today.*'

Lazaridis showed off a forthcoming device at the 'vision meeting' following the iPhone's launch, which 'had a shedload of features packed into it that we'd never considered for a device before', recalls another ex-employee, 'every one of which was tagged with "which is better than the iPhone"'. Lazaridis insisted to the staff that, 'We're not making a "me too" device.' One at least agreed: 'As it turned out, it wasn't a "me too" device. It was worse.'

In summer 2007 the US operator Verizon, and its partner, the multinational operator Vodafone, having failed to get the exclusive contract to sell the iPhone in the United States and Europe, contacted Lazaridis and told him that RIM needed to develop an iPhone competitor right away so the carrier would have a competitor to sell. RIM had to develop an entirely new touch interface, something Apple had spent years over, in months. In late 2008 the first BlackBerry Storm finally appeared in the United States and European markets, with a 'touch' screen which had to be pushed hard enough to click – an odd sensation – but no Wi-Fi (Lazaridis said there 'wasn't enough room' for it on the main logic board). But it had a very slightly better camera and slightly more storage, and was the same size and weight as, with better (claimed) battery life than, the second-generation iPhone 3G with which it now competed. On a spec-for-spec basis, the Storm won. The user experience, though, was terrible. The Storm was a flop, to RIM's great surprise. 'This again was indicative of RIM's ethos at the time,' explains an ex-employee, 'that if we make it people will buy it because it's got bigger numbers in the specs, that no one cares about usability or functionality as long as it's BlackBerry and their friends haven't got it yet. For RIM the biggest shock was people actually liked the iPhone's easy-to-use touchscreen.'

Although RIM's business was still growing, the iPhone's arrival would have a dramatic effect because it ushered in the mobile web. The BlackBerry's browser was, in contrast, pitiful; websites either looked wrong or didn't load. On the iPhone, web browsing became useful. And the ability to 'pull' or tap parts of a screen to magnify them was a revelation. The keyboard-driven BlackBerry was still great for e-mails. But Apple had added a new dimension.

Inside Nokia, there was less discomfort – as Dediu had forecast. Nobody, besides him, saw anything threatening.

Within Google, the iPhone caused much more action. Plans for a keyboard-based device had already been well advanced. Rubin's team saw the arrival of the iPhone as setting a new bar. Internally, the team immediately dropped development of keyboard-based Android interfaces (although the one being developed was continued to its fruition) and began working on a touch-based interface – codenamed 'Sooner'. Touch, Rubin could see, was the future. Apple had really changed everything. Nobody had ever made it possible to stroke the internet before.

The other group for whom the iPhone presented disruption was the mobile carriers. They were intermediates between the handset makers and the users: they controlled pricing of devices and data contracts, the timing of software updates, device branding, everything. Within Nokia and other handset makers, the thinking had become more about keeping the carriers happy than delighting the customers who would make calls. To Jobs, they were both ripe for disintermediation. The deal that he negotiated with Cingular (soon to be renamed AT&T) was unprecedented in the history of mobile networks: Apple would control the iPhone's branding and marketing and the timing of software updates. It was the expression of Jobs's desire to control the presentation of every item he sold – *you can't let just anyone sell your ties.*

Free as in data

A crucial aspect of the iPhone that Steve Jobs didn't talk about in his Macworld speech that January, because it hadn't been settled, was the iPhone's data plan: how much data users would be able to get each month on their contract. Carriers saw data contracts as the next in a long line of golden egg-laying geese, after voice calls, text messaging (aka SMS) and multimedia messaging (MMS). The advent of 3G data offerings (which moved to a faster packet-based connection) had not been met with equal enthusiasm by customers. People were wary of the data charges that the carriers slapped on connections. To those now used to broadband connections at home, 3G data charges felt like a return to the medieval days of the dial-up internet, when every minute online would cost you. But data charges were worse than dial-up, because you couldn't be entirely sure how big an e-mail or web page was.

In a series of negotiations with Cingular, Apple cut the Gordian knot: the iPhone would come with unlimited data. The plans weren't cheap, but – unlimited? 'Holy cow. This is really cheap,'[27] Shaun Parvez, an analyst at Cowen & Co, blurted when the plans were announced, with unlimited data typically for about $20 more per month than a voice contract. (According to Vogelstein, Apple and AT&T had a complex revenue-sharing system: AT&T got some payment from iTunes downloads, while Apple got a cut of each AT&T iPhone subscriber's monthly contract payments.)

That $20 turned out to be the price of the networks' disruption. Though Sigman wasn't to know it, he had begun the transformation of carriers from the gatekeepers of the mobile world to 'dumb pipes' – a simple conduit for a commodity (internet packets) from which they couldn't easily extract any extra value. It was a position from which they would subsequently spend years trying to extricate themselves. Given enough data, why would you buy a map service from your carrier if you could get Google's maps free via the web on your handset – as iPhone users with unlimited data could? Even if the first iPhones didn't have GPS chips, users could figure out their location by entering the name of the closest road on Google Maps.

For carriers hoping to charge people for electronic map access, iPhones plus Google Maps plus data equalled calamity. They had been cut out of the revenue stream; instead of selling data plus maps, they were selling just data. It was worst for Nokia, which had bought the mapping company Navteq for $8.1 billion in October 2007 in the expectation of selling it back, a dollar per month per head, to carriers around the world. (Things would become even worse when Google Android phones began arriving.)

Even so, analysts were, like Ballmer, dubious about the iPhone's $599 price, pointing out that only 15 per cent of phone buyers in the United States spent more than $100 on a new handset. (Parvez forecast that Apple would sell 3 million iPhones in 2007 and 10 million in 2008; in fact it sold 1.3 million and 15.3 million. Like Dediu, he was over-optimistic in the short term, but pessimistic in the longer term.) They were proved right: on 5 September 2007 – the start of the new financial quarter – Apple killed off the 4GB version of the iPhone and cut the price of the 8GB model from $599 to $399 – making the quarter of a million who had bought it look suddenly foolish. 'In June, they were calling it "the God Phone",' noted the *New York Times*. 'Yesterday, it was the Chump Phone.'[28]

The next day, in response to 'hundreds' of aggrieved e-mails from the people who had bought at the higher price in the just-finished quarter, Jobs wrote a marvellously passive-aggressive note: 'This is life in the technology lane. If you always wait for the next price cut or to buy the new improved model, you'll never buy any technology product because there is always something better and less expensive on the horizon.'[29] He offered an apology and a concession: a $100 credit to buy more Apple products. It was a cheap piece of PR, costing at most $27 million when Apple had billions in the bank. It left some people wary of rushing to buy the iPhone until the company could convince them it wouldn't pull the price rug out from under them. (By the start of 2008, when there had been no more pricing surprises, with no post-Christmas price drops, the concerns subsided.)

The iPhone's arrival was pivotal for the mobile industry, and for Google. The iPhone became the fulcrum, and Apple pushed hard to change the industry to its way – so much so that by 2010 it would be the carriers that were cowering at its behaviour, when an executive at one UK mobile phone carrier told me: 'Apple's like the big kid in the playground, and everyone wants to be its friend. And some days it likes you, and some days it doesn't, and you have to go and sit out in the cold while the other ones are in its favour – getting price cuts, or extra supplies, or whatever.'

Another says now that the arrival of the iPhone effectively validated all their investment at the start of the century in 3G services. 'The business was – let's say – heavily pregnant with data services,' he commented. The data provision was all there in the networks, but nobody had managed to find a way to tempt people to use it. To the average person, setting up e-mail and the web on a feature phone was a bamboozling nightmare of settings, APNs and passwords. On a smartphone, it was all done already.

The iPhone became a very effective midwife for data pregnancy. UK networks, which had effectively written off the £22.5 billion they had spent buying 3G access in 2001, really needed a phone that would get lots of people interested in accessing data services.

Wasn't the BlackBerry doing that, though? Or Nokia's phones? Or Windows Mobile phones? No, says one industry insider (who asked not to be named because it could affect his company's working relationships). The iPhone did.

It was the browsing experience. That's what made the difference. If you're trying to look at a web page and you can't make out the text, well, what's the point? The iPhone brought pull-to-zoom, and that made all the difference. That, and apps. Plus the iPhone was the only phone that didn't come with a manual. Apple's very clever: they can sell you services even while you don't really realize that you're buying them.

The gulf in usability and desirability was crystallized for one mobile executive who visited Nokia late in 2007 under its then management, led by Olli-Pekka Kallasvuo, and suggested that the iPhone was doing something remarkable to the market. 'Look,' he said, 'I can even give it to my three-year-old and he knows how to use it.'

'We don't make smartphones for three-year-olds,' Kallasvuo shot back contemptuously. The visitor left convinced that Nokia now had a serious problem: not only was a rival grabbing its potential market, but it didn't realize how dangerous that rival was. Dediu had tried to raise the same alarm inside the company, with a similar lack of success.

Apple, meanwhile, began courting and was courted in return by mobile networks from around the world. The beauty contests were based on a combination of capability, willingness, but also cultural fit. O2, in the UK, was helped by having a large parent, Telefónica, which had a European spread; the parent handled the principal negotiations, and its customer-oriented approach won.

For anyone who hasn't worked in the mobile industry, it's hard to express how complete that reversal was from any period before 2007, when no handset maker would dare dictate terms to a carrier. Nokia, the only one that might have tried it, had learnt from trying to introduce a music phone in the United States that tried to gather data about the phone owners for its own systems, bypassing the carriers. The carriers had told it in no uncertain terms to stop. Nokia had become a compliant bureaucracy, turning out incremental improvements on what had gone before while tightening its supply chain wherever it could. And it saw those two processes as sufficient.

The drawer of broken dreams

At the end of July 2007, Bill Gates spoke to the *New York Times* as he prepared to step down finally from the company. He dismissed the idea of Google succeeding in the mobile phone business with its own software and services. Rather like Ballmer with the iPhone, he accepted the idea, but dismissed the prospect. 'How many products, of all the Google products that have been introduced, how many of them are profit-making products?' Gates asked rhetorically. 'They've introduced about 30 different products; they have one profit-making product.' (Strictly, two: AdWords, on searches, and AdSense, on non-search properties such as Blogger.) 'So, you're now making a prediction without ever seeing the software that they're going to have the world's best phone and it's going to be free?'[30]

There was that word again: free. In Microsoft's world, there is no free software lunch. In Google's world there is; it acts as the waiter, being paid by retailers putting tempting offerings beside the meal.

Gates emphasized the importance of software quality to success. 'Why do you like your iPod, your iPhone, your Xbox 360, your Google Search?' he asked. 'The real magic sauce is not the parts that we buy for the Xbox, or the parts that Apple buys for the iPhone, it's the software that goes into it.'

And phones were going to demand even better software. 'The phone is becoming way more software intensive,' he said. 'And to be able to say that there's some challenge for us in the phone market when it's becoming software intensive – I don't see that.' In other words, Microsoft was fine: Windows Mobile was going to be able to cope with whatever came along.

Yet even then there were huge debates, Knook says, about whether Microsoft should pursue a vertical integration strategy, as it had with the Zune and Xbox, and try to own (in Jobs's words) the whole widget. 'Robbie [Bach], J Allard [who had pushed the Zune through to fruition] and Steve [Ballmer] really favoured that route. Bill did not, but by that stage Bill really was already checking out.'

There was also a growing problem with Windows Mobile: if a handset maker wanted to add an extra button or an extra feature, Knook was happy to get the Windows Mobile team to comply and customize their baby. More tweakability meant more sales, surely, especially to enterprise customers?

But it also meant bigger problems trying to keep the Windows Mobile codebase in sync, as each different stock-keeping unit (SKU) – or identifiably different available version – imposed a load on the developers in Redmond. Soon there were hundreds of SKUs for Windows Mobile, which for every update had to go through regression testing to make sure that the new code wouldn't break existing functions, involving more tweaking if it did.

'There was no standard screen size, so manufacturers made up their own, in all sorts of form factors,' one former Microsoft employee told me. 'There were various amounts of memory and processing power. This was especially painful; many manufacturers saw applications as extra and put in cheaper, lower-grade processors and the bare minimum of RAM, which often made apps very sluggish.'

That led to a hideous diversity of products, each of which was a valid version of a Windows Mobile implementation, but each of which was different. 'Somewhere in Redmond they used to keep a drawer full of all sorts of different makes and models of Windows Mobile devices,' the ex-employee recalls. 'It was called "the drawer of broken dreams".'

Choosing between them wasn't much fun for the carriers either; their sales staff began shying away from Windows Mobile. And the code problems led to grumblings within Microsoft's Entertainment and Devices (E&D) division.

That was one problem. The other, as Ballmer and a team from the division recognized, was that they simply didn't have a consumer offering in mobile phones. Windows Mobile might win corporate contracts, but it would never win a popularity contest with users. And they'd realized back in 1999 that they needed more consumer focus.

The idea that emerged from E&D was for Microsoft to build its own consumer-focused phone. J Allard was keen to push forward with the idea – for which the Zune had been the starting point – of a cloud-based device that would do much more than just play music. In 2007 the Zune business manager Rick Thompson and Allard began a project codenamed 'Pink' to create a smartphone to access music in the cloud. The underlying operating system would be the same Windows Mobile, but aimed at young 'connected consumers', and would have its own music store, just like Apple's iPod (and, now, iPhone).

The problem, Knook says, was that Ballmer and Allard seriously underestimated the cost, difficulty and timing of entering into the smartphone business – just as the senior managers had with the Xbox, with search and in 2006 with the Zune MP3 player. 'With the Zune, the plan went from a worldwide launch to a North American launch and then to just a US launch,' says Knook, 'because they realized how much the working capital and manufacturing costs would be.' He points to the Zune's failings – incompatible with all the music that people had ripped to Windows Media Player, and the existing music stores Microsoft had worked with – and says that he felt he and Melvyn Flowers, the financial officer for the Windows Mobile division, had the arguments they needed to prevail in the argument with Ballmer against greenlighting Pink.

Knook and Flowers lost. Allard, now in charge of the new Premium Mobile Experience (PMX) division, pushed Pink along – and soon had his eyes on Danger, which Rubin had founded in 1998 before he left (to set up Android). Danger's Sidekick and Hiptop phones were hip: users included celebrities such as Paris Hilton. Allard wanted to buy Danger for its proven relationships with carriers and knowledge of operator billing, which his team didn't have; and the Danger team knew how to make handheld hardware – something the Xbox group had realized was a special skill when they had tried to build the Zune.

Allard argued that Microsoft needed to have its own ecosystem – an idea that had worked with the Xbox – and most of all needed to be selling the hardware, because that, not software, was where the profits were in mobile. Buy Danger, he told Ballmer.

Knook and Flowers disagreed: it was too expensive, it would require difficult integration of an entire company, and building hardware wasn't Microsoft's skill. Also, Allard's plan would lead to incompatible user experiences between Pink and Windows Mobile, even if the underlying software was the same. If Microsoft was going to invest so much money in mobile, shouldn't it go into the core platform?

Ballmer gave the nod to Allard.

Developers and the iPhone

Developers, meanwhile, had been looking at the iPhone and drooling. Whereas the idea of writing applications to run on the iPod had looked like an interesting idea, the iPhone was clearly a computing platform. The separate 'apps' – Mail, Safari (for browsing), the Address Book, Calendar (for calendaring), Google Maps, YouTube and so on – meant it had an operating system, so you could write programs for it, just as had been done by third parties in a limited way with games on the iPod.

That was really all that it was: an internet-connected handheld computer that ran one program at a time and happened to make phone calls as well, and that sometimes used the phone network to connect to the internet. Mail, Safari: they were just programs. That was the thinking that was so different about the iPhone compared to the previous devices such as Nokia's or the BlackBerry.

Developers wanted to join in, far more urgently than they had with the iPod. Where, they asked, was the software development kit (SDK)? Where was the guide to the application programming interfaces (APIs) so they could dream up new apps for this wonderful machine that you could *stroke*? Just using what was on it would be like using existing feature phones – closed and dull.

Other platforms already offered apps: Symbian phones had calorie counters and pedometers, panic alarms, exercise monitors, biometrics, ID and face recognition, electronic wallets and – just to finish it off – 6GB of music.

Jobs was initially wary. In January 2007, just after the iPhone launch, he told *Newsweek*: 'You don't want your phone to be an open platform... Cingular doesn't want to see their West Coast network go down because some application messed up.'[31] He seemed to have unwound a little by May: 'We'll find a way to let third parties write apps and still preserve security on the iPhone. But until we find that way we can't compromise the security of the phone.'

Drance, with his role as 'developer evangelist', says reaction after the iPhone announcement was like night and day:

> For the first five and a half years of my career at Apple, I couldn't sell Objective-C [the programming language for developing Mac applications] to anybody. Nobody wanted to talk about developing for the Mac; nobody wanted to learn this new obscure programming language – obscure is their word, not mine. It was a real hard sales job. Then all of a sudden this iPhone comes out, and people are furious that they can't write Cocoa [the programming language used to create programs on Apple's Macintosh computers] apps.[32]

The first formal request to develop third-party iPhone software was logged before Jobs finished his original iPhone presentation in January, Drance says.

In June, Steve Jobs said he'd found a way to do it. At Apple's Worldwide Developers Conference (WWDC) in San Francisco, days before the iPhone was to go on sale, he told the audience of developers:

> We have been trying to come up with a solution to expand the capabilities of the iPhone so developers can write great apps for it, but keep the iPhone secure. And we've come up with a very... sweet... solution. Let me tell you about it.

An innovative new way to create applications for mobile devices... it's all based on the fact that we have the full Safari engine in the iPhone.[33]

The developers waited.

The wonderful apps, Jobs explained, would actually be on the web, and users would access them via the browser:

You can write amazing Web 2.0 and AJAX apps that look and behave exactly like apps on the iPhone, and these apps can integrate perfectly with iPhone services. They can make a call, check e-mail, look up a location on [Google] Maps... don't worry about distribution, just put 'em on an internet server. They're easy to update; just update it on your server.

The silence was almost threatening. The audience knew they were being short-changed. Apple's developers, after all, had obviously written apps, and Jobs had boasted about the software. So clearly APIs existed. And an SDK must exist for the developers to have written the apps. Afterwards John Gruber, an independent (and professional) blogger whose Daring Fireball site is regarded as a nexus for thinking about Apple (and other) news, called the suggestion 'insulting, because it's not a way to write iPhone apps',[34] and said that developers could not be fooled. Jobs, he suggested, should just have said that Apple was working on it but did not have anything to announce yet. In fact Jobs was still being lobbied by Schiller and Forstall, who insisted that apps were essential; he saw apps as an intrusion, an imperfection, and liable to spoil the machine.

Drance was in the WWDC audience. 'I got plenty of earfuls after that one,' he laughs. But it got worse: he then had to go on the road and encourage developers to write those web apps. Was he aware then that Apple was building an SDK (for it was) to allow third-party apps? 'I'd need to rack my brain. That was a crazy year,' he hedges. How about another question: when did he become aware that an SDK was being prepared?

'I think I probably shouldn't answer that,' he says, laughing. 'I'm not sure I can answer that without giving away too much of the timeline. But let's say I knew before the announcement happened.'

In October, a statement by Jobs appeared on Apple's site: 'Let me just say it: we want native third-party applications on the iPhone, and we plan to have an SDK in developers' hands in February [2008].'[35] He explained that the delay was 'because we're trying to do two diametrically opposed things at once – provide an advanced and open platform to developers while at the same time protect iPhone users from viruses, malware, privacy attacks, etc. This is no easy task.' Nokia, he noted, had already taken steps to prevent just any app being loaded on to a Symbian phone. Apple would only make available some of the APIs for the iPhone (and iPod Touch) so malware couldn't overrun iPhones as they had Windows PCs. 'While this makes such a phone less than "totally open", we believe it is a step in the right direction,' he wrote. 'We think a few months of patience now will be rewarded by many years of great third-party applications running on safe and reliable iPhones.'

But the October statement didn't quite tamp down the annoyance: there was only the announcement of a forthcoming SDK, not the kit itself. 'So now we were doing these WebApp shows and we were saying, so, yes, we announced our SDK the other day, but I'm just talking about Safari today. Everybody would go "Ah",' Drance recalls. 'So that was a fun month.'

While the software developers waited for the iPhone SDK, the hardware ecosystem that had built up around the iPod swung into action around this new piece of kit. Griffin, and the other accessory makers, soon had products that once more pushed a secondary wave of advertising for Apple, bringing the brand to people's notice; even if you didn't want an iPhone, you might see a pointer to it in a non-phone store.

Free as in lunch

In November 2007, Google launched the Open Handset Alliance (OHA) – a grandiose naming that for a while also obscured the fact that Google was proposing to make its mobile operating system available to any handset maker absolutely free. In all, 34 companies backed it, including HTC (which had formerly worked exclusively with Microsoft making the majority of Windows Mobile handsets), Motorola, T-Mobile and Qualcomm (essential for the phone software), saying how pleased they were at the idea. The vice-president of China Mobile – the biggest carrier in the world – said that an open mobile platform would accelerate China's smartphone adoption.

Page and Brin emphasized that this was not a 'Google Phone': it was a Google phone *platform*. 'Is there a Google phone coming?' asked *USA Today*'s writer. Andy Rubin replied: 'Another way to think about the G-phone is that there will be thousands of Google phones – some you like, some you don't.'

The OHA was a method to build a phone that would have Google at its core – in search, apps and so on. It was part of a dual mobile strategy on phones: get apps such as Google Maps on to phones through 'handset partnerships' (principally Apple); and provide 'a whole new mobile experience'. The licence would be 'the most open': manufacturers would get access to the OS source code, the stuff that Apple and Microsoft guarded most closely. And the first part of what was shipping was an SDK, a week after the press announcement.

Marc Hedlund, an entrepreneur blogging at O'Reilly at the time, thought that this would be the classic repeat of history: Apple would get run over by an open platform that was talking first to developers. 'I think [Apple will] repeat history – they are already repeating history – by not doing whatever they can to bring developers to their platform. I wonder if Google will teach them what they should have already learned from Microsoft.'[36]

Analysts were cautious. 'While I believe the effort by the Open Handset Alliance will have a significant impact on the market, I think it will build slowly over time', Forrester Research's Golvin told CNET. 'Even if there is a tidal wave of new devices using the Android platform, they will still represent a relatively small portion of the overall market.'[37]

And what did Microsoft think of the OHA? In November, Ballmer was dismissive. 'Well, of course, their efforts are just some words on paper right now. It's hard to do a very clear comparison,' he replied.

Windows Mobile is available on over 150 different handsets, is available from over 100 different mobile operators around the world. We will probably license about 20 million Windows Mobile devices this year – which is really quite dramatic, at least amongst smartphone systems – so we have great momentum... We'll have to see what Google does. Right now they have a press release. We have many, many millions of customers, great software, many hardware devices, and they're... they're welcome in our world![38]

As he spoke, Windows Mobile licence sales were growing quickly: for the fiscal year (ending in June 2007) Microsoft had sold 11 million, almost double the 5.95 million of the previous fiscal year. My calculations, based on publicly stated numbers from Microsoft, suggest that in October 2007 just over 1.4 million Windows Mobile licences were sold, growing by 77,000 every month. (When I showed my figures to Knook, he didn't disagree.) An annual total of 20 million was in sight, and Windows Mobile licence sales were growing faster than the smartphone market; Microsoft would impose itself on the mobile internet and control the ecosystem, just as it had done with the desktop PC. Certainly, Nokia and Symbian had the lion's share of the market, but Windows Mobile had third-party developers building applications to link to enterprise systems.

The mobile handset makers, however, were growing worried. Knook recalls that even in 2002 they fretted that Microsoft would win and they would lose. Visiting Motorola, he says, 'We got into the classic discussion we got into with almost all the other device makers, which is how do we control our destiny? How do we manage differentiation? What do we do that's not going to play just into your arms and turn our mobile business – where we make a lot of profit out of the handset – into the PC business, where we've seen what's happened with Dell and HP? We don't like it.' Knook had a ready response: 'My first dare to them was, OK, show me a product if you think you can do this all yourself. But if you think you want to have an alternative – why don't we work on a project together and we'll go do something?' Symbian didn't appeal to handset makers as an alternative, because Nokia dominated it. For handset makers trying to get into the booming market all that was left was Linux, which was simply too messy – although it suited some Chinese handset makers.

Into this web of distrust between Microsoft and the handset makers came Google and Android. Its model immediately appealed: no licensing cost, no certifying how many handsets had been made. Make a reference device, get it approved by Google, and they could make as many as they could sell to retailers, carriers or customers. The source code was available too, so they could modify the interface, and add or subtract as they wished to achieve differentiation. Google was commoditizing what Microsoft charged for. Even as Ballmer was speaking, carriers and handset makers were edging away from Windows Mobile. Not that they had ever really embraced it before. Microsoft itself let a small cat out of the bag in February 2009, when Andy Lees told Mobile World Congress that Windows Mobile had sold more than 50 million licences; and then HTC's chief executive Peter Chou joined him on stage and said that HTC had sold more than 40 million Windows Mobile phones worldwide. Clearly, Samsung, Palm, Motorola and other licensees had made up the remainder; which meant their reliance on Windows Mobile was minimal. And licence sales don't necessarily translate into handset sales.

That's borne out by Mary Jo Foley, a journalist who has covered Microsoft in minute detail for years, and her experiences with Windows Mobile – or, more precisely, her lack of experiences with it. Despite it being her patch, she never ended up using a Windows Mobile phone. 'I was a prime candidate for one,' she says,

> and the reason I never did [get one] was that every time I'd go to my carrier and say 'I think I want a Windows Mobile', they'd say: 'No you don't... it doesn't work, there's millions of returns

and they're overly complicated. They don't do what they're supposed to do.' The list [of problems] just went on and on, and they talked me out of it every single time I was going to buy one. [The carrier in question was Verizon, the second-biggest carrier in the United States.] Even though there was a loyal base [of users and developers] who loved that platform, and who were developing for that platform and were loyal to it and backed it, they never did really get outside their own kind of niche.[39]

Instead she would end up getting a feature phone ('mostly from LG'). She recalls the Verizon staff telling her that it was pointless to try to work with smartphones: 'They'd say, "It would be nice if you could do your e-mail and all that, but it doesn't work". They kept saying don't do it, you're going to return it, you're going to hate it.'

That disdain extended inside Microsoft, she says: 'Even talking to Microsoft people who were using the phones, or people who had them, they'd be like "They're OK. They're not great. I don't really like them. I wish I could dump them."' This perplexed her: 'I'm like wow, OK, they must know that people don't like this platform, and not just Verizon but other people. I thought: "They must be hearing this, because they love to do these surveys, going out and talking to people about what they think of Microsoft products."'

She felt Knook wasn't hearing that:

> Every year he'd get up on stage at the Microsoft Partner Conference, and at TechEd, and all these different Microsoft shows, and he'd show off: 'Look at all these handsets we have. We have so many, and this is the proof that everyone loves Windows Mobile!' But every year it felt like they were just showing the same thing over and over – there wasn't a feeling of progress, or a feeling that they were gaining any ground in features, or functionality, or ease of use.

On 11 February 2008, Microsoft announced that it had signed a deal to buy Danger. Allard had got his way. At exactly the same time, Knook was speaking at the Mobile World Congress (MWC) in Barcelona, and had good news: 'Up until the December 31, we sold

14.3 million units of Windows Mobile, which puts us handsomely ahead of both RIM and of course by a significant margin ahead of Apple iPhone,' he said. 'That puts us on track to reach our 20 million unit goal for the full fiscal year, and we're very excited to share that number with you.'[40]

Of course, the figures conflated the calendar year (during which the 14.3 million had been sold) and the fiscal year (which was looking good, but nothing like the sure thing it would have been had Microsoft really sold 14.3 million licences in six months – which would have been a hit rate of more than 2 million licences per month, or around 25 million in a year).

Knook's speech turned out to be the moment Windows Mobile licences hit their peak – by my estimates, at around 1.75 million per month. After that, they flattened. For the 2007/08 fiscal year, Microsoft in fact sold 17.8 million licences.

Why, I asked Knook recently, did the numbers peak there? He had a simple answer: Steve Ballmer.

Not long after MWC 2008, Ballmer called Knook to a one-to-one meeting. 'I'd been doing the mobile business by that stage for about six years. Steve said "Look, you've done a great job. It's time that you considered other things. Come and run the Windows business, or come and run the Services business." He had all kinds of ideas for what he wanted me to do next.'

But Knook didn't have the same ambitions, or at least not on the same schedule as Ballmer: 'I said to him, I kind of like this mobile stuff. I find it interesting. It's exciting. It's grown a lot. I've had a big impact.' Knook was also suffering the frustrations of success at Microsoft:

One of the challenges I faced at Microsoft was, having grown [Windows Mobile] from zero to close to 20 million units, you get a lot more focus and attention from the rest of the business. So there were regular reviews with Steve and Bill [Gates] and Craig Mundie [the cross-divisional chief technical officer] and Robbie Bach [head of Entertainment and Devices, whose division subsumed Knook's], and everybody had a say. We'd gone from being the people who just sucked up their revenue to being the ones getting 'Now we want to tell you what to do', and there were 15 different voices telling you what to do. You can't rationalize that. Even Bill and Steve didn't agree. You'd go into a review, and then Bill would be called out on a phone call, and Steve would tell you one thing, and then Steve would get called out on a phone call, and Bill would come back in and tell you exactly the opposite. My whole team would sit there and we'd say: 'We don't know what they want us to do.' So we'd make up our own minds.

Meanwhile the Danger acquisition had gone ahead, which meant that he would have the political challenge of getting Allard and a new team to integrate and cooperate with Windows Mobile even while they tried to plough their own furrow, with the aim of producing something that would compete with the main product. It would be a nightmare if he stayed. Equally, he didn't want to move inside the organization.

For Knook, Ballmer's request that he give up the mobile business was a turning point. In March 2008, soon after the meeting, he left to join Vodafone, one of the largest international mobile companies in the world; it wanted someone with his experience to help its diversification into software.

At that point Windows Mobile licensing began to slow down – and went into a decline that would never be reversed, even though Knook was replaced almost immediately. He puts the decline down to the discontinuity: Andy Lees, who took over, had spent four years heading the Server and Tools marketing and solutions group; phones weren't in his blood. And Lees's focus, driven by Ballmer, was different. In line with Ballmer's general intent, he decided that the focus should be on consumers, who far outnumber the businesses at which Windows Mobile had been aimed.

'There was a pretty major reset,' Knook says. 'All the senior leadership team was changed, and I think it's that factor more than anything else that stopped things, because then the sales side starts to get discombobulated.'

The handset makers also sensed a lack of direction, leaving the door open to a newcomer – Google. Previously, Knook suggests, the manufacturers could call him to ask for guidance. Now, he says, their attitude was, 'The new guy won't tell me anything because he says he needs time to go and figure out what he wants to do. So what does that mean for the device I'm about to launch? Maybe I should just go easy and not launch this device.' So, he says, 'the natural by-product of all this change is that ODMs [original device manufacturers] take their foot off the gas, operators take their foot off the gas, everybody takes their foot off the gas and that's kind of what happened. It isn't whether it would have been me or anybody else. [It was] just the change.'

So it was the arrival of Android, rather than the iPhone, that killed Windows Mobile. Google had flummoxed Microsoft again, this time by undercutting it. Because how do you compete with free? Apple benefited, though: during Windows Mobile's glory year – July 2007 to June 2008 – Apple sold 5.41 million iPhones. In the next July–June period, 20.25 million iPhones were sold, outselling Windows Mobile by more than 2 million.

Websites also began noticing that, while Apple's iPhone might be only a drop in the mobile ocean in terms of absolute numbers, iPhone users were very active mobile web users. Compared to the tens of millions of BlackBerry and Windows Mobile phone users, iPhone users seemed to spend enormous amounts of time browsing the web. The mobile internet really had begun to take off – and Apple had taken control of it. Google's deal to make itself the default search engine in the Mobile Safari browser soon looked like one of its smarter decisions: on Christmas Day 2007, people unwrapped iPhones and internet-enabled iPod Touches, turned them on and started using them. In the next 24 hours, despite being only a tiny fraction the mobile devices in use, they drove more searches through Google than any other mobile. Inside Google – where information is treasured – it was more confirmation of the power of the mobile platform. And it meant that Rubin's Android project assumed more significance inside Google than ever.

It would also drive a wedge between Apple and Google.

Apps for all

The announcement of Apple's SDK for the iPhone created a storm of excitement among developers. The news that Apple would distribute 'apps' through a new segment of the iTunes Music Store – the iTunes App Store – and that it would vet every app first, and take 30 per cent of any purchase price, wasn't initially popular. But the alternative was to create a web page that you'd have to hope would display well, and run fast enough compared to native code, and also (if you wanted to make money) have some sort of effective payment system. Developers already knew they didn't want to develop web pages; that was what had driven the demand for an SDK in the first place. As for speed, a web page would rely on connectivity, while an app could store and cache images locally and just download data if needed – though many games wouldn't need a connection (and many developers were keen to write games). Just as games developers try to get 'as close to the silicon' as possible – that is, write in code that can be run directly by the processor, rather than having to be interpreted by other software – so with iPhone developers. The 70/30 revenue split was viewed as 'liveable', if not totally desirable.

The enormous merit of the App Store was visibility: it would be the only place to find apps, and anyone who had registered to buy songs or videos there would also be able to buy apps there in a zero-friction experience; they could even do it over the air, without going through their computer. The cost of entry was $99 for a listing, and the development software was Mac-only (which helped drive Mac sales; they began growing faster than the rest of the PC market, boosted by new would-be developers).

Apps faced many restrictions: they couldn't carry on running if they weren't directly on the screen – a move to save on memory and battery (but also, arguably, to prevent 'spy' applications that might watch your keystrokes and pass them off to a distant website). The user had no way to control which tasks or apps were running, because essentially there was only ever one app – the one the user was looking at – working at any time. In theory, you'd want a smartphone to be doing just as many things at once as you could. But this was reality, as Gruber observed:

> The iPhone is severely resource constrained. Battery, RAM, and CPU cycles are all severely limited. If third-party apps could run in the background, all three could suffer. RAM would suffer for sure; all running apps consume memory. The iPhone has just 128MB of RAM, and no swap space. CPU performance and battery life would suffer when background apps do something – and if they're not doing anything, what's the point of keeping them running?[41]

Would-be developers weren't discouraged. Gruber's sources at Apple told him that 10,000 people and companies applied in the first fortnight. There certainly hadn't been anything like 10,000 'web apps' created in the iPhone's first two weeks on sale – nor since.

Android was also attracting widespread developer interest via a $10 million fund to seed developer ideas; by April 2008 it had almost 2,000 applications, two-thirds from outside the United States. They used the Android connectivity – Google's certainty that 'the cloud' of the internet would always be there – to offer photo-enhanced driving, on-the-fly mash-ups with maps, and passive surveillance on your family's whereabouts. Even though there wasn't yet a phone running Android on sale, it already had half as many apps as RIM's BlackBerry, and a tenth as many as those available for Windows Mobile on the Handango download site. Android was big even before it got started.

Money in apps

Apps for the iPhone started appearing in July 2008, and quickly demonstrated that there was serious money to be made. Sega's Super Monkey Ball game, which used the inbuilt two-axis accelerometer to detect how the iPhone was tilted, saw 11,000 downloads within the first day – racking up about $110,000 in sales (of which $76,000 would go to Sega and $34,000 to Apple).

Developers could hear the distant sound of cash registers, but exposure suddenly became essential, and Apple began behaving in odd ways: it would ban apps for seemingly random reasons, such as 'duplicating the functionality of existing iPhone apps'. Mail programs, browsers, podcast downloaders – those would be rejected. Developers howled, and howled even more loudly at being told they couldn't howl publicly because of Apple's non-disclosure agreement on rejections.

Still, the lure of money was enough to bring developers flocking. In July 2008 Apple launched the iPhone 3G, cutting its prices in half while also adding 3G connectivity (and so faster data access) and GPS capability. The aim – to capture market share – worked: from July 2008 to June 2009 – the period covering the arrival of the 3GS and apps on the iTunes App Store – iPhone sales quadrupled to 20.25 million compared to the same 2007/08 period, while the smartphone market grew by less than 20 per cent (and, amid the credit crunch, the overall mobile market actually shrank). By July 2009, the 65,000 apps had had 1.5 billion downloads. The investment in building the iTunes Music Store all those years ago was clearly paying off; apps downloads were running at the same rate as song downloads and, while there were many more sources to deal with, as well as the extra work for Apple of approving apps to be published (a non-trivial task for which it employed around 40 people working full time), they brought clear benefits. Smartphones weren't just for e-mail and web browsing; now they were doing all sorts of other functions too. Where the feature phone had swallowed functions from other devices – calculators, torches, cameras, recording, music playback, calendars – the smartphone could swallow anything that could be programmed. Maps had only been the beginning.

Flash? Ah

One thing was quickly noticed about the iPhone: it didn't play Flash video – found in many advertisements and games all over the web.

(Those advertisements that jump up and twirl around on your desktop browser are Flash-based animations.) Games that on a desktop PC would engross someone for hours would instead be represented by an unmoving blue cube or a black screen on an iPhone. Flash is a format owned by Adobe, and its pervasiveness in browsers is the result of the company's assiduous work: 99 per cent of desktop browsers have the Flash plug-in (not to be confused with flash memory, which is hardware) installed. Because the vast majority of those desktops run Windows, Adobe tuned Flash to run well on them. The browser plug-in was free, while Adobe charged for the software used to create and serve Flash-based content – a model rather like Microsoft's Windows Media Audio strategy.

But on smartphones the story was different. Flash was processor-intensive – which meant it used up battery life. Apple's software team also found, from the crash reports received automatically from users, that many browser problems – especially crashes and lock-ups – were caused by pages using Flash, even on powerful desktop computers. On phones using far less powerful processors, a lock-up or crash would be calamitous, and a terrible user experience (especially for the ur-user Steve Jobs). Also, a company making its first phone wanted to avoid battery-draining programs. Flash could be included in the iPhone only if it abruptly became much more efficient and robust. By 2006, it was obvious that wasn't going to happen in time for the iPhone's launch.

Apple also had a separate argument about Adobe and Flash: Adobe controlled its development. Jobs had already been frustrated by what he saw as Adobe's intransigence over the rewriting of its Photoshop and other software to run on Mac OSX: graphics designers, a core market, wouldn't upgrade their computers until it was ready. The same applied with Flash. If the iPhone included Flash and the performance was terrible, that would be hard on Apple, but Adobe might choose simply to concentrate on improving Flash on larger platforms – perhaps Symbian or Windows Mobile – instead of the iPhone. Apple would be constrained by Adobe.

The whole of Apple's corporate culture resists being straitjacketed by other companies. When Jobs returned in 1997 and laid waste to internal projects, he espoused building on open source projects rather than trying to reinvent the wheel. 'The wisdom is to know what 10 per cent of stuff we should invent, and what we should use that's just out there', he said to that year's WWDC, stunning outside developers who were used to Apple developing worthy but minority technologies that never got wider use. 'This whole notion of being proprietary in every facet has really hurt us,' Jobs continued, focusing on what he saw as the key distinction: 'I don't think it's important that Apple's perceived as different – I want it to be perceived as much, much better.'

Dropping Flash posed a problem though: most of the video on the web, and particularly the most-used video site on the web, YouTube, encoded video in that format. If the iPhone couldn't play YouTube videos, a significant part of its appeal would be lost.

But Eric Schmidt was a board member at Apple and chief executive at Google. Even though the Android project was progressing rapidly, he could see that the iPhone presaged an enormous shift in smartphone use. YouTube began a huge project to convert its content to the H.264 video format – a broadly licensed one, in which Apple owned patents – so it could be played directly in the iPhone browser.

Some commentators scorned the iPhone's lack of Flash. Online advertisers saw a problem: if they built advertisements that used Flash, people using Apple's device wouldn't see them. Apple, meanwhile, was encouraging developers to use HTML5 – the emerging next-generation version of the web's 'mark-up' language HTML. HTML5 offered many of the same capabilities as Flash – moving objects, video, sound, curved corners, shadows – but without being proprietary. Google too was pushing ahead with HTML5 compatibility in its new Chrome browser.

Gruber suggested that Apple would never put Flash on the iPhone. 'The mobile market is wide open in ways that the desktop market is not,' he wrote on Daring Fireball.

In the mobile OS market, Microsoft isn't even in first place, let alone a monopoly. And, in the mobile world, Flash is rare, not ubiquitous [compared to the desktop]. Why would Apple help Adobe establish Flash as a de facto standard for the mobile web, too? If Flash does turn into a major force in the mobile world, Apple can always add it later. But why shouldn't Apple push for a Flash-free mobile web future now?[42]

Apple controlled the entire software stack; if Google was prepared to provide video in H.264 format, as it had, then the biggest obstacle to video viewing was gone. It would now be a question of how quickly other sites with video content would transcode their content to an HTML5-friendly H.264 format.

The row over Flash may be one of the most important in indicating where the 'mobile internet' is headed, and how the balance of power can be swayed. Android phones did run Flash: Rubin, Page and Brin decided early on that the improvement in phone hardware computing power – roughly doubling every 18 months, in line with Moore's law – would make early problems go away. It's not only with Flash; many software subsystems within Android, such as fast scrolling, which functioned poorly on early phones have become highly effective as faster hardware has made up for them.

Apple's decision emerged from a fundamental choice: it could either retain full control over the user experience or make the operating system open to anyone who wanted to enhance it in some way. The first choice is the one it made in the 1980s with the Macintosh; the second choice is the one Microsoft made with Windows. The two are incompatible. It means that Apple necessarily limits the user experience on iPhones and iPads: it decides Flash won't run. The Windows and Android choice, meanwhile, inevitably means that not all users will get the best possible experience from their handset or computer, but it does mean that a lot of handsets or PCs will get sold, and the customer can figure out (with the help of advertisements, reviews, friends' recommendations and so on) which is the best.

The first Android phone to support Flash in the browser, rather than having it as a separate app, was the HTC Hero in July 2009; the review on the gadget site Engadget indicated that it wasn't a pleasant experience. Without hardware acceleration – that is, being able to use spare processing capacity on the graphics chip for calculations – the Flash software had to run on the main CPU, fighting for valuable processor time with other processes such as formatting the page being displayed. 'It's actually kind of maddening waiting for pages to load,' remarked the reviewer, Joshua Topolsky.

In the UK, the BBC followed the 'open' line, developing an H.264-based iPhone-friendly version of its iPlayer watch-again TV and radio service, which it released in December 2007, while keeping the Flash version for desktop systems. The iPhone was clearly getting special treatment, but that was because it was used so much for mobile browsing. Owners of Android phones, meanwhile, fumed that they didn't seem to be favoured in the same way; an Android version of the iPlayer app didn't appear until February 2011.

Google shies away from answering why, when it has been keen to back the use of open standards and open software in so many areas (not least its own servers and on its Chrome browser), it was happy to go with Flash as the video platform for its mobile phones – meaning that it ceded control of its progress. The answer is complicated. It rests on the fact that the video codec (the software for compression and decompression) most widely used in HTML5 video, called H.264, is patented, and has to be licensed from the companies that control it – one of which is Apple. Google doesn't belong to the group.

Google anticipated success for Android, but if that happened and every handset used H.264 in HTML5, rather than Flash, then that would mean the handset makers could be liable for H.264 patent payments; if H.264 decoding were included in the software, Google might even be liable for a per-handset licence payment. Better to hand the problem on to Adobe. Meantime, it sought its own patent-free codec, buying a company called WebM, which had a codec called VP8, in order to avoid the licensing costs of H.264. It also announced that it would stop including a plug-in to play H.264 in its Chrome browser – a quick way to lower costs. In May 2010, it announced that it was making WebM open source.

But, as Apple's experience with Flash on the desktop showed, having a codec that worked with the horsepower of a dedicated computer wasn't the same as getting a good experience on a mobile handset. WebM was barely ready for the desktop. There was no way it could be for the mobile. So Flash remained – and improved with Moore's law.

In April 2010, the cold war turned hot when a commentary written by Jobs appeared on Apple's 'Hot News' slot on its web page. The tone of the piece was classic Jobs. He'd tried, he really had, but Adobe just wouldn't tidy its room:

> We have routinely asked Adobe to show us Flash performing well on a mobile device, any mobile device, for a few years now. We have never seen it. Adobe publicly said that Flash would ship on a smartphone in early 2009, then the second half of 2009, then the first half of 2010, and now they say the second half of 2010. We think it will eventually ship, but we're glad we didn't hold our breath. Who knows how it will perform?

The key paragraph said:

> We know from painful experience that letting a third party layer of software come between the platform and the developer ultimately results in sub-standard apps and hinders the enhancement and progress of the platform. If developers grow dependent on third party development libraries and tools, they can only take advantage of platform enhancements if and when the third party chooses to adopt the new features. We cannot be at the mercy of a third party deciding if and when they will make our enhancements available to our developers.

Apple later stripped Flash from its laptop computers too: if you needed to run Flash content, you had to download a browser plug-in. It was like 1995, when a fresh plug-in for the Netscape browser (always requiring a download and restart) seemed to sprout every week.

Tactically, the rejection of Flash was part of Apple's view of how the mobile internet would develop: that it would be app-driven, but those apps would be built to its own standards.

To some people, the refusal to include Flash in favour of HTML5 indicated that Apple was a closed platform. Jobs, and Apple, argued that it was giving people the chance to rely on the open standards of the web (harking back to Jobs's mid-1997 speech to developers). The corollary of this dispute was the question of whether the future of smartphones lies in apps or in 'web apps' (websites that offer the same functionality as a phone-installed app).

Developers faced a conflict in trying to decide on this. If they chose the app route, they would have to write for multiple platforms, tweaking or even rewriting their code to work on iOS, Android, Windows Phone, and RIM'S BB6 or 7 or QNX. The advantage for 'native' apps was to be able to use all the power of the phone and feel integrated into it. A web app – a page viewed through the browser – would have the benefit of looking the same (or similar) on every platform, but without the functionality of a native app. There was no single answer. Matt Gemmell, a British iOS developer, summed up the conflict in a blog post in July 2011: the problem is always, he noted, that 'Apps, by virtue of running on devices which we're physically interacting with, have two frames of interaction: the app, and the device. You're reaching through a window to do whatever you're doing.' He compared running a calculator app (running on the machine) and running a calculator web app (running in a browser window): in one you are dealing almost directly with the app; in the second you have to reach through a window to touch the app. 'No matter how commonplace and mundane computers have become, we still exist in a physical world – and our experience continues to teach us that the best tools are dedicated,' he noted, before concluding: 'Native apps are the fortune of an ecosystem, and thus of a platform.'[43]

For Apple, which has rebuilt its fortunes by building an ecosystem around its newest two platforms, that seems to be the lesson to apply: native apps are what bring people to the platform. By the middle of 2011, it had more than 450,000 apps available in its App Store. There's no way to count web apps; but, in terms of revenues earned on mobile, there was no indication that they might catch up.

In November 2011, amid the announcement of 750 job cuts, Adobe announced that it would cease the development of Flash for mobile. Mike Chambers of Adobe put it bluntly: 'given... the fact that one of the leading mobile platforms (Apple's iOS) was not going to allow the Flash Player in the browser, the Flash Player was not on track to reach anywhere near the ubiquity of the Flash Player on desktops'.[44]

By contrast, he said, HTML5 'on mobile devices... has a level of ubiquity similar to what the Flash Player has on the desktop'. And keeping mobile Flash updated was consuming resources in dealing with handset makers, OS companies and graphics card makers. Adobe wanted to focus. Flash on mobiles was dead. Apple had won.

Envy

Something else became noticeable about coverage of Apple and the iPhone. Where once the company had attracted indifference – of which Michael Dell's 'just shut it down' remark was the distilled essence – now Apple was the object of two extremes of feeling among the public: desire and hate. Either you thought iPhones were marvellous or you thought they were for posers. Either you thought Apple had wreaked a miracle or you thought they had pulled the wool. I asked Don Norman about this peculiar polarization, more familiar from football teams or games console users (where similar rows rage between Microsoft Xbox and Sony PlayStation users). He recognized its roots immediately. 'I have trouble convincing companies about this,' he explained.

While great design will really convert people, it will also put off other people, some people. So you have to be willing to offend people, to make things that you know a lot of people are going to hate. So many people try to make a product that *everybody* will love. Microsoft is a good example. If you make a product that everybody loves – you do all your market surveys, and when people don't like something about it you change it – you end up with a bland product that everybody will accept, but nobody truly *loves*.

Apple was different, he explained. 'Apple says "We're not going to even worry about it. We're going to make something that we ourselves love. We just assume that anything that we really love, lots and lots of people will love. And if other people really dislike it and hate it, so what? Tough on them."'

It wasn't only design, though; Apple's desire to control the app market, to take a cut of sales and to prevent others deciding how the iPhone would look (by adding logos to it, as carriers often desired) was cited as evidence of a 'control-freak' approach, and further reason to hate it. Everyone in the company, right up to Jobs, simply repeated their aim: make something that gives a really good customer experience. Being 'open', having the biggest specification list, having the whole staff blogging their every move – those might be nice for some companies, but Apple didn't see the point if it conflicted with its aims.

The losers

It was hard to argue with the results. Beginning in 2008, the iPhone quickly captured a sizeable share of the profits – even if not sales – in the smartphone market. It came in like a lawnmower, chopping off the top end of the business for many rivals by grabbing customers willing to pay $600 (and up) for a phone. Nokia wasn't the only one to suffer. Sony Ericsson (which also used the Symbian operating system) and Motorola, which had been two of the other biggest phone makers outside Asia, saw their revenues and profits begin to wobble after the iPhone's arrival. At the end of 2007, Sony Ericsson's profits turned to losses, and the average selling price of its handsets collapsed. It began bleeding cash, profit and sales.

Dediu notes that making a loss is a danger signal for a mobile phone business. 'Any company in the mobile phone market that ended up losing money has never recovered its standing in terms of share or profit.' Why?

> Profitability is the canary in the coal mine. It causes a brand to be tarnished in the eyes of distributors who, because of sales cycle times, are extremely sensitive to obsolete inventory. A loss maker is seen as a maker of damaged goods. It then turns off the tap of incentives, promotions and hence visibility in the eyes of consumers. It's a vicious cycle from which few (if any) can recover. Past greatness offers no succour.[45]

Sony and Ericsson, the joint owners, were forced to pour in millions of euros to keep the company afloat while it restructured and cut thousands of jobs. By the first quarter of 2011 it had made an aggregate net loss in the 15 quarters since the iPhone went on sale of €169 million. Motorola's mobile phone division had to rely on finance from its parent.

Palm's profitability was also destroyed. As soon as the iPhone hit the market in June 2007, even though it began selling more smartphones, its revenues started trending downwards. By December 2008, it had been loss-making for six consecutive quarters and was burning through its cash pile. Colligan – who had insisted that 'PC guys aren't just going to walk in' in late 2006 – announced 20 per cent cuts in costs, and job losses. One of them turned out to be his own: by July 2009 he was gone, replaced by Jon Rubinstein, who had joined in 2007 (after leaving Apple in March 2006). Palm was now staking its future on a new smartphone design – the Pre, launched in spring 2009 – and a new operating system, called webOS.

At Microsoft, meanwhile, Ballmer had problems brewing in the mobile division. It had been obvious that the integration of Danger was never going to be simple: absorbing a working company that made hardware into one whose entire ethos is built around the primacy of software involves a culture shift for one or both. Even though the Danger team (in Allard's new PMX division) were nestled among the people who had built the Xbox, both organizations were suffering from the upheaval. The other challenge was internal and political: Lees logically saw himself as the head of mobile; why then should Allard be running a parallel project in the same space?

Such organizational niceties can be make-or-break for an acquisition inside Microsoft. A power struggle began between Lees and Allard: one to take control of Pink, the other to retain it. Meanwhile the Danger team struggled with organizational priorities. There were still millions of Sidekicks in use, but the team were also trying to rewrite the interface to fit Allard's dream. The idea was that there should be something available by the middle of 2009.

Android rising

The mobile business began a rapid evolution. At the beginning of 2007, the top five handset makers – Nokia, Motorola, Samsung, Sony Ericsson and LG – sold 85 per cent of all phones. Smartphones were less than 7 per cent of sales. ('The smartphone didn't really exist before 2007,' Dediu comments.) Even by the first quarter of 2009, phones using Android barely made a dent in worldwide sales figures; Gartner calculates half a million were sold. Yet even though Symbian dominated the smartphone market – with more than 40 per cent of the smartphone sector – it's notable that handset makers such as HTC didn't turn to it when mobile operators sought something to compete with the iPhone. Why? Symbian had similar licensing to Android: open source, but each required certification from its parent to be able to run particular services (Nokia and maps for Symbian, Google and Google services including the Android Market access to apps for Android).

Android, though, built on the huge popularity of Google. The first Android phone, the G1 (built by HTC of Taiwan), released in October 2008, was nothing special in hardware terms: a slide-out portrait keyboard, rather like some Nokia models; and limited touch functionality on the screen. But it was tightly tied to Google's services: you had to create an account with Google to activate it, upon which you'd be directed to Google search, maps, e-mail and calendars. 'This is a phone that Steve Ballmer would hate,' I noted in my review. The growing number of apps was interesting too.

By the fourth quarter of 2009, Android had begun to take off. Gartner's worldwide figures for the period show that a shade over 4 million Android phones were sold – only 7 per cent of the 53 million smartphones sold that quarter, but neck and neck with Windows Mobile, which had a last high before beginning its final fade. (The iPhone made up 16 per cent of world smartphone sales, snapping at the heels of RIM's 20 per cent.)

Android phones found a particularly receptive market in China, where upwardly mobile buyers liked having something that looked to all intents and purposes like an iPhone, but was a lot cheaper; the Chinese grey market importers who would throw down hundreds of pounds (or more usually dollars, as the exchange rate was more favourable) in Apple Stores in the UK and the United States for an armful of iPhones couldn't keep up with demand.

As Apple sliced off the top of the market, different Android phones from various manufacturers began to chew, termite-like, at the bottom. This wasn't a problem for phone manufacturers nimble enough to change their plans and swap quickly enough to a different operating system. LG, Motorola and Samsung all began offering Android phones in 2009; Sony Ericsson did not offer them until mid-2010. But for the companies wedded to their own OS – Nokia and RIM – it was, to say the least, troubling. At worst, it could be life-threatening.

Nor was Apple unaware of the threat that Android posed to its own nascent business. Vogelstein's account suggests that Steve Jobs initially thought that his good relationship with Larry Page, Eric Schmidt and Vic Gundotra – the latter coordinating mobile work between Apple and Google – would stop them using Android to compete on features, and that the iPhone would be allowed to retain its special interface elements such as 'pinch-to-zoom', double-tap-to-zoom, and that Google would at least give it feature parity on its services.

Rubin wasn't about to cooperate, and once Gundotra saw the potential of Android's growth, he switched from being agnostic to an enthusiastic backer, Vogelstein records. By August 2009, Eric Schmidt had left Apple's board. Google's refusal to give Apple turn-by-turn voice directions on maps, and its incorporation of interface elements Apple's executives were sure they had patented for the iPhone, put the two at loggerheads. In the space of less than three years, Apple and Google had gone from being cooperative to deadly rivals. A new front had opened up in the digital wars.

Meanwhile, inside Microsoft, the Pink project was running into problems. Lees had decided that Windows Mobile could not compete against the new generation of smartphones – the touch-based iPhone and Android. The whole platform was being rewritten using a new set of code – called Windows Phone – incorporating a touch interface, dubbed Metro. Lees had won the power struggle over Pink: being a mobile project, it now came under his division – and he decided that it, too, should use the same underlying code as Windows Phone. Danger had been written using Java, the programming language developed by Sun; but Microsoft is insistent that its products should use its technology.

This was good company politics, perhaps, but it had a disastrous effect on the project's timing. Rewriting Pink to run on Windows CE, the 'embedded OS' version of Windows, put the project 18 months behind its original schedule. Verizon, the carrier partner that had signed up to the plans that Lees and Allard had laid out, became impatient. It was losing customers to Cingular – now AT&T – which was the only carrier with the iPhone. (In Europe, Vodafone had agreed to take the Pink phones: it too wanted something that teenagers could afford that might compete with the iPhone.)

As 2009 wore on, the problems piled up. Features had to be ditched just to get the phones to be tolerably late. The Windows Phone project fell behind schedule, forcing Lees to deploy some of his team to write another update for Windows Mobile so that it would not fall calamitously behind competitors, especially the iPhone and Android. Because Pink needed to be out before Windows Phone, to keep Verizon happy, it was hurriedly rewritten in Windows CE, the ageing basis of Windows Mobile.

Everyone outside Microsoft had been expecting it to roar back against the twin threats of the mobile world's upstarts, Apple and Google. Instead, Windows Mobile was dying on its feet, and there didn't seem to be any response.

Eventually, Pink – now renamed Kin – was announced in April 2010: Verizon would offer two models in May 2010. The concept of the 'total cloud' device had been pared back substantially: now it was just music, via a subscription. There was no way to install third-party apps, no app store and no games. The contact list could be copied from another phone only by a Verizon employee. There was no calendar app, and it couldn't synchronize with cloud services such as Microsoft's Outlook or Google's Calendar. It didn't offer instant messaging – one of the most-used functions among US teens. There was no memory expansion. There was no navigation.

Verizon, angry at the delays that had seen continued lost customers to AT&T's iPhone, withdrew the subsidies. The phones would have to sell on their own merits, with a voice plan costing $40 per month, and an additional Zune Pass music service for $15 per month. It was a horrendously bad deal compared to the fast-growing number of Android phones; making data an additional cost simply made the attraction even smaller. On 30 June, after just 48 days on sale, the Kin was killed.

As it sank, Bach, who had headed the Entertainment and Devices division, and Allard both left. (Allard's departure was linked more to a frustration over tablets, as will be seen.) Bach was not replaced; the Xbox team, and Lees with the mobile team, now reported directly to Ballmer.

Furious ex-Danger staff inside and outside Microsoft headed over to the blog run by Mini-Microsoft, an anonymous manager whose agenda is a slimmer, less bureaucratic Microsoft, to vent their anger – much of it directed upwards at Lees. 'Personally I quit because of the frustrating management and autocratic decision style of Terry Myerson [corporate vice-president of Windows Phone engineering] and Andrew Lees', wrote one.

> The only exec in the team myself and other folks respected was Tom Gibbons [then head of Mobile Device Strategy and Commercialization] who is now sidelined. Lees and Myerson don't know consumer products or phones. Gibbons at least knows consumer product development. We often talk about how Andrew Lees still has a job but Microsoft's loss is a gain for the rest of us.

Another wrote about how demotivated the previously eager team had become:

> When we were first acquired, we were not taking long lunches and coffee breaks. We were committed to help this Pink project out and show our stuff. But when our best ideas were knocked down over and over and it began to dawn on us that we were not going to have any real affect [sic] on the product, we gave up. We began counting down to the two-year point so we could get our retention bonuses and get out.
>   I am sorry you had to witness that amazing group behave so poorly. Trust me, they were (and still are) the best group of people ever assembled to fight the cellular battle. But when the leaders are all incompetent, we just wanted out.

The remaining staff conceded that their hearts hadn't been in it. 'The remaining Danger team was not professional nor did we show off the amazing stuff we had that made Danger such a great place,' wrote one.

> But the reason for that was our collective disbelief that we were working in such a screwed up place. Yes, we took long lunches and we sat in conference rooms and went on coffee

breaks and the conversations always went something like this... 'Can you believe that they want us to do this?' Or 'Did you hear that IM [instant messaging] was cut, YouTube was cut? The App store was cut?' 'Can you believe how mismanaged this place is?' 'Why is this place so dysfunctional?'... we went from being a high functioning, extremely passionate and driven organization to a dysfunctional organization where decisions were made by politics rather than logic.

But the anonymous writer had an even more stinging verdict to pass: that Danger had done far more, with far less, far more quickly:

Consider this. In less than 10 years with one-tenth of the budget Microsoft had for PMX [the division created for the Pink project], we created a fully multitasking operating system, a powerful service to support it, 12 different device models, and obsessed and supportive fans of our product. While I will grant that we did not shake up the entire wireless world (à la iPhone) we made a really good product and were rewarded by the incredible support of our user base and our own feelings of accomplishment. If we had had more time and resources, we would of come out with newer versions, supporting touchscreens and revamping our UI. But we ran out of time and were acquired and look at the results. A phone that was a complete and total failure. We all knew (Microsoft employees included) that is was a lacklustre device, lacked the features the market wanted and was buggy with performance problems on top of it all.

Excoriation apart, Microsoft still didn't have anything to compete with the iPhone, or with the multiplicity of Android phones now appearing. The challenge wasn't just from phones: apps had become part of the landscape. Development houses set up with the sole purpose of writing apps for the iPhone platform. (The appearance of Apple's iPad in April 2010, after being shown off in January so that developers could rewrite their apps for its larger screen, accelerated that process.) Android was attracting more and more developers and apps too, though it found it far harder to charge directly for them. Google didn't have the juggernaut of the iTunes Store, with its millions of users who had handed over credit card details; instead it had to rely either on its Google Checkout system or on operator billing, where it had very few alliances. Alternatively, it simply relied on getting a cut of advertising (served by Google).

Inside Nokia, by 2010 things were moving only slightly ahead of Dediu's forecast memo (from 2007), where year three suggested: 'Realization that iPhone is a threat from new dimensions (user experience). Planning begins on reshaping the software base as a market-driven (not technology-driven) asset (five-year cycle). Apple begins to be evaluated as a competitor in devices and services, although still not compliant with current market definitions.'

To their credit, Nokia's directors got ahead of that schedule. They had woken up to the challenge and recognized that whatever their segmentation exercises might have told them – particularly that the proportion of the population who would pay $600 for a touchscreen phone was too tiny to bother with – it was wrong. Nokia's share of the smartphone market was falling dramatically, while Apple and the Android battalions were growing relentlessly. They began pressing the chief executive, Olli-Pekka Kallasvuo, for faster change. By the summer he was embattled, and issued a stark challenge to his board: back me or sack me.

In the first week of September, they sacked him. Directors I spoke to afterwards declined to expand on the press statement saying that 'the time is right to accelerate the company's renewal'. Dediu suggests that Kallasvuo's failing was not directly down to a failure to hold off the two challengers; instead, it was the spiralling complexity of the business plan he was enunciating. 'What Nokia had in mind was to offer various value-added, billable services to operators which would be enabled by Nokia handsets. The types of services included music subscriptions (Comes With Music), e-mail (several acquisitions), photo sharing, and navigation,' he wrote on his Asymco blog the day after Kallasvuo's ejection. 'The idea was that since many operators would not be capable of rolling out own brand services and could not do the heavy back-end lifting or the integration with handsets, someone could step in and roll out white-labeled solutions world-wide. Third parties would also find it impossible to integrate and would lack the relationships Nokia had with operators worldwide.' Nokia could help carriers offer another service such as e-mail to their customers for a little extra; the two could then do a revenue share. 'Anyone can see that this is a complicated business plan and is therefore unlikely to be successful. But what makes it a complete failure is the realization that most buyers will resist the idea of paying for individual services separately. $1/mo for e-mail, $2/mo for music, $3/mo for maps, etc. is repulsive.' Instead, people headed for unlimited data plans, and smartphones – which could do all of those things over the internet.

Kallasvuo was replaced by Stephen Elop, a Canadian who had most recently been head of Microsoft's enormously profitable Office division, and previously been at Macromedia (makers of the Flash video format, subsequently swallowed by Adobe). Elop had dealt with Nokia before, setting up a deal to put a form of Office on its phones. Now he had to take an enormously dysfunctional, overstaffed company and turn it into a slimline fighter in an entirely new world. In some ways, Elop's task in September 2010 was like that facing Steve Jobs on his return to Apple in 1996, except that he was taking over the market leader, which was still supremely profitable. The trouble was that it was rapidly running out of road. The 'feature phone' market was being reduced to a commodity market, as everyone offered near-identical features (camera, video, and music playback, but no useful e-mail, web browsing or apps). In the smartphone business, demand at the high end for the iPhone left everyone else scrabbling for share in the mid-range.

But Nokia had a more serious internal problem, enunciated by any Nokia engineer you could get to talk: the software teams designing the user interface and other systems were beholden to the hardware teams, who might abruptly reduce the specifications of a phone in order to hit a selling price – regardless of the effect on the software. The idea that software was the key to the phone experience – something Apple had always insisted on – had been drowned.

As Elop was appointed, Microsoft finally had Windows Phone on track: at the start of September the final code got its release to manufacture (RTM) for phone makers. The Windows Phone team celebrated by holding a 'funeral parade' in the Microsoft grounds for the BlackBerry and iPhone, which looked like instant hubris: 'I remember cringing,' says one ex-Microsoft employee. Those on board included well-known handset makers HTC, Asus, LG and Samsung – and Dell, which had decided that it wanted to get into the smartphone business (via contract manufacturers), and offered Android phones as well. Carriers had grown frustrated by Microsoft's delays, and the lack of attention to Windows Mobile, which in the summer quarter sold just 3 million licences; the decline was clearly terminal.

As the October launch was international, which attracted plenty of media coverage, carriers – sweetened by good terms from Microsoft – were on hand to show off the handsets. Everyone agreed that the Metro interface was attractive and different: it showed eight large 'tiles', when the iPhone and Android layout (of 20 icons, four of them fixed) seemed a de facto standard. Customers didn't seem enamoured of the new devices, though; sales were slow. By the end of the year Microsoft said 2 million devices had been 'shipped'; Gartner estimated only 700,000 of them had actually sold, and another 1.6 million in the January to March quarter. Microsoft, which would have known the true figures, consistently refused to move beyond the '2 million shipped' statement. In January Steve Ballmer garnished it by saying that Windows Phone had the highest satisfaction rating of any smartphone, while in May Achim Berg, the corporate vice-president of Windows Phone marketing, added a little sprinkle by saying that in the UK it had the lowest return rate of any smartphone OS. (This may have been true in aggregate, but wasn't true for every UK operator, according to my inquiries.)

Windows Phone looked dead in the water: Android was running away with the market in the West, while Apple was nipping at RIM's market share everywhere. But Ballmer had an ace in the hole. In October 2010, around the time Ballmer was touting the benefits of Windows Phone's 'glance and go' interface, Stephen Elop had made a decision. He'd concluded that Symbian was a zombie: it would never attract enough developers to rival iOS (as the operating system for the iPhone, iPod Touch and iPad was now known) or Android. In the future he saw, the feature phone would be dead, smartphones essential, and only a strong ecosystem of developers could guarantee success. Symbian simply couldn't compete in the new touch-based era. It was the same decision Lees had reached two and a half years earlier, after about the same period in charge of Microsoft's mobile division.

An in-house OS called MeeGo, being developed with Intel, held out some promise – until Elop asked hard questions about preparedness, and learnt that it wasn't ready, or battle-hardened, and so couldn't be the basis of Nokia's future smartphone strategy.

That left one choice: get a third-party operating system. Apple and RIM weren't going to offer theirs, so clearly it would have to be Android or Windows Phone. He called Ballmer and told him he was ready to explore 'strategic options'. He also got in touch with Schmidt at Google, who got him together with Rubin.

Ballmer knew that, if Elop was talking to Microsoft, he must be talking to Google as well. Yet the talks almost broke down, Elop later said,[46] because even by January 2011 Microsoft was still trying to treat Nokia – the biggest mobile phone maker, the one that had become slang for 'mobile phone' across entire continents – as just another handset partner. The stakes were far higher for Nokia, and Elop let Ballmer know it. If Nokia went to Android, that would effectively be the end of Windows Phone; it would be left eking out an existence at the margins of OS share, in the badlands where such disregarded blemishes as handheld Linux lurked. Or, as Elop put it, 'At that point, the race is over.'

Ever the dealmaker, Ballmer saw the sweetener that would turn Nokia his way: a big cash payment, plus ongoing royalties. Microsoft would pay to use Nokia's Navteq mapping service – the one on which it had spent $8.1 billion but that had been turned into a financial albatross by Google's free mapping offerings. Since its acquisition, Navteq had lost a total of €722 million on revenues only three times greater. It was a money pit comparable with Microsoft's Bing, but Nokia didn't have Microsoft's cash reserves. Getting some per-phone or per-search money for it – Kallasvuo's plan so long before – might fill the pit a little faster, at least.

Elop also got two other useful pieces of information. Microsoft was, he learnt, about to go after Android in a big way through the courts: it would claim the implementation of Android in handsets infringed its patents. The handset makers didn't have Google's resources to fight a lawsuit. Secondly, from Google he learnt that Rubin would continue providing certain handset makers with the first version of new Android releases to showcase them, and perhaps slow down the release of source code, to try to control the almost viral spread of companies, especially in China, making Android phones. (Some had tweaked them so they used China's Baidu, rather than Google, for searching; that wasn't helpful.)

That the deal hadn't gone Google's way became clear two days ahead of the announcement, scheduled for 9 February 2011, when Vic Gundotra, a former Microsoft executive who had joined Google in 2007 as a senior vice-president, tweeted succinctly: 'Two turkeys don't make an eagle'. It was a reference to the same comment, made by a former Nokia executive, Anssi Vanjoki, in 2005 about BenQ buying Siemens's handset business. (BenQ filed for insolvency a year later.) It was a neat sideswipe by Gundotra, insulting both rivals and making it plain that the Android deal had failed. The race was on.

Speaking in London, Elop confirmed the deal – and Ballmer turned up too to emphasize its importance. Elop said Nokia's Windows Phone would build the 'third ecosystem' in the mobile market, alongside Apple and Android. Where, I wondered, was RIM in this picture? In Elop's opinion, not in the race. He also announced a huge reorganization involving thousands of job cuts. For a company as deeply woven into Finnish society as Nokia, the announcements struck deep. Not only was its heritage being abandoned for foreign software, but its workers were being thrown out of their jobs. Elop and Microsoft weren't popular. Yet the blame lay with Nokia's slow-moving executives, its dysfunctional teams, and the challenge from the iPhone and Android – which had joined the mobile business less than four years earlier.

It also quickly became plain that Nokia wouldn't join the race for a while. Elop promised Windows Phone handsets 'this year'. As quickly became clear, that actually meant 'by the end of the year', with shipments in volume in 2012. Symbian sales fell off a cliff as carriers, realizing that Symbian was dying, demanded deep discounts. Nokia began staggering. Profits and revenues fell. In May, Elop had to admit that the mobile division might actually make a loss. In July, he announced that it had, of around €250 million, as revenues and phone sales dropped about 20 per cent for the quarter (compared to 2010). Dediu, noting his comment about falling into loss being a one-way street, observed: 'It's only natural to question its fate as an independent company.' His words would turn out to be prophetic – and what could be dubbed 'Dediu's Law', that an independent phone company which makes a loss even once is doomed, would become a touchstone for understanding the industry.

Patently

Almost as soon as the iPhone went on sale, Nokia filed a number of patent infringement cases. Apple was accused of infringing Nokia's intellectual property on touchscreens and a myriad of other elements in the use of mobile technology. The detail of the case was mind-numbing, but added up to a simple aim: either stop sales of the iPhone or make sure that Nokia got a significant cut of the sale price of every handset.

In the mobile business, patents – novel ways of doing things that, in the judgement of the patent examiners, aren't 'obvious' and so deserve legal protection against being copied – are a way of life, because there is so much scope for invention. Methods of saving power, or communicating more efficiently with cell masts, or combining functions – they're all fair game. And every wrinkle gets patented, because if you can get money from a competitor's sales then it's almost as good as having part of its market.

The question becomes stickier when it comes to software, where an obvious question is: can you really patent software processes? 'Obviousness' is a test for method by which an output is reached. In the pharmaceutical industry, where the output is molecules, if the final product can be duplicated without using the same processes that's what is required. In software there are many ways to achieve the same output, but the US Patent Office in effect supports the patenting of the output. (The European Patent Office is stricter, and doesn't.)

Nokia's patents almost all related to hardware and processes. Apple hit back with its own set of patents and claims, while also seeking to have Nokia's dismissed as irrelevant or not even patentable. The war rumbled on for almost four years before being settled in June 2011, with Apple agreeing to make a one-off payment and ongoing royalties and to cross-license a number of patents with Nokia ('but not the majority of innovations that make the iPhone unique', Apple pointed out).

Apple didn't have to give in completely to Nokia, because despite its short life in the mobile business it had learnt its lesson well when Creative Technologies had sued it on the basis it had patented the iPod's menu: patent early; patent often. (Jobs was bitter: 'Creative is very fortunate to have been granted this early patent,' he said as Apple handed over $100 million in August 2006.) Being a 35-year-old hardware company also gave it the advantage of a sizeable patent portfolio. In the mobile business, it's important to be able to lay claim to some intellectual property when disputes arise. Otherwise you'll get steamrollered.

And Jobs was quick to use that patent set when, as he saw it, Android began 'copying' the iPhone. When HTC released a phone running the new Android 2.1 software in January 2010, which included features like pinch-to-zoom and other elements familiar from the iPhone, he exploded. 'I will spend my last dying breath if I need to, and I will spend every penny of Apple's $40 billion in the bank, to right this wrong,' Jobs told Walter Isaacson, his biographer, at the time. 'I'm going to destroy Android, because it's a stolen product. I'm willing to go thermonuclear war on this.'[47] Apple filed a suit against HTC and, soon, a number of other Android handset makers.

Schmidt was summoned to a meeting at a café in Palo Alto in March, where Jobs began by being charming, and then – as the biography retells – turned angry. 'I don't want your money,' he told Schmidt. 'If you offer me $5 billion, I won't want it. I've got plenty of money. I want you to stop using our ideas in Android; that's all I want.' (Schmidt has declined to discuss the meeting.) Lawsuits against Motorola and Samsung soon followed. But patent litigation moves extremely slowly; Jobs never lived to see the Android ones finally resolved. HTC finally capitulated in November 2012, signing a 10-year 'licence agreement' with Apple – its conditions unspecified. Motorola fought longer but the two sides began settling, also in November 2012. Samsung, though, fought through and beyond the bitter end; after a Californian jury awarded $1.05bn in damages against it for essentially copying the design of the iPhone 3GS with various models, and copying the way some Apple functions worked, it contested the decision, and sought delays. Not all to its own benefit; in June 2013 a Samsung executive suggested to one at Nokia that he knew all about the terms of the deal between Apple and Nokia – which had been provided, under court seal, to an expert witness for Samsung. The company's trustworthiness came under a spotlight as it emerged that the licence details, appended to an e-mail, had been accessed by scores of Samsung executives who were not meant to see it. Samsung, and its lawyers, denied wrongdoing.

Microsoft meanwhile had been patenting software for as long as it was able; it also owned Danger, which had brought its own set of patents with it; and it had acquired intellectual property from a number of other phone companies along the line. So, when Android began eclipsing everyone else in the phone market, and Windows Phone wasn't getting any traction, Microsoft took the alternative route to winning: it began filing lawsuits on the basis that Android handsets infringed its patents by embodying the code into hardware.

By October 2011 Microsoft had signed up 10 Android manufacturers to pay licences against its patents. HTC was rumoured to be paying $5 per Android handset sold (HTC declined to tell me the number); Samsung and Microsoft signed a deal in September 2011 rumoured to be worth around $8 per Android handset (though rumours suggested it could be as high as $15). At the latter price, it would be almost as expensive in licensing terms to make an Android handset as a Windows Phone one. Google called Microsoft's lawsuits against the handset makers 'extortion': 'Failing to succeed in the smartphone market, they are resorting to legal measures to extort profit from others' achievements and hinder the pace of innovation.'[48] (Frank Shaw, Microsoft's PR manager, delighted in offering his version of Google's statement, 'boiled down from 48 words to 1: "Waaaah".')

That, of course, was the idea: Microsoft offers patent protection to Windows Phone licensees; if they get sued, it will go to court for them. As it was making abundantly clear, Google doesn't do the same on Android. Microsoft could conclude the deals without long-drawn-out litigation like Apple's because it was willing to license – at a price. Ironically, that was more effective at getting Android licensors to ponder its value than Apple's head-on approach.

Google meanwhile was facing its own legal demons, with a brain-frazzling lawsuit from Oracle over whether the code in Android is copied, borrowed, licensed or re-imagined from Java code developed by Sun Microsystems. After Oracle bought Sun in mid-2009, it demanded $6.1 billion in damages for infringement. (Then again, Google had $36 billion in the bank.)

Android was thus under attack on two fronts. But Google saw a chance to regain its position: a bankruptcy auction of 6,000 patents from the Canadian telecommunications company Nortel. Many related to mobile and future mobile technologies including Long Term Evolution (LTE), also known as 4G – a next-generation high-speed mobile connectivity system. Armed with them, it should be able to fend off attacks on handset makers from the likes of Microsoft and Nokia; it could simply decline to license them for future phones, or demand insanely high licence fees – or demand a cross-licensing deal that made the other problems go away.

As the bidding opened on 27 June, Google was arrayed against a number of other bidders: Apple, Intel and another called Rockstar Bidco (in fact a front for RIM, Microsoft and Sony). The bidding opened at $900 million and quickly escalated; after five rounds, Rockstar Bidco dropped out, leaving just Apple, Google and chipmaker Intel in the race.

Apple then invited the Rockstar Bidco trio to form an alliance with it, to keep bidding. (One reason may be that the US Department of Justice had previously expressed antitrust concerns if Apple were to win the auction outright.) One round later, Intel dropped out – and then teamed up with Google. The two sides upped the stakes in $50 million increments – with Google's team making mathematical jokes by bidding $3.14159 billion (a billion pi dollars). Earlier in the bidding they had put in what to the layperson looked like strangely precise bids, of $1,902,160,540 and $2,614,972,128; they're actually obscure mathematical constants related to prime numbers, multiplied by a billion. The bidding rose to $4.5 billion, at which point Google and Intel dropped out. Schmidt dismissed the outcome, saying the next week that 'the price exceeded our value threshold'. (Google has a full-time economist, Hal Varian, to advise on auction tactics.)

But Rubin had recognized that Google needed a serious patent portfolio to defend Android. Weeks later at the start of July, Rubin and Page sat down with Sanjay Jha, chief executive of Motorola Mobility (MMI), which had only existed as a separate company since January, to talk about acquiring its huge raft of patents, many of which covered essential mobile functionality.[49] (To start with, Motorola invented the mobile phone.) The topic of the meeting was 'the protection of the Android ecosystem'. Jha, though, thought that selling the patents would be disposing of the family silver. By the end of the month the two sides had begun discussing prices. Jha knew he had the whip hand: in an earnings call at the end of that month, he hinted that MMI might start going after other Android handset makers for patent infringement. Why not, if Microsoft was?

The tactic forced a Google bid on 1 August of $30 per share, valuing MMI at nearly $9 billion, one-third above the market value, and twice as much as the Nortel patents. Jha, sure he could do better, persuaded his board to reject it. Frank Quattrone, an investment banker then acting for MMI, told Google that a $43.50 offer would be accepted.

Early on Tuesday 9 August, with the negotiations offer still secret, the following things happened. Page came back with a $37 offer. Jha responded by saying he'd accept $40.50. Jha made a speech at a public conference where he reiterated Motorola's patent strengths, threatening again to sue other Android makers and suggesting that MMI might even follow Nokia and go wholly with Microsoft's Windows Phone if it could get the same deal – billions upfront, marketing assistance, customization.[50]

Page upped the bid, to $40, but demanded Jha's signature by 14 August. Whether the first and second bids preceded or bracketed Jha's speech isn't clear (Google declined to tell me), but Jha turned the thumbscrews, recognizing Google's need. Even though his 5 million share options had leapt in value over those nine days from $112 million to $150 million to $200 million, Jha didn't rush. He took another six days before finally signing the deal early on 15 August. It had taken six weeks and would cost $12.5 billion, but Google had the patents it thought it needed to defend Android.

Richard Windsor, then the sector analyst at Nomura Research, saw the MMI deal as the outbreak of peace: 'The patent situation is clear. The have-nots in the world of [Android] handset intellectual property will now enjoy the benefit of Motorola's portfolio of 17,000 patents.' He saw no chance that Google would become vertically integrated like Apple or RIM; it was much better to help Samsung and HTC, far bigger in the Android business, to compete against the predations of Apple and Microsoft. 'Now that everyone is fairly well armed when it comes to patents, we expect amicable arrangements to be reached with less recourse being made to contentious litigation.'[51]

That analysis, though, overlooked the fact that many Motorola patents were 'standards-essential' – that is, they underpinned standards such as the wireless broadband Wi-Fi or the video encoding system H.264. Owners of SEPs, as they're known, have to pledge to offer licences to their patents on 'fair, reasonable and non-discriminatory' (FRAND) terms; they can't refuse a willing licensee. And they can't charge wildly different amounts for the same patents. Nor, according to legal theory which came to prevail, could it charge 'hold-up' amounts for the patents. They were worth only what the intrinsic process of the patent was worth – which, given that many SEPs described particular mathematical functions, wasn't much at all. In one long-running court row over Wi-Fi and H.264 SEPs which it owned, Motorola demanded the equivalent of $4bn per year from Microsoft; a US district judge pared it down to $1.8m, or just 0.04 per cent of Motorola's demand. That suddenly made the patents side of Motorola look worth very much less than the $5bn Google had valued it at in July 2012 in an SEC filing.

Google didn't indicate what it would do with the handset business. Sell it? Close it? But Page and Rubin had what they wanted – though Page had also revealed, inadvertently, how easily he could be hurried in a negotiation.

Meanwhile Android was beginning to look like a better business for Microsoft than Windows Phone; it didn't even need to write code. One calculation suggested that, with Android's current growth trajectory, by the end of 2012 the patent royalties could be a billion-dollar business.[52] And that would be almost pure profit. In July 2013, a financial statement from Microsoft said that its Windows Phone division had generated $1.2bn in the 12 months ending June 2013; but in the same period, only 26 million Windows Phone devices had shipped. At $15 per licence, that would be less than $400 million – meaning that Android patent payments were generating around $800 million in revenue for Microsoft. And the Android market was expanding at a healthy clip, with more than a million devices being activated each day. Microsoft wasn't winning in handsets, but it certainly was in patents.

Google's failed bid for the Nortel patents may also have carried a sting in its tail. In November 2013, the Rockstar company (now a standalone patent licensing entity with offices in Ottawa, Canada and Pano, Texas) filed a lawsuit in Delaware alleging that Google's AdWords infringe a patent filed in 1997 – before the company existed. It was as though the ghost of Overture had returned – but this time, backed by bitter rivals.

App patents

The patent licensing business cut both ways, though. As smartphones took off, two US companies with software patents granted in the United States – Lodsys and MacroSolve – began suing developers in the United States and beyond, claiming infringement of their intellectual property. Apple and Google had licensed the patents involved – for Lodsys, it involved in-app purchases, a function available only through Apple's own SDK – and said their protection extended to the developers. By mid-July 2011, British developers were withdrawing their apps from sale in the United States across all platforms. Shaun Austin, a British developer based in Cheltenham, tweeted: 'selling software in the US has already reached the non-viable tipping point'. The United States, though, is the largest single English-language market; cutting yourself off from that market limits potential clients. But independent developers began to see it as dangerous territory.

If there is a single threat to the future of the smartphone, it is patents – and particularly software patents, which allow the patenting of an outcome rather than a process. If developers get too scared to develop, the apps market will become the province only of the well-funded and legally protected; the long tail of tiny developers with great ideas will be stunted. The outcome of the patent wars won't be decided within a year or even two years. Yet, for Apple and Google and Microsoft, anything that dissuades developers from writing software for their platform (and so reduces the number of apps, which reduces the reliance on a particular OS) is bad. Whether lobbying can turn the supertanker of software patents in the United States around is questionable, but the experience of app developers like Craig Hockenberry, whose Twitterrific app was one of the reasons that thousands of people joined Twitter, and who found himself being targeted by not one but two patent-holding companies, is not encouraging. On Twitter, he groaned: 'I became an independent developer to control my own destiny. I no longer do.' Patents have begun to look like a greater burden than benefit.

The biggest mystery surrounded the identity of those behind Lodsys and MacroSolve. Lodsys acquired its patents from Intellectual Ventures, a company set up by former Microsoft executive Nathan Myhrvold with the sole purpose of acquiring patents and exploiting them; it had won millions of dollars in venture capital funding on the basis that it could exploit its patent portfolio. In that case, though, why had it transferred the title for exploitable patents to what looked like (in Lodsys's case) a one-man band? Why would a well-funded company, set up to exploit patents, pass valuable patents to what looked like a start-up?

My questions to Intellectual Ventures about any financial or other relationships with Lodsys were politely answered:

> When it makes sense for our business we sell patents – either to companies who can use them for defensive purposes or to buyers who monetize them. Sometimes based on the structure of the sale we have a financial interest in the

outcome of those efforts, but we never have control over, or are involved in, the path to monetization that these companies pursue once we sell the patent.

Some suggested that Lodsys and MacroSolve were shell companies, set up by Intellectual Ventures to profit from lawsuits, while risking nothing if cases collapsed. (Intellectual Ventures declined to comment.) In the long term, some worried, US-based software patents might turn app development from a potentially huge cottage industry into a business only for the largest corporations.

And apps are important. Dediu calculated from Apple's stated figures – a total of $11 billion paid to developers by the end of June 2013 – that apps would soon be a more valuable business, month by month, than music sales. By June 2013, he was sure: Apple's figures showed that on average each of its 575 million iTunes users spent $12 per year on music – and $16 per year on apps.

Tipping

By the end of 2010, the top five sellers across all phone types were Nokia, Samsung, LG, RIM and Apple – but they only constituted 59 per cent of the total. Chinese manufacturers making 'white box' handsets and others made up 30 per cent of the total. The old order, and more importantly the primacy of the biggest sellers, was being eroded. The presence of two smartphone-only makers (Apple and RIM) in that top five also indicated how the business was changing.

Late in April 2011, Apple announced its quarterly results for the first three months of the year: 18.6 million iPhones sold, generating $12.3 billion of revenues. The next morning, Nokia announced its results for the same period: 24.2 million smartphones, 84.3 million feature phones – but their revenues were only €7.1 billion (then equivalent to $10.3 billion). In under four years, Apple had become the biggest mobile phone company in the world by revenue, and almost certainly the most profitable, as the iPhone's average selling price was $660, against Nokia's €147 ($213) for smart-phones, continuing a general downward drift; two years before it had been getting around €190 ($275). Three months later, Apple announced that it had sold over 20 million iPhones; Nokia had sold fewer than 17 million. Android handsets, meanwhile, had around 40 per cent of the market, by Gartner's calculation (though only Samsung approached Apple's standalone share).

The smartphone market had tipped into one vulnerable to sudden shifts and disruption. Apple's concentrated attack on the top end had paid off; Android's assault on the low end was destabilizing the previous incumbents. The threat to Nokia and RIM looked more serious than ever. Commenting on the results, Chris Lawton, writing in the *Wall Street Journal*, observed that Nokia was trying to get rid of its 'stone age' Symbian operating system, and added: 'it must be frustrating for the Finns to see their diamond slowly turning back into a lump of coal'.[53] Nokia had a trump card up its sleeve though. With the woeful results, it announced it had finally signed the deal to replace Symbian with Microsoft's Windows Phone on high-end phones. The arrangement, it added, would mean it would be paid 'billions of dollars'. Symbian's flame was going out, but Windows Phone was getting ready to carry Nokia's torch onwards.

Yet, despite Android's success, Paul Griffin thinks its manufacturer diversity (while helping to push prices down) and consequent lack of uniformity among phones will always be a drawback in the consumer's eyes. 'I think if you were to have common connectors, and if things all were to work the same – even if they had slightly different form factors and slightly different features, if they generally worked the same, I think you'd see a greater installed base of accessories, and that really helps the market,' he says. 'I think that [Google] would help themselves if they were to standardize [Android] enough to make the accessories all interchangeable. Some things can't be standardized – cases have to be specific, for example – but speakers don't have to be.'[54]

The standardization of the 30-pin dock and the base of almost every iPod and iPhone model since April 2003 is what gives Apple its hardware ecosystem, worth around a billion dollars per year in licensing fees from accessory companies (a special chip is needed to work with the dock). By contrast, Android phones have chargers on the bottom, or left, or right. The shape of the base varies. No accessory company would commission an Android speaker dock, because there's no such thing as 'an' Android phone. The rate of change is bewildering. The 'best' (meaning fastest processor, most features or best advertised) changes from month to month, even week to week. No manufacturer wants to standardize beyond what it must (generally, the micro-USB charger) for fear of having its accessories market stolen by a rival. Without a hardware ecosystem, there's less potential for 'lock-in' – or, if you prefer, loyalty – to the device. Ensuring someone stays with that maker and platform rests then on the handset software itself – and the software ecosystem of apps.

Even so, smartphone numbers were growing fast. By mid-2011, they constituted 25 per cent of all phones sold worldwide. Of 5.1 billion mobile users worldwide, 800 million had mobile internet connections. The number of 'fixed-line' internet users had fallen from 1.5 billion in the middle of the decade to 1.2 billion as people began to migrate to mobile. Only Japan, which had been first with 3G data, was resisting smartphones, which made just 10 per cent of sales. Feature phones there have all the capabilities of the smartphones used in the West – except downloadable apps. Japan turns out to be a smartphone desert.

Dediu calls the date when half of users in a market own smartphones 'the tipping point', and suggests that 'that's the point where we'll stop using the word "smartphone"'.

Get lost

In December 2009, version 1.6 of Android introduced 'turn-by-turn' navigation with Google Maps: choose a destination, and the screen would show you the directions, augmented by voice direction. It was functionality of a dedicated satellite navigation system which would easily cost £100 or more made free. Google had commoditised another web service, using its investment in mapping and routing – which it had offered through the desktop browser since February 2005 (having acquired the company making it in October 2004).

But though Apple used Google's maps service as the default on the iPhone, including directions, Google didn't make voice direction available to Apple or its users. The instructions would appear silently on the screen – hardly helpful, or safe, for a driver, who would have to look back and forth from road to screen. Apple's executives, already angry about what they saw as Android's incursion into interface features (tap-to-zoom and others), began pressuring Google for voice navigation; Google replied that it didn't make that available through its API (application programming interface, used by outside programs to connect to services). And it wasn't making an exception for Apple.

The competition between the iPhone and the growing range of Android phones was beginning to heat up. Google also had designs on branding and advertising inside the Maps app on the iPhone. It also wanted to implement its Latitude system, which let people track each other (with mutual consent) via Google's location servers. Apple refused.

Inside Apple, frustration at Google's flat refusal, which left iPhone users reliant on expensive add-ons, brought comparisons with Flash. Apple couldn't be at the mercy of Google in deciding how quickly and in what way its maps offering evolved. Nokia had been right in one way: mapping was now an essential offering for smartphone users, along with an app ecosystem. Mix in the frustration as Android began winning users – because it had feature parity but often lower prices – and you had the recipe for a huge split.

The gap between Android and iPhone mapping kept growing. In December 2010 Google added 'vector' maps to Android. A 'vector' file stores the relationship between the elements of the map – roads, locations, intersections – as a mathematical set. Earlier versions, and those available for the iPhone, used 'raster' systems: each screen was effectively an image, which had to be knitted together with its neighbours to give the impression of a single map. A key difference: a vector map, once downloaded, would still work without a data connection. A raster image would draw a blank – and used much more data continually.

Maps were becoming a wedge between Apple and Google, and the iPhone and Android. Apple began quietly buying mapping companies, beginning in July 2009 with one called Placebase (for overlaying datasets). The pace accelerated in 2010 and 2011, Rumours grew; in June 2012, Apple confirmed them by unveiling its own Maps offering at its Worldwide Developers Conference. Google Maps would be gone from the iPhone and iPad when iOS6 arrived in September.

But developers who had access to the early version, mainly sourced from Holland's TomTom, noted that it didn't offer public transport directions. The maps weren't as clear as Google's.

Even so, Google stood to lose out if Apple really did dump it. Location data from peoples' phones is enormously useful for generating data such as traffic reports and route navigation: if someone's phone position (provided anonymously and with permission, of course) indicates they're on a road, and they don't seem to be moving, and other phones in the same area report the same, you can conclude there's a traffic jam, and use that data to calculate the best route for people who hadn't even set out yet. Phones running your Maps app, and reporting it, are hugely useful, especially for a data company. If Apple dumped Google, it wouldn't get that data.

And there was a lot of data. In April 2012, data from the research company ComScore, based on panels of thousands of users, found that in the United States there were 31.4 million iOS users of Google Maps, and 34.8 million on Android. iOS users were heavier users – 9.7 million daily on iOS against 7.2 million on Android. Monthly use pegged at 75.5 minutes per month on iOS, against 56.2 for Android. And finally, 90 per cent of iOS users used the maps at least once a month; only 71 per cent of Android users did.

Google was set to lose its most eager users in the United States – and, likely, the world, since the general pattern of maps usage on the different platforms was similar: in March 2012 ComScore found that in Europe, 53 per cent of iPhone users access maps, against 40 per cent of Android.

Google's best hope was that users would rebel against Apple's decision. Its developers could see that Apple's maps weren't as good as theirs. Since Apple seemed to have made its mind up, and Google wasn't going to provide turn-by-turn, perhaps people could be told about the important differences – and change back.

Ahead of the launch of iOS 6, Google provided Alexis Madrigal, a writer for The Atlantic, access to its 'Ground Truth' mapping program. It explained how it combined its Street View camera imagery with logo recognition to pinpoint the locations of Kentucky Fried Chicken outlets; how hundreds of people are needed to tweak and improve the maps of each country. 'The sheer amount of human effort that goes into Google's maps is just mind-boggling,' Madrigal wrote. He added: 'The geographic data Google has assembled is not likely to be matched by any other company.' The secret was its preparedness to throw human effort at the task, he suggested. If anyone was looking for a warning, this was it.

With iOS 6 in September 2012, Apple dumped Google. It introduced vector mapping, voice-driven turn-by-turn directions, 3D photographic and schematic views, satellite and hybrid and simplified views. But when the millions of iPhone and iPad users began using the new maps, they found error after error. An Irish city farm called 'Airfield' was described with an airport symbol. Satellite pictures were clouded or missing. Despite a gigantic laundry list of contributing sources, Apple's Maps was clearly a rushed job, rolled out to match the annual timetable of iOS releases, not its readiness. And while it was correct for huge amounts of the world's roads, in some it was so wrong as to be laughable; in others, potentially lethal. The latter was the case with the town of Mildura, in the Australian Outback, which was shown miles from its correct location; Australian police issued a warning to people not to use Apple's Maps to find it lest they die of heatstroke in the arid land. (The error was tracked down to a difference in the official Australian gazetteer, which gives place locations, between 'Mildura', the town, and 'Mildura Rural City', the nominal centre of a 22,000 square kilometre area including the town. Apple had used the latter. It was corrected within days.)

A week after the release, and with Apple's maps a laughing stock, Tim Cook – who had now been in unquestioned charge of Apple for a year – surprised the media with an effusive apology posted on the website. Maps 'fell short' and he was 'extremely sorry for the frustration' users had experienced. He outlined what Apple had wanted to bring – 'turn-by-turn directions, voice integration, [3D views] and vector-based maps. In order to do this, we had to create a new version of Maps from the ground up.'

In other words, Cook was making it explicit that Google wouldn't play ball. One senior Apple executive later said to me – through gritted teeth – 'they [Google] went back on their word' to provide turn-by-turn navigation. Separately, I asked a senior Google executive who had dropped whom. 'Not us!' he shot back.

Even more surprising than the fact of Cook's apology was its following paragraph, suggesting that people use alternative apps – Microsoft's Bing, Mapquest, Israeli startup Waze – or Google's or Nokia's services, via the web. (The latter two quickly developed apps; Google's rapidly became the most downloaded on the App Store.) Apple suggesting rival products? It was a clear break from the past.

It looked like game over for Google. Except Apple Maps remained the default on millions of iOS devices – and continued to provide anonymous data to Apple. Plus, Cook acted. In October he fired Scott Forstall, who had been the driving force behind iOS; in a subsequent interview with Bloomberg *BusinessWeek* magazine he suggested it was a combination of failure to collaborate, and 'politics': 'There can't be politics. I despise politics. There is no room for it in a company,' Cook said. Soon after, Richard Williamson, who had been given the key (and arguably impossible) task of building Apple's maps and making them as good as Google's, was also fired.

Slowly and entirely silently, Maps improved. A year later, the most noticeable flaws (and many smaller unremarked ones) had been fixed.

But Google's maps were still far more detailed, and the representation – exaggerating the width of roads – more user-friendly. However, people also noticed that it had begun to insert paid results into searches, and at the bottom of maps – or 'more ways to interact with paid content', as Google put it.

The map wars produced Pyrrhic victories for each side. Apple suffered a significant blow to its reputation. But Google lost a lot of users. It never announced how many regular iOS users it had – although it must have known how many API calls it was getting.

ComScore showed that Google Maps hit a high in the United States of 81.1 million mobile users at the start of September 2012. Then iOS 6 arrived: the next month Google Maps had lost 9 million users, even though the total number of Android users had grown by 2.5 million, and of iPhone users by more than half a million.

By August 2013, ComScore's data showed that Google Maps on mobile had just 66.8 million users – fewer than a year before – even while the number of Android users had grown by 12.2 million, and of iOS users by 18.1 million, cumulatively reaching 133.8 million.

Apple's Maps, though, were the 10th most-used smartphone app that month, despite only being available on the iPhone; ComScore reckoned they had 39.9 million users. All were customers lost to Google. Extra data provided to me by ComScore suggests that there were about 7.8 million users of Google's maps on the iPhone – and only about 2.6 million who used it exclusively. Apple users hadn't rebelled.

And the total number of maps users on both platforms in the United States alone was 101 million. Google could probably have had them all if it had allowed Apple to have voice-driven turn-by-turn access. The argument that its API licence forbade that doesn't hold. Big companies can, and do, make exceptions.

No wonder Google didn't talk about how well its Maps app had done on the iPhone; it hadn't. For a data-driven company, losing access to all that information from peoples' smartphones – and fewer users than a year before – was not success. Worse, it had brought the struggle with Apple – which was also being played out in parallel in the patent courts – to the notice of everyone. Apple had suffered a bloody nose over maps. But Google had lost what it craves: users and their data.

The revolution will be handheld

In the fourth quarter of 2010, 100 million smartphones were sold worldwide, according to both IDC and Gartner. This is an impressive number, but even more impressive given that they had, for the first time, outsold PCs, which hit their own world record of around 93 million (the two companies offer slightly different figures: 93.5 million and 92.1 million). The trend continued in the first quarter of 2011: the PC market, it became clear, had begun to slow down, especially in the United States and western Europe. The only bright spots were in China, India and Latin America. In the first three months of 2011, PC sales actually fell year on year by 2 per cent to 84 million; smartphones kept roaring ahead, with another 100 million sold. It's an inflection point that won't be reversed. PC shipments overall peaked in the third quarter of 2011, at 96.1m, and then began to slide. By the end of 2013, they had fallen for six quarters in a row, and IDC and Gartner both expected 2014 to bring no recovery.

For Apple, getting more and more iPhone customers every quarter, the growth in smartphones is good news, and similarly for Google, whose Android customer base almost always opts into Google accounts and services (except in China, where it is effectively banned on mobile; local services dominate). But for Microsoft it's bad. PC sales are one leg of its profits – the others being Office and Server sales. If PC sales dwindle, so does Microsoft's Windows income. If smartphones forestall PC sales in places the PC has not yet reached – particularly developing countries – then Microsoft's future revenues and profits are endangered. The difference between a Windows licence on a

PC (bringing in about $55, which generates about $40 of profit) and a Windows Phone licence (bringing in about $15, and very much less profit) is large – large enough for Microsoft to need new revenue streams from mobile to compensate for any loss to its PC and Office business.

One was its search business: in 2011 it did deals with RIM and with Nokia to make Bing the default search engine on their handsets. But the traffic acquisition costs there would take a long time to pay off. For now, only Apple and Google look like winners of this part of the digital war. Apple has the money, and Google has the search. Microsoft is left with Nokia's future success, an unknown quantity.

But why do smartphones matter? Why does it matter whether any of these companies succeed or vanish? The first question is easier to answer. Smartphones are the evolution of the mobile phone. With tablets they're also the future of the computer. They are the ultimate battlefield for the digital wars.

The first mobile phones transformed how people worked and lived. For those with peripatetic lifestyles – travelling salespeople or tradespeople whose earning prospects were enhanced by being contactable at any time – the mobile phone was a godsend. This applied not only in rich countries; a 2006 study by Uppsala University showed that fishermen in Tanzania – a country where the daily income of half the population was below $1 – benefited substantially from having mobile phones on board: they could phone ahead to prepare for trips and contact markets to determine where to land their catch. One fisherman said his income had gone up by 30 per cent since getting a mobile phone.[55]

Feature phones – adding cameras, then audio and then video recording – had a similar effect, but more broadly spread. Shoppers could send photos of clothes to friends; in London, women getting into taxis would ostentatiously send a picture message of the cab number to friends, just in case they came to harm; using phone cameras to record violence by the authorities became a feature of the 2010 Iran election protests, and the 2011 Arab Spring uprisings. The feature phone proved that a device could be much more than the sum of its parts if those parts could interact and communicate simply enough. It qualitatively changed the experience of owning a mobile phone.

The smartphone takes that another step forward, to embrace the internet. Until the smartphone, your details – friends' numbers, pictures, texts, notes – had to stay on the phone, held on its SIM or in its memory. If you had a sufficiently advanced phone, you could synchronize your contacts and sometimes pictures with a computer, but most people who lost their mobile phone faced a tedious couple of weeks re-entering friends' mobile numbers, and sometimes telling their friends that they had a new number and transmitting that to them.

Smartphones change that. It's perfectly possible to borrow someone's smartphone, wipe their settings and set up your own – downloading them from the internet. Apple, Android, RIM and Windows Phone all allow that because the operating system is not an endpoint, but a platform that leads through to services held in the cloud. The only thing that would remain unchanged would be the phone number, tied to the SIM. Otherwise, you would see your e-mails, your web bookmarks and your apps. The process is automatic when you sign into a new phone. Any individual smartphone – the most high-tech expression of telephone technology – is *more*, not less, disposable than its predecessors. If yours is stolen, you can wipe it remotely yourself – something that the mobile networks once had to do. Consumers are in control, just as Ballmer and Lees had seen they would be. (The actual item is more valuable, of course; Mac developer Cabel Sasser's iPhone was stolen from him on a street in San Francisco. Two weeks later he detected it – in Vietnam.) As the phone is being wiped, you can load another with your contacts – phone numbers, e-mails, pictures – from Apple's, or Google's, or RIM's, or Microsoft's servers (and the pictures perhaps on Yahoo's Flickr service). You can re-download your apps. Within half an hour of being taken out of its packaging, a brand new replacement will be indistinguishable from the old one.

With that fungibility, smartphones bring the internet to places it might never have reached before; they are handheld computers that are also (most of the time, data connections permitting) connected to the internet. In sub-Saharan Africa there are 14 mobile phones for every PC; as smartphones become cheaper, that ratio will grow. Broadband connections are cheaper to provide wirelessly, from cellphone towers, than via expensive copper lines to buildings. And, while even a laptop PC battery will run out in less than a day, a smartphone will last at least that long, and needs less energy to recharge. A smartphone also requires far less capital cost than a PC.

Once a developing population has a smartphone, then the device can come into its own. Video calls, apps to advise on medical conditions, financial information, banking, education: all come in reach through the screen of a continuously internet-connected device. Making phone calls becomes almost incidental. It's the connection to the web and the rest of the internet that matters.

That makes smartphones a radical departure from the feature phones that preceded them. The signal that the iPhone was the first generation of this radical change was in the server logs on all the websites that started seeing the devices pinging their pages as soon as it went on sale.

The iPhone made mobile web browsing far simpler than any device before it. StatCounter, which measures hits on websites, shows Apple's iOS (which powers the iPhone and the iPod Touch, effectively an iPhone without the camera or phone function, but with Wi-Fi) as the dominant OS used to browse sites in North America and Europe from 2007 onwards; and, when combined with viewings via the Wi-Fi-enabled iPod Touch, iOS was the most used in the world by the end of 2008, ahead of Nokia's browser, installed in millions of people's hands.

That's the first-generation smartphone effect. But inside Google they have their eyes on bigger possibilities in future. Marissa Mayer is a graduate in artificial intelligence who was one of the first 20 employees at the company, where she led its search products, user interface and more recently location and local services. When I spoke to her in July 2009, before she left to head Yahoo, she was thinking ahead to the sort of data and the sort of search that smartphones could enable: 'I think that some of the smartphones are doing a lot of the work for us: by having cameras they already have eyes; by having GPS they know where they are; by having things like accelerometers they know how you're holding them.' The trick would be to gather the data:

> We think the real-time search is incredibly important and the real-time data that's coming online can be super useful in terms of us finding out something like, you know, is this conference today any good? Is it warmer in San Francisco than it is in Silicon Valley? There's a lot of useful information about real time and your actions that we think ultimately will reinvent search.

Voice, she felt, was heading towards being a solved problem: speech-to-text was coming in reach of the processors used in phones. Images were more difficult – though in 2010 Google offered Google Goggles, an Android app to compare pictures taken on your phone's camera with landmarks (based on your location), text, books, contact information, artwork, wines or logos. (Eric Schmidt felt it should hold off at faces over privacy concerns.) Medical applications were already plentiful on the iPhone – for recording blood sugar levels, measuring heart rate and offering advice.

Carolina Milanesi, who worked at Gartner following the progress of smartphones, thinks their effect will be radical. 'There used to be a huge difference between a normal phone, which was just voice, and something which could do much more,' she told me.

> But in the future you're going to have different degrees of 'smartness'. There will be smartphones which have a known operating system and app ecosystem. Then there will be others at different price points which will bring

different features and experiences to the user. It's similar to the PC market, where you go all the way from a desktop machine with a really fast processor and 27-inch screen to a little 10-inch or 12-inch laptop optimized for battery life.

She adds: 'People see the predictions for smartphones, where we're talking about 1.1 billion sales in 2015, and think they're all going to cost $600. But the way that you get to that 1.1 billion is by having some which cost $75.' Chinese phone manufacturers such as ZTE already make Android phones at that price point; one went on sale in Kenya in late 2011.

For the manufacturers competing in such a scenario, the question becomes: what does 'winning' mean? With Android becoming the dominant platform on mobiles, the usual media construct of 'winning', in which one company or product 'wins' and the others 'lose', as in an Olympic event, has a pat answer. Android is the winner. Apple, RIM, Nokia and Microsoft are all losers.

To the companies themselves, such scenarios matter enormously, of course: slipping into twilight just as the mobile phone business achieves a wide-ranging marriage with the internet would be a terrible failure, not just of management but of opportunity. The smartphone business offers riches beyond belief, which will accrue not only to handset manufacturers and software developers, but also to the carriers and their customers, who will find their lives enhanced and ultimately enriched by them.

Yet is the standard dialogue of 'winners' and 'losers' really a sensible way to view a world where the players may seek different outcomes? As presently configured, Google simply wants to dominate the mobile search business; it doesn't actually care which platform dominates, as long as its search engine (and so advertising system) is the most used. Apple, meanwhile, doesn't necessarily care about selling the most phones, if it can corral a substantial profit from those it does sell, and boost it from the surrounding software and hardware ecosystems. And Microsoft – while wanting the Nokia deal to turn it into the world's most widely used mobile phone platform – can nevertheless profit handsomely if mobile users become more closely tied to the Windows PC platform and Office products, with their operating profit margins of 75 per cent. (There's also the money from Android patents.)

Dediu thinks talk of the mobile race being 'over' with Android's arrival in the top spot is premature – and misses the point:

> What 'winning' is, is having sufficient numbers of users. It's not percentage. There's a critical minimum that you need for an ecosystem which makes it attractive to [software] developers. So an operating system could be a winner with 5 per cent of the market, as long as there's a million users. After all, what did Windows need for critical mass on PCs, compared to the Macintosh? And now we're talking about 'losers' such as iOS having half a billion users on the current growth roadmap. If Apple does nothing but follow the script, it will get to half a billion. And Android is likely going to get to a billion first. But that doesn't mean that Apple loses. No way that the platform will wither.
>
> The counterpoint is [Nokia's] Symbian with 250 million users – but they're pulling the rug. It wasn't sticky enough.

Symbian was unable to form a protective moat – that combination of hardware accessories and software ecosystem – to hold its users close and prevent defection to other platforms. In addition, of course, Nokia didn't react quickly enough, as Dediu had forecast. 'You have to quantify the network effects [of being on a platform],' he continues. 'Apple's iOS is sticky.'

And that's where the simplistic 'winning' or 'losing' idea breaks down. 'Each platform has a different position. I think Microsoft will buy its way in – $2 billion will buy a way in,' Dediu says. (That's the minimum amount Microsoft spent on its partnership with Nokia; the true cost is likely to be very much higher.)

The position exists for Android to rush ahead and plant a flag in all new markets, and then Apple can skim the best customers. I don't want to make this into a winner-takes-all; it's not like that in mobile. They have complementary elements. [Apple and Google] don't have symmetry in how they benefit from their ecosystems. The world is big enough for more and more. With 5 billion people [already using mobiles] before this decade is out, then 4 billion people will move to smartphones. Twenty-five per cent of that is a billion people. Is 100 million big enough to stay alive? Sure it is. And let's not forget local, provincial systems... They're rooted in politics, and the way this industry works it's about having plenty of opportunities, which require decisions from adults. It's not going to be the Wild West everywhere. We're going to see some balance. Even commodity markets have obstacles.

Nor does he think that the evolution of input – and therefore interaction, and so application – of mobile phones has finished with the touchscreen. 'Look at what Jobs described when he put up that slide [in January 2007] showing the iPhone: he said "We've had these three revolutions in input – the mouse, the scroll wheel and now the touchscreen." That's three new industries. A thesis I have is that touch isn't the end of it.' Given that he forecast how Nokia, the world's largest and most impenetrable mobile phone company, would react over a four-year period, correct to within six months, one has a suspicion he might just be right.

New input methods will emerge, and new user interfaces and ecosystems and players will emerge. I suspect it will be Apple, with maybe Google as a 'fast follower' [just as it was with multi-touch on Android]. Will it be about gestures? Motion-sensitive? Causes interaction by seeing us? Recognizes our intentions? I'm not willing to draw a line and say that 'this' or 'that' marks the end of innovation.

The addition by Apple of voice commands across the iPhone 4S in October 2011, competing with Google's voice input systems, suggests one path for future inputs.

Knook thinks that it's pride, more than anything, that keeps some of the companies fighting a battle that they cannot possibly dominate. Moreover, he thinks nobody is ever going to make money purely from a mobile operating system. 'I don't think there's space for much variety,' he said briefly.

> It's different in the PC environment, in the sense that none of these [mobile] players are in it to make money out of the OS itself, so if you'd done the analysis based on the business merits of being in these [mobile] OSs, you'd long ago have decided that everybody should accept that Apple's putting a ton of money into iOS and getting no return – they get all their gross margin out of the hardware. Google is getting a ton of mobile searches – very good news for them, but they're losing all this money on the Android team. Microsoft's losing money on Windows Mobile – always has, always will – but none of them seem to want to get out.
>
> So the first one to get out is Nokia, which was my prediction, and HP's still in with webOS, which was not my prediction. [Soon after we spoke, HP killed webOS.] The rationale for why people are sticking in there and fighting this operating system battle has absolutely nothing to do with the commercial nature of that business, and has everything to do with 'How does it help me with some other business?' In the case of Google, how does it help me suck people into my search crowd? With Microsoft, how do I keep Windows relevant? So everybody's got different alternatives. None of them will give up easily.

It's a truism that was quoted back to Stephen Elop at the announcement of the Nokia–Microsoft tie-up that 'today's smartphone is tomorrow's feature phone' – that relentless improvements in computing technology mean that eventually everyone will be using something that we would today class as a smartphone. Even since the iPhone's introduction, the computing power contained in an iPhone has grown from 7.75 megaflops (million floating point operations per second) in 2007 to around 34 megaflops in the iPhone 4 of 2010, putting it slightly ahead of Moore's law. In 2013, the iPhone 5s hit 171 megaflops, neatly fitting an exponential curve.

At that rate of change, functions we might find remarkable and unusual today – GPS, voice recognition, cloud synchronization, TV streaming – will become commonplace within a few years, and available to anyone in 10 or 15 years. When Tanzanian fishermen can make video calls showing the size and quality of today's catch, we'll know that the smartphone has reached its most valuable frontier. And then the triumph of the internet will be complete.

The downward spiral

In March 2012, RIM did something surprising: it announced that it had made an operating loss in the quarter from December 2011 to February 2012. During the previous quarter it had written off $485 million on an estimated 2 million unsold PlayBooks – yet still made a profit. But the Christmas period had created problems, including another writeoff, this time of $267 million on its older BB7 handsets.

Thorsten Heins, the chief operations officer (equivalent to Tim Cook under Steve Jobs) who had taken over from Balsillie and Lazaridis in January 2012, announced that it would in future focus on its 'core strengths'. Balsillie resigned from the board, later revealing he had fought to make BlackBerry Messenger – the app which let BlackBerry phones send data cheaply and quickly between each other – a standalone, cross-platform app that would generate necessary income.

But the core had gone away. Within months Heins had to admit the company would lose money for another quarter. It became evident that Apple had taken away its clothes in the enterprise, and Android had done the same with low-end consumers. With its new BB10 software delayed to some time in 2013, the company had fallen into a downward spiral: it kept losing old customers, and couldn't gain enough new ones.

Nokia, meanwhile, didn't have it easy either. Elop's decision to announce Symbian's forthcoming death in January 2011, yet not have any Windows Phone handsets to sell, had a dramatic effect on the company's primary customers – the carriers. Six months after that announcement, and three months before it had any Windows Phone handsets to sell, Nokia too made an operating loss on its handset business. The next two quarters were profitable; then the money began bleeding out again.

By the end of 2012, both Nokia and RIM were trapped in a financial gravity well. According to Dediu's rule of thumb – which was quickly taking on the force of a law of nature – it was only a matter of time before each would succumb, either to a takeover, merger, or breakup.

Nokia's response, as it tried to pull itself out of the dive, was to differentiate itself through phone features such as wireless charging and high-quality cameras. At the launch of one handset, I asked Jo Harlow, its head of Windows Phone, why people should buy a Lumia device (its Windows Phone brand) rather than any other brand. She replied that the usage data Nokia collected indicated that people who bought them did so to use the camera – a feature where the company excelled.

I mentioned this later to a senior Apple executive, who guffawed quietly, and said: 'That's because they don't have any apps.' Even three years after its launch, Windows Phone still didn't have some of the most popular, and many of the less popular (but fringe), apps. Among them were a native version of the photo-sharing service Instagram, now owned by Facebook, and Snapchat, a photo sharing service whose wrinkle made it hugely popular with teenagers: you sent the photo to a recipient – and then it wiped itself. Windows Phone had no native version, and had to rely on third-party bolt-ons.

So if Nokia thought the smartphone was about photos, what did Apple think the smartphone was for? 'A computer in your pocket,' the executive replied at once.

In mid-July, Nokia hit one mark: sales of Lumia phones for the three months to June outstripped those of BlackBerry. But it would be premature to call Windows Phone the third ecosystem; BlackBerry (as RIM had renamed itself in January, launching new phones with new software derived from the PlayBook's) still had around 70 million users. Nokia had sold fewer than 27 million Lumias over seven quarters. And the handset business was still losing money.

The spiral tightened. At the end of August 2013, Heins announced that BlackBerry's board had formed a special committee to examine options, including selling the business. The chairman, Prem Watsa, resigned in order to put together a bid – which emerged a few weeks later as an unfinanced, tentative $4.9 billion offer. Watsa had until 4 November to finance it. Other would-be buyers circled – though none could see a better solution than dismantling the handset business and selling the remaining pieces. Cerberus, a private equity company, and China's Lenovo all indicated interest.

Nokia was in trouble too. In September, Microsoft announced – at 4am in the morning – that it was buying the Finnish company's handset business. The €5.4 billion deal was complex: it was licensing the 'Nokia' brand, buying the 'Lumia' name, and licensing a portfolio of patents – which observers suspected would be used against Android handset makers to extract more licensing fees. Microsoft also offered €1.5 billion of 'immediate financing', repayable on the deal's conclusion in early 2014 – suggesting that Nokia had hit a serious cash flow problem. Microsoft turned out to be the deus ex machina to pull it out of its black hole. BlackBerry was left, alone, to drift towards the singularity of oblivion. Dediu had been right.

Apple and Google, meanwhile, had gone from close cooperation to open warfare. Of the two, Google and Android were the clear winner; and Google search's position as the default on the iPhone browser meant the overwhelming majority of all mobile search went through Google. Apple – and Microsoft, trailing badly – needed a new battlefield.

Chapter Six
Tablets

'Within five years'

'Within five years, I predict this will be the most popular form of PC sold in America,' said the middle-aged man, wearing his customary glasses, and hefting aloft an unusual new product: a computer that relied on a touch-sensitive screen, instead of a keyboard, for its input. He continued: 'We just finished some of the prototypes of that device, and I have to say there's been more fighting over who gets to use those prototypes than any new thing that we've ever done. I think that's a good sign,' he told the audience, adding that the design was 'the ultimate evolution of the laptop'.

Bill Gates turned out to be wrong. The audience at the Comdex in Las Vegas on that November day in 2000 wasn't getting a vision of the future – at least, not Microsoft's future. Five years later, Windows-based tablet computers were the tiniest of niches in the computer business. They were heavy and expensive, and had modest battery lives; you needed a stylus – a hostage to absent-mindedness – to operate them. A few people swore by them. More swore at them. Most ignored them.

Inside Microsoft, the tablet design had already been the focus of a bitter battle involving Richard Brass, whom Gates had given the job of turning tablets from a really nice laboratory idea into the next-generation devices to take Windows and Office into the future. Brass, who had joined the company only in 1997, had been appointed vice-president of emerging technologies, with a brief to develop new concepts.

In March 1999, Gates gave him and his team the task of developing a tablet computer – an idea that had echoed around Silicon Valley for decades: a letterpad-sized, portable computer without a keyboard that you could write on directly. (Its forebears are seen on the original *Star Trek* series, and the Etch A Sketch.) As Gates explained to the *New York Times* that August, 'We're trying to see if we can produce a tablet PC and the software for it that will be sufficiently powerful and intuitive and inexpensive to capture the imagination and the marketplace.'[1] He thought handwriting or speech recognition might replace the keyboard.

Brass already knew he faced a huge challenge. It wasn't over the quality of the idea; it was getting the right backing inside the company. He had experience of that already: when the group invented a system for displaying text on-screen with greater legibility, which they called ClearType, he was told by the Windows group that some of the colours made the display break, and by the Office group that the display wasn't sharp, but 'fuzzy'. The head of the pocket devices group offered to support ClearType if Brass's group transferred to work for him. (Brass demurred.) Not for nothing has Microsoft's culture been likened to the Mafia, with its strict rules and promotions and 'strong' internal culture.

Brass, a New Yorker with an aggressive style, described in a profile in *BusinessWeek* as a 'force of nature' who 'can grab the attention of an entire room just by walking in the door', who 'often bellows to make a point or interrupts people to redirect the course of a conversation',[2] was up against the inertia of a gigantic organization. His task was getting tablets to happen. Powerful forces inside Microsoft weren't so eager. Brass later recounted, in an article in the *New York Times* in 2010, how the vice-president in charge of Office had decided he didn't like the styluses needed to control the tablet; he preferred keyboards. He therefore wouldn't devote developer resources to rewriting Office to work properly with a tablet. 'So if you wanted to enter a number into a spreadsheet or correct a word in an e-mail message, you had to write it in a special pop-up box, which then transferred the information to Office. Annoying, clumsy and slow,' Brass growled.[3]

He felt the tablet initiative had effectively been sabotaged. Without Office support, the tablet was stillborn. And, even in 2001, laptops were only just becoming popular; more than three-quarters of PC sales were desktops.

Apple didn't take much notice until, according to Jobs's biography, in 2002 he was at a dinner with Gates, and a senior Microsoft executive who was working on the tablet. He insisted it would revolutionize the market and that Apple should license the stylus-driven software.[4] Jobs, however, detested pen-driven computers: he thought fingers could do the job far better – and unlike a stylus, you'd never lose them. Soon after, Apple's design team, headed by Jonathan Ive, was given the task of investigating it and coming up with an implementation of a finger-driven touchscreen.

The problem then with touchscreens was the resistive technology they used (where pressure from a stylus, finger or fingernail changes the resistance of two or more screen layers; connectors along the top and side sense the change, and the processor calculates the point where it happened). They could respond to pressure only at one point. You couldn't swipe them – the pressure wouldn't be transmitted evenly through the motion – or use other gestures.

Also, Jobs realized, handwriting is too slow: 'You could never keep up with your e-mail if you had to write it all out. If you do e-mail of any volume you've gotta have a keyboard. We looked at the [Microsoft] tablet and we think it's gonna fail,' he said in April 2003. It might work as a reading device, he allowed: 'If you've got a bunch of rich guys who can afford their third computer: they've got a desktop; they've got a portable; now they're going to have one of these to read with – that's your market. And people accuse *us* of niche marketing.'

Apple's team realized that sometimes you did want to touch the screen at multiple points, or swipe it as if you were directly manipulating a mouse pointer (to move around a web page, say). Doing that required a capacitive screen, which has a single layer and detects the conductance of something touching it; usually, it's tuned to that of a finger.

After some experiments with the then-newest generations of capacitive screens, the teams came up with some designs that they thought could work. They used a version of Mac OSX and proved the concept. But there was one insurmountable problem: capacitive screens were up to 50 per cent more expensive than resistive ones, and even those were expensive. Marketing said there was no market at the price. The tablet idea was shelved. Still, the design team had learnt some useful lessons from working on a touchscreen. They put it to good use in another product – the iPhone.

Within two years of launching the iPhone, Apple was buying such large areas of capacitive screens that prices had fallen significantly. There was already a stripped-down Mac OS for touchscreen (now named iOS). The tablet project was dusted off. This time, it looked more promising: gestures worked. The software worked. There could also be apps for it, just as there were for the phone. One thing that was different from the phone: at arm's length, the tablet took about as much of the field of vision as a TV screen. Typing was feasible, but the main thing that would make a difference was content.

Apple began working on it, and also began – as secretly as it could manage – meeting media companies such as Time Warner and Major League Baseball about producing content that would fit on a sort of iPhone… except with a much larger screen. Word leaked out, so that, just as with the iPhone three years before, by the end of December 2009 the noise that Apple was about to launch a tablet was unmistakable. Typically, Apple's tight secrecy meant that all that was unknown was its name, size, weight, specifications and price. Some of that data – about the shipment estimates and screen orders – was leaked in December 2009 by a Samsung employee, Suk-Joo Hwang, to a US research executive and a hedge fund manager at a lunch in Mountain View, California. A nearby Apple employee overheard the conversation; ruthless as ever, Apple terminated the contract it had to buy more screens from Samsung soon afterwards in favour of Seiko, Epson and LG.

Inside Microsoft, the noise about Apple's plans was also being heard. Just as they had recognized even before the iPhone that Microsoft needed a smartphone aimed at consumers, a team led by J Allard could see opportunities in the tablet market. Allard was once more espousing the benefits of vertical integration: build it all; control the experience. His team devised a book-style e-reader with two 7-inch screens which could be operated by a stylus or fingers in multi-touch mode. The 'device' was mostly conceptual, involving lots of drag-and-drop operation; concept videos from the project showed it operating rather like a pair of large iPhones, with apps, photos, mapping, contacts, calendars and projects.

Towards the end of 2009 Allard took the idea, called Courier, to Ballmer and the chiefs to get it approved. Though it was a 'whole widget' project – where Microsoft made the hardware as well as the software – he'd succeeded with the Xbox, the Zune MP3 player and the Kin phone (then being ramped up for production); why not a tablet? But unlike those two projects, which stepped on the toes only of projects inside Entertainment and Devices, the Courier did computing: address books, maps, pictures.

The relentless logic of Microsoft's survival took over. The Courier wasn't running Windows, nor even apparently running Windows Phone, the next-generation phone operating system then in development. If it didn't run Windows, it wouldn't run Office, which would deny Microsoft the profit from the Windows licence and the chance of an Office licence. If it didn't run Windows Phone, it didn't fit into the longer-range scheme for phones. No Windows meant development costs and also lost revenues: on average Microsoft makes $56 of revenue and $40 of profit per PC sold running Windows. If Courier were a hit but subtracted from PC sales, each one would have to generate $40 of profit – or it would damage Microsoft's bottom line.

Ballmer told Allard he would think about it. Still, he didn't like the idea of Steve Jobs stealing his tablet thunder, and in the week ahead of the Apple announcement he used his spot at the keynote speech of the Consumer Electronics Show (CES) in January to imply that Dell and HP, two of the world's largest PC manufacturers, would have their own tablets coming out in 2010. Windows 7, he said, was 'touch-enabled' – an intriguing phrase. You could run Windows 7 on a tablet, but the experience was dire: icons were too small, and fingers too large to operate the standard Windows interface.

Ahead of the launch, Apple's detractors lost no time in pointing out that Microsoft had tried tablet PCs, and they sold about a million per year, so Apple – with an even tinier share of the PC market – was clearly on course to sell only a few thousand devices. John Gruber, a self-described raconteur (more precisely, a Philadelphia-based blogger who has developed wide and deep connections inside and around Apple), responded: 'The hype isn't about Apple possibly unveiling the first tablet computing device; it's about Apple possibly unveiling the first *great* one.'[5]

Third category

A few weeks later, with CES all but forgotten, Steve Jobs took the stage at the Yerba Buena Center in San Francisco to announce a new product – the iPad. But rather than a product for mobility – like the iPod or iPhone – the iPad seemed to be for immobility. The stage set included a large armchair, in which Jobs sat for large parts of the presentation. He browsed. He e-mailed. He flipped back and forth between screens of photos. He didn't seem to be doing *serious* computing. This was someone on a break. Although there were also versions of Apple's 'productivity' apps, what Jobs demonstrated suggested the devices weren't necessarily for work.

He suggested that this was a 'third category' of device, and said that it would have to be 'far better at doing some really important things – things like browsing the web. That's a pretty tall order', he said. It would have to excel at e-mail, listening to music, playing games and reading e-books. 'If there's going to be a third category of device, it's going to have to be better at these kinds of tasks than a laptop or a smartphone; otherwise it has no reason for being.'

In some ways it echoed his introduction of the iPod just over eight years before: define the categories; suggest which one this should fit into. But here there were competitors – principally the netbook, a category created in 2008 by Taiwanese laptop manufacturers trying to boost sales by creating an ultra-low-priced, smaller laptop that would be extra-portable with a longer battery life. (Apple had stolidly refused to build a netbook: Jobs had said at one analyst call that he didn't know how to build a laptop for that price that wasn't rubbish.)

Jobs continued explaining where the iPad would fit into the new world: 'Now, some people have thought that's a netbook. The problem is netbooks aren't *better* at anything. They... they're slow, they have low-quality displays, and they run clunky old PC software. So they're not better than a laptop at anything – they're just cheaper. They're just cheap laptops. And we don't think they're a third category of device. But we think we've got something that is, and we'd like to show it to you today for the first time.'

Just as with the iPod, he didn't show the full-frontal shot first; he began with the side view. 'And we call it... the iPad,' he said.

Analysts found it hard to decide whether the iPad was the next iPod and iPhone, or another Cube – the minimal computer that Jobs had proudly unveiled in July 2000 and killed off within a year owing to poor sales. Forecasts ranged from complete flop to runaway success. Anders Bylund of TMF Zahrim opined: 'The Apple iPad is not unique, nor necessarily the best of breed in the media tablet sector it is spearheading. And it ain't gonna help Apple shareholders any.'[6] Horace Dediu, the former Nokia executive now running his own consultancy, forecast after the announcement that 6 million units would be sold in the year. (I forecast 5 million in its first nine months, a couple of days before the device was unveiled.)

What the doubters overlooked was that the iPad was the result of very careful work inside Apple. In April 2008 it had absorbed a chip design company, PA Semi, which specialized in processor design using the ARM architecture – the one used in all smartphones for its low-power characteristics. The iPad processor was a custom build, with an in-house team, making problem solving simpler than for a company building hardware, using someone else's processors and someone else's software. Internal teams developed and tested multiple prototypes – with different screen sizes, battery weights and aspect ratios – which then competed against each other. One ex-Apple employee told me this is done all the time – but the teams do it without animosity; the aim is to get the best design, not to win. Jobs and Ive settled on a 10-inch screen, enough battery for 10 hours, and a 4:3 height-to-length ratio. Meanwhile a team of a few dozen – tiny by Microsoft's standards, average for Google, large for Apple – worked on converting the iPhone's operating system and software such as the e-mail and browser program to work on the larger screen.

It went on sale at the start of April. People queued outside stores. But others couldn't see the point of a tablet running a phone-like OS – especially at Microsoft. Ballmer had run the numbers, and the Windows division, led by Steve Sinofsky, had prevailed. In mid-April, Ballmer drove up to the separate laboratory where Allard's team had been working on the Courier and told them it was over, just as the iPad began flying off the shelves. Allard was furious. He and his wife, Rebecca Norlander, left Microsoft soon afterwards.

'A big lesson is that it may be easier to go into your quiet space and incubate. But when you want to get bigger and get more resources, you want to make sure you're aligned,' one Courier team member told the journalist Jay Greene, who did an in-depth investigation into the Courier's demise: 'If you get Sinofsky on board from the start, you're probably going to market.'[7]

Almost exactly as Allard was getting the bad news, a group from the Windows division was giving a presentation to some of the larger PC manufacturers, including HP and Dell. One of the slides included a comparison against Apple, titled 'How Apple does it: a virtuous cycle', which commented that:

- 'Apple brand is known for high quality, uncomplicated, "it just works".'

- 'Product UX [user experience] is designed to help people realize value.'
- 'Realized value leads to product satisfaction, which in turn feeds brand loyalty.'
- 'This is something people will pay for!'[8]

For Microsoft to mention Apple's perceived advantages in a discussion about the future of Windows indicated how differently Sinofsky, who had taken over the division in September 2006, was prepared to think. The reality of the PC industry was that Apple made more profit per computer (estimated at $370 per $1,300 machine) sold than HP or Dell (which managed about $40 per $800 machine). With PC sales growth now slowing dramatically in the West, and shifting to the Far East, where piracy was rampant, Microsoft was seeing average per-PC revenues and profits fall year by year. It needed to be able to offer PC makers a new format that would drive loyalty such as Apple saw, and revive its sales and margins.

Sinofsky, born in 1965, was a Microsoft veteran who joined the company as a software engineer in 1995 – four years after Allard, despite being a few years older – and worked his way up the ranks through the Office division. Where Allard was radical, Sinofsky was an organizational thinker, who says his first experience at the company was of spending a year on a software project that was 'a pretty colossal failure'[9] – but that what he learnt from it was that 'Microsoft holds no grudges. The boss said "OK, you made a mistake. Let's get moving and don't make that same mistake."' Having led the Office division's development of its radical 'ribbon' interface in 2007 (which inspired hate and love in roughly equal measure), he was put in charge of the Windows division, where it was struggling with Vista, its next version of Windows later that year. He got that untangled as best he could, then drove through Windows 7, a far more polished version of Windows, and with that done, in summer 2009, he began a 're-imagining' of Windows.

The slideshow shown to HP indicated that Microsoft was thinking that the next version of Windows would run on slates (keyboardless tablets, like the iPad) as well as laptops and desktops. That was nothing new; but, inside Microsoft, Sinofsky was leading a radical plan of which Allard's defeat was only part. The project was nothing less than the unification of Windows across all platforms – mobile, tablet and desktop. The purpose was to protect the most valuable thing the company had – its Windows monopoly – in perpetuity. And part of that meant making it run on the same low-power processor architecture as the iPad and smartphones: ARM, designed by a British company based in Cambridge.

Apple dominant

At the end of May 2010, Apple announced that it had sold 2 million iPads in less than 60 days. That was only in the United States; it had just begun shipping to other countries – Japan, Germany, France, the UK, Italy, Spain, Canada, Australia and Switzerland. Yet in less than one quarter it had sold more than twice as many tablets as had previously been sold in a year.

While many commentators kept dismissing the iPad as a fad, rivals scrambled to build their own. The problem was: what operating system should they build it on? Windows 7, despite being 'fully touch-enabled', really wasn't suitable: the icons were too small for finger control and the interface unwieldy. And hardware makers who used Windows 7 would have to pay the full licence cost of about $50 per device. A tablet that sold as well as the iPad would cost the maker $100 million in licensing fees before any profit.

What about Windows Phone? Despite the fact that the Metro interface looked like the perfect form for a tablet, and would cost only $15 or so per machine, Microsoft turned requests down flat. It wouldn't say why. It didn't hint that it had a grand plan, and junior staff who interacted with the press weren't told there was a grand plan. It simply stonewalled.

So manufacturers turned instead to Android. In the race to manufacture, Samsung had a head start: having supplied some of the screens, it knew the specifications. Its first tablet, the Galaxy Tab, used Android 2.2 – the same as on many mobile phones – and a 7-inch screen (a 7-inch screen has half the area of a 10-inch one: the measurement is on the diagonal). Half the cost of the device is in the screen, so chopping that in half cut costs. Even so, it couldn't match Apple's price; despite being smaller, the Tab was more expensive.

Despite the price gap, as more companies announced tablets there was the expectation that the tablet market would be a rapid repeat of the PC market: horizontal would beat vertical. In June 2010 Shantanu Narayen, chief executive of Adobe, told the AllThingsD conference what he expected: 'What you saw with smartphones hitting an inflection point with Android, you'll see it again with tablets,' he said. 'There will be another 20 tablets that will come by the end of the year that will push the industry in different directions.'[10] He cited HP's webOS (the result of purchasing Palm in mid-2010) and RIM's PlayBook – a 7-inch tablet being developed in a crash programme rather like that for the BlackBerry Storm, whose hardware development was mostly outsourced to the Taiwanese computer assembler Quanta – as others that would certainly get enterprise take-up. Because it was enterprise adoption that had decided the PC's success, so it would surely be for tablets – wouldn't it?

The importance – or not – of Flash became a fresh topic of debate, just as on the iPhone. It was the only element separating Apple from rivals – that, and the fact that the iPad was selling in huge numbers. Did Flash matter? Apple said not. Adobe and the tablet manufacturers said yes: without it, videos on many news websites wouldn't play, advertisements wouldn't play, but YouTube and most other video sites would play fine, and news sites began converting their video output to work with the iPad too.

By the end of 2010 Apple completely dominated the tablet space; it had sold a total of 14.3 million, adding $9.5 billion to its revenues. And the hardware add-on ecosystem welcomed it with open arms, building iPad music docks, covers, sleeves and add-ons. Android tablet shipments (though not necessarily sales) were estimated at 2.5 million. By January 2011, the Consumer Electronics Show in Las Vegas, where Ballmer was once more giving the keynote speech, had acres devoted to Chinese manufacturing companies that seemed to be doing nothing but turning out iPad-compatible products. One company even had a profitable line in dummy iPads for displays; they were everywhere.

Always on

The iPad, and the tablet idea, wasn't important only for Apple. Along with the smartphone, it has profound implications for how computing might look in the future. Even a casual study of how people used iPads showed that they used them in places and at times where they wouldn't dream of using a laptop: in brief snatched moments between meetings, on short rides between locations, pulled quickly from a bag to check on something. Key to this use was the iPad's ability to be 'instant on' (more precisely 'never off, always asleep') because the machine state could be preserved for days, just as with a phone, and it had a long battery life – around 10 hours if used for computing. The 3G versions were in effect constantly connected computers, but with the advantages of portability. For people whose lifestyles meant they were expected to be always available, or constantly finishing something, it slotted in perfectly.

Three other things helped its popularity. First was the huge number of quality apps, as developers stepped up to the challenge of designing for a larger screen (and were in turn rewarded by people buying apps through Apple). Second was the fact that no Android tablet maker could match its price. Although some Chinese companies managed to turn out Android tablets – and even 10-inch tablets – that undercut the iPad, the user experience was gruesome: old and therefore slow processors, inaccurate touchscreens, software that crashed and batteries that drained in less than an hour. Even a serious upgrade to Android by Rubin's team aimed at the 10-inch tablet, called Honeycomb (officially, version 3.0), failed to make a dent. Despite behaving much more like a tablet-designed operating system, with larger icons, it still revealed its phone origins in various places (such as the system information setting saying 'About this phone').

Apple's trump card, though, was the galaxy of content from its store – apps, music, film, TV shows, books – that people could download directly. Alternatively, they could read newspapers or sites such as Twitter in new, more visual ways via apps created for that purpose. Other Android tablet makers, which didn't have the same content offering, had to pitch Flash as their unique selling point; they certainly couldn't do it on other paid-for media content.

Once again, the horizontal model wasn't looking as healthy as theory suggested it should. To some people, this suggested that it was practice, not theory, that was wrong. The iPad's perceived limitations from an IT worker's perspective included lack of access to the file system, inability to attach an SD card or USB memory stick, and inability to run Flash video. Clearly, then, people must be buying it as a 'toy'. As one commentator, Aaron Habgrove, put it in June 2011:

> Actually, the iPad succeeds because it enables you to read websites whilst sitting on the toilet and play casual games in bed. It's a toy. You can't eliminate complexity when there was never any complexity in the first place – Apple went and threw a 10-inch screen on the iPod Touch and iPhone and called them the iPad and iPad 3G, respectively.[11]

Obviously it couldn't be for any serious computing ends.

Evidence to the contrary kept turning up. One day I asked a man on a train what he was using his iPad for: he explained that he ran a chain of restaurants, and used it to view spreadsheets of the business's performance, as well as his e-mail and web browsing. Any serious keyboard work he did on the laptop in his office. But the idea of carrying both around didn't make sense.

Airlines began testing it for pilots in cockpits, to replace huge manuals and pages of navigation charts. Schools began buying them to replace textbooks and give children direct access to the web. In Apple earnings calls, Cook would reel off statistics about the number of Fortune 500 companies 'testing or deploying' iPads, of banks and brokers that were trying it, and of serious apps being written for it. Apple was going, ever so quietly, after the business computing market – the one that had belonged for years to Microsoft.

The extent of the iPad's acceptance – and applicability – was brought into focus most clearly when Greece, facing an economic calamity which required the renegotiation of €146 billion worth of bonds, decided to solve it using iPads. Each of the 135 principal bondowners was issued with an iPad with a custom app, built by Bondcom, a London-based company.

The previous largest comparable bond restructuring was in Argentina, in 2005: it involved more than 200,000 investors, and took 90 days as clerks entered responses on paper to tally the total.

The Greek restructuring was for three times the debt – and had just 30 days to complete it. Using a standard Excel spreadsheet, 'There would have been close to 100,000 rows and dozens of columns...scattered over 135 separate worksheets,' a Bondcom representative told me.

The idea of doing the restructuring with PCs was thrown out. They would be liable to viruses; banks wouldn't allow them onto their networks; they weren't portable for bankers who would be travelling to and from meetings. The iPads, though, could be encrypted, remotely wiped, connected to the phone network, and tracked via GPS.

A convenient four-month delay for political wrangling let the developers refine the app; by the time the crunch came, all the bondholders had an interactive display showing precisely how much had been restructured, how much remained, and how much time remained. They could call virtual meetings. And at the end, the restructuring was successful. Greece avoided a gigantic default that could have had a knock-on effect on the European and world economy. Not bad for a toy.

The iPad was eating into Microsoft in another way. Each of those $9.5 billion worth of purchases in 2010 – the majority by consumers – represented money not spent on a PC. The absence of a viable Microsoft tablet, effectively neutered all those years ago by the power of the Office division, was ceding cash to Apple. As iPad sales grew, the research groups Gartner and IDC revised their forecasts for PC sales downwards; by the end of 2010, 15.2 million fewer PCs were sold than had been forecast in January. For Sinofsky's Windows division, that represented $850 million of lost revenues and $610 million of lost profit.

Sinofsky was aware of the importance – but wouldn't be hurried. During 2010, he had thrown the Windows team into a focused effort to produce a version of Windows that would run on tablets using the ARM processor architecture. Intel chips chew up batteries; none of its efforts to make a low-power processor matched ARM's ground-up low-power designs. As a result almost every smartphone uses ARM, despite years of wheedling and chip design by Intel.

The ARM-based Windows computers would use the Metro interface. But the really important point was that they would use Windows at the full price – not the cut-price Windows Phone, or some new Courier OS. Allard's idea had been killed because it risked the future income stream from Windows, and Microsoft would never do that. But Sinofsky's plan – a Windows for two different architectures – had huge implications for the challenge of keeping the versions synchronized.

Interviewed in October 2010, Ballmer was asked what his riskiest product bet was. His reply: 'Next release of Windows.'[12] He didn't elucidate.

Sinofsky finally showed the first fruits of the effort in January 2011, at the Consumer Electronics Show, though in a hotel far from the madding crowds of iPad cases and accessory makers. It was brief, showing Windows and Word running on an ARM-based system.

Windows 8 was not released until October 2012. Its ARM variant, called 'Windows RT', was launched in parallel. Although apps had to be recompiled to run on ARM rather than Intel, Microsoft assured developers it was simple. The RT devices could only install programs from a Microsoft app store – an idea it had handily borrowed from the world of smartphones. It had however overlooked one key point: app stores offer leverage both to those who control them and those who write for them if the latter is large enough.

The theory – from Microsoft's point of view – was that Windows would now permeate through the whole processor market, across both Intel and ARM devices.

But it didn't. Third-party computer makers offered ARM-based PCs running RT; buyers shunned or returned them as soon as they realized that they couldn't run standard desktop software. In January 2013 I happened to be standing beside a middle-aged man who was returning an RT computer – one of Microsoft's own Surface RT tablets.

Why? 'The salesman told me it would run iTunes,' he complained. 'It doesn't.' The software that Steve Jobs had hesitated about, iTunes for Windows, was now on hundreds of millions of computers, and turning out to be a serious stumbling block for Microsoft's desire to escape the past. Apple showed no inclination to recompile iTunes for Windows RT. Nor did Google with its increasingly successful Chrome browser, which now challenged Internet Explorer as the most used. RT was a dead end. By the end of 2013, sales of RT devices were minimal – perhaps a few million, against a PC market of around 350 million Intel-based machines (even though that was slipping). RT seemed to have taken Microsoft down an expensive cul-de-sac: in July 2013 it wrote off $900m on unsold Surface RT tablets, while admitting it had sold just $833m worth in the nine months they had been on sale – equivalent to a couple of million (though no figures were given).

Hermann Hauser, a co-founder of ARM, claimed that Intel's microprocessor business was 'doomed': 'If you look at the history of computing there was mainframe, which was dominated by IBM, then came the minicomputer dominated by DEC, then came the third wave with workstations dominated by Sun and Apollo, then the PC, and now it's the mobile architecture that is going to be the main computing platform at least on the terminal side,' he said. 'There is no case in the history of computing where a company that has dominated one wave has dominated the next wave and there is no case where a new wave did not kill the previous wave – as in obliterate them.'[13] And, he summed up, 'the people that dominate the PC market are Intel and Microsoft'.

Post-PC

In March 2011 Jobs turned up – despite being on his final bout of medical leave from Apple – to launch an upgrade to the iPad. Compared to the previous year, he could be confident about the possibilities for the iPad. His message was that this was the start of a new shift in computing, and that the iPad was the forerunner of a 'post-PC' world, where computing would be freed of many of the restrictions that had burdened the computing experience so far. Most of all he was critical of the idea that this would be like the 1980s again, where any hardware and any software would do.

'Our competitors are looking at this [tablet market] like it's the next PC market. That is not the right approach to this. These are post-PC devices that need to be easier to use than a PC, more intuitive,' he said, pacing the stage. 'The hardware and software need to intertwine more than they do on a PC. We think we're on the right path with this.'[14]

There was a curious echo in his words to what someone else had written, in a company-wide memo that offered both promise and warning. He had also been thinking about life after the PC, and suggested this:

Imagining a post-PC world ... at this juncture, given all that has transpired in computing and communications, it's important that all of us do precisely what our competitors and customers will ultimately do: close our eyes and form a realistic picture of what a post-PC world might actually look like. How would customers accomplish the kinds of things they do today? In what ways would it be better? In what ways would it be worse, or just different?

The words were in a company-wide e-mail sent by Ray Ozzie as he stepped down from the role of Microsoft's chief software architect – the role that before him had been held by Bill Gates – in October 2010. Ozzie, it was clear, had tired of the political infighting necessary to effect change within the corporate culture where Windows and Office stood like the legs of the biggest statue to software's profitable success. Ozzie had stepped down, and Ballmer had chosen not to replace him.

As 2011 wore on, Apple didn't cede any ground. By mid-year nearly 12 million more iPads had been sold, generating almost $9 billion of revenue. By contrast RIM's much-heralded PlayBook saw 500,000 shipments in its first quarter – and then 200,000 in the next. The company became bloated with as many as 700,000 unshipped tablets, and began offering 40 per cent discounts to buyers to try to make them shift. HP put the TouchPad on sale in June – and then killed it in August, apparently because of uninspiring sales. HP ran a fire sale of the machines for $99 and sold its entire output within weeks, at a loss of millions of dollars. Samsung, the most promising of the Android rivals, fought a number of increasingly bitter patent and court battles with Apple around the world, but sales of the Galaxy Tab remained mostly unquantified, though some research put it at 6 per cent of the market compared to Apple's 75 per cent; even so it was the largest Android maker, with dozens of others having a handful of the share.

The iPad market was beginning to look more like the iPod market than the PC market. Could Microsoft change that?

Grand unified theory

In June 2011 Sinofsky appeared at the AllThingsD conference, where he was quizzed by the veteran writer Walt Mossberg. 'You missed the first wave of super smartphones, consumer tablets and so on. What's going on? I know you have smart people,' said Mossberg.

'There are always things we are doing well,' Sinofsky replied. 'You picked two of the things we didn't do particularly well. We're not out of the game.' He denied the suggestion that there was a systemic issue with Microsoft.

And then he showed off the new interface for Windows 8, which immediately answered why Microsoft hadn't licensed Windows Phone for tablets. Sinofsky was using Metro as the new interface for Windows 8 on tablets.

As a strategy, it couldn't be faulted. Microsoft would preserve its licensing revenues, yet it would also reach down towards the 'post-PC' form factor that Apple was making popular. Writing on a Microsoft blog, Sinofsky said that Windows 8 had been planned since summer 2009 – before its predecessor Windows 7 was shipped (though after it was complete) – with the intention of 'reimagining Windows, and to be open to revisiting even the most basic elements of the user model, the platform and APIs, and the architectures we support. Our goal was a no compromise design.' But of course user interface design always involves compromises, and Windows 8 would be either compromised or complicated. You can't do the same things on a tablet that you can on a desktop. You don't use them the same way: tablets are for touch, where desktops are for keyboards. So Sinofsky set out a further bifurcation in September 2011, explaining to the annual conference for external developers writing Windows programs that they would have to recompile and perhaps rewrite programs to run on ARM-based tablets running Windows 8. In that sense, it isn't the 'same' Windows they had been using and for which millions of programs exist. But, he told them, 'those apps don't take advantage of all the things that make ARM a unique offering'. He didn't expand on what made ARM a unique offering – though the implication seemed to be its low power demands and hence longer battery life for a given power input; ARM designs trailed Intel substantially for processing capability.

He announced something else: to get apps on to ARM-based Windows tablets, they'd have to submit them to Microsoft, which would vet them and place them in an online store for download. For paid-for apps, Microsoft would take a 30 per cent cut. And, in a final twist, Dean Hachamovitch, head of the Internet Explorer team, noted that the version of browser on ARM (and Intel) tablets wouldn't run any plug-ins, including Flash.[15] It would all be about HTML5, because that was becoming mainstream.

An ARM-based version of its principal operating system? A controlled app store? A ban on Flash? By the end of 2011, Microsoft had suddenly begun to look a lot like Apple. The only thing it didn't have was the product – yet: Windows 8 was expected to go on sale towards the end of 2012.

Analysts puzzled too over how Microsoft would get the message across that one breed of tablets (with Intel chips) would be able to run old Windows apps, while another (with ARM) wouldn't. What would consumers make of it? That uncertainty, mixed with Apple's juggernaut, led Carolina Milanesi at Gartner to forecast that the iPod-like dominance would continue as far as 2015, retaining a market share of over 50 per cent. 'Apple delivers a superior and unified user experience across its hardware, software and services,' she observed. 'Apple had the foresight to create this market and in doing that planned for it as far as component supplies such as memory and screen.'[16] Windows 8's timing was a 'late arrival'; the best chance would be in business.

She also forecast that the number of tablets sold would grow from the equivalent of 5 per cent of PC sales in 2010 to 60 per cent by 2015. Half of PC sales are in North America and Europe, and are slowing dramatically, so if those figures are correct there might then be more tablet sales than PC sales in the

West, although in her model less than 10 per cent of them would be Windows devices.

That would certainly be a post-PC era. Gates's prophecy would have come true – just a decade late.

Yet as so often with predictions, Milanesi was too pessimistic in some parts, too optimistic in others. Tablet sales blossomed, so that by the final three months of 2013 another company, IDC, was forecasting they would outsell PCs, 84.1m to 83.1m. (They fell short, 76.9m to 82.1m.) Apple did not retain its share; in the third quarter Apple's share fell to around 30 per cent as sales of small, cheap Android tablets took off in China and elsewhere in Asia.

Yet those tablets didn't quite seem to be replacing PCs, or forestalling PCs' purchase. Though PC sales kept slowing, especially in Asia, they seemed to be substituted by large-screen smartphones – dubbed 'phablets' – with screens of 5in diagonally or more. Many were produced at ultra-low prices – $50 or so – and sold in the Far East. Though classed as 'Android', they weren't running Google services because they were sold in China. A substantial proportion seemed to be used purely for 'content consumption', as had been expected early on.

Apple and Microsoft, though, had bigger ideas for the tablet. Microsoft wanted it to be a branch of the PC: its Surface Pro line, with Office onboard and a 'full' version of Windows, was intended to capture business interest. The iPad, meanwhile, gained more and more apps to make it useful in business and education. Schools began buying iPads for students to use; airlines and insurance companies followed suit. (Pilots could put huge amounts of paper documentation onto a single tablet; claims adjusters could take photos of damage with the tablet and upload a claim within minutes over the mobile network.) In some ways the tablet did less than a PC; in some ways, especially by integrating the camera and mobile functions, it could do more. What was clear was that it was not going away.

Chapter Seven
China

For years in the 20th-century China was a byword in the west for cheap and unreliable items: childrens' toys that fell apart within hours of being used, toxic paints, fakes. That began to change when the Chinese government decided that it should pursue economic growth, and the rise of factories and cities began to create a middle class as the population shifted from rural to urban areas, as had happened in the 1700s in Britain and the rest of Europe and North America with the Industrial Revolution.

By the late 1990s, China was competitive in a number of areas – and the burgeoning middle class meant that there were people who would require the new computing power on offer from PCs. The idea of a PC on every desk – or in every household – in a nation of a billion people was a mouth-watering thought for Microsoft. As with every company looking for fresh growth, it eyed China as an untapped market.

Microsoft was not the first big western company to perceive potentially huge benefits there. Nor was it the first to be disappointed by the reality of dealing with another culture and legal system than that prevalent in the West. Arguably, though, the only damage it suffered was financial – unlike the other two, which suffered internal tensions and reputational damage.

Microsoft

Microsoft's first efforts in China began in 1992 – the same year that its first properly stable version of Windows, 3.1, appeared. But it stumbled for a decade until it realized that its approach in the West – high software prices, indifference to government, a tight grip on intellectual property – would not work there. 'We were a naive American company,' Bill Gates told Fortune in 2007[1] as he visited the country.

By 2004, the state of Washington in the north-east US was the second-biggest state exporter to China – through Microsoft, and neighbour Boeing, and Starbucks. China was the world's second-biggest market for PCs, behind the United States. But in terms of software revenue, it was 25th, because piracy – especially of Windows and the Office suite – was rife. Even so Gates and Ballmer kept on pushing. During a visit to Microsoft and Gates's house in April 2006, then Chinese president Hu Jintao said he was 'a friend of Microsoft' and that he dealt with 'the operating system produced by Microsoft every day'. Back home, his government had told four Chinese PC makers that they could no longer sell machines without an operating system already installed.

So-called 'naked' machines were Microsoft's worst nightmare, because they could be loaded up with anything – usually, a copy of Windows which had had its protection removed, or which had been authorized via a duplicate key or one granted to large organizations (and so capable of activating huge numbers of machines without question). Revoking a key would cause problems to the legitimate user. In 2005 Microsoft had tried offering users of bootleg versions a 50 per cent discount on a legitimate version if they could explain where they got their pirated version. It wasn't a great hit. Even by 2007, Microsoft's revenues in China were an estimated $700 million or so – about 1.5 per cent of its global sales. Windows did fine on market share: it ran on about 90 per cent of the 120 million or so PCs in China. But Microsoft didn't make any money from it; it cut its own prices to $3 for a legitimate copy of Windows and Office for students. Even so, software pirates were still able to offer new versions of Windows before it had been officially released; and the official copies were 15 times more expensive. The company tried a campaign in 2008 where owners of pirated versions of Windows XP would see a black screen every hour. Irate users switched to free software[2] such as that made by Kingsoft, which has been running since 1989 and makes Office-compatible rivals. China was at best a limited success for Microsoft's desktop business.

And what of the censorship that China's government imposed on its citizens and publications, the Fortune journalist asked Gates? The silence stretched on and on. Eventually, Gates replied: 'I don't think I want to give an answer to that.'

Google: ethical challenge

Google, meanwhile, was riven by internal tension over China. Eric Schmidt, then chief executive, suggested that it was the next big, and obvious, growth area in internet use. Logically, the company which wanted to gather and process and learn everything about peoples' use of the internet should be active in the country where people were joining it more quickly than anywhere in the world. It made everywhere else look pedestrian. Even by 2006 it had 50 million fixed broadband users, more than the UK, and 140 million internet users in all; by 2009 it had hit 384 million users and was growing at 29 per cent annually. Almost all was on the desktop. China looked like green fields waiting to be conquered.

There was a problem: China's government implemented hefty censorship on internal discussion and external connections over the net. Known as the 'Great Firewall', its systems – staffed by thousands of government apparatchiks – used a combination of automatic searches and human-powered observation to stifle free speech and debate. Its ferocity, and the risks for western companies, was already known: in 2005, Yahoo was revealed to have provided information to the Chinese authorities which helped them identify Shi Tao, a Chinese journalist who was subsequently sentenced to 10 years' imprisonment for 'divulging state secrets abroad'. His crime had been to disseminate a message the authorities had sent to his newspaper which had been marked 'top secret', about risks posed by 15th-anniversary commemorations of the

Tiananmen Square killings. When Yahoo's role in Shi Tao's arrest became known, the company was heavily and publicly criticized by US politicians.

In an authoritarian state, control of information flow is all. Search engines risk undermining that. Hence the strict rules that Google had to operate under in China. People who searched for 'forbidden' phrases (such as 'Falun Gong') would get the enigmatic message that 'the connection has been reset' – which in the West would mean that there had been a brief problem at the server. In China, it meant the Great Firewall had blocked it. The Chinese government had been blocking Google.com since 2002[3], apparently to prevent people viewing cached versions of 'subversive' pages.

If Google were to enter the Chinese market with a local version of its world-beating search engine, it would have to submit to Chinese censorship. But doing so went against the grain; in fact, it was contrary to the idealism on which the company had been set up by the duo who had met at a university in a country which enshrines freedom of speech in its First Amendment. Censorship was authoritarian, undemocratic, top-down. Google had always tried to be the opposite.

The company's top triumvirate, and chief legal counsel David Drummond, argued furiously over whether they should enter China. Asked in 2004 (in the Playboy interview which almost upended the company's flotation) about China, Brin called the topic 'difficult questions, difficult challenges'.

Brin, the child of parents who had effectively been forced out of their native Georgia by discrimination over their Jewish ancestry, was insistent that the company should not do deals with dictatorships. Drummond, who happens to be African-American, agreed. Schmidt, while less adamant, said that it was unreasonable to miss out on the opportunity; without Google, the search business in China would still grow, and local rivals would get the chance to dominate and leave Google trying to catch up. Page, in effect holding the casting vote, sided with Schmidt. Google began offering a search engine sited inside China in January 2006 at google.cn.

Already known for the 'Don't be evil' slogan, Google came under intense scrutiny over its decision. 'We felt that perhaps we could compromise our principles, but provide ultimately more information for the Chinese... and perhaps make more of a difference,' Brin suggested in a press conference afterwards.

But Irene Khan, then Amnesty International's secretary-general, was unimpressed: 'Whether succumbing to demands from Chinese officials or anticipating government concerns, companies that impose restrictions that infringe on human rights are being extremely short-sighted,' she said, adding: 'Internet companies justify their actions on the basis of Chinese regulations. In fact, such agreements and the resulting self-censorship violate both international standards and China's own constitution, which protects freedom of expression.'

Western commentators experimented with what they could find, and not find, on the google.cn website when they carried out searches. Those for the Chinese characters for 'Tiananmen Square', they discovered, turned up nothing about the events of 1989 when a student protest in favour of democracy was brutally crushed. Picture searches on the same topic outside China gave prominence to an iconic picture of a lone man standing in front of a row of tanks; inside China, the results only included happy tourists and visitors at the giant location.

But Google was only making the same compromises as every other search engine inside the country. It even tried to thumb its nose at the giant, by offering link text which would explain why searchers were getting incomplete results – and appeared to get away with it.

But it turned out the Chinese government had other ideas unconnected to the search results Google was or wasn't offering. The popularity and security of its e-mail service (in which since 2008 all connections to the e-mail server could use an encrypted, 'secure' connection) meant it was widely used by dissidents seeking to evade the watchful eye of the government.

While Google worked on its search results, a hacking project by state-sponsored Chinese hackers used a flaw in Microsoft's Internet Explorer 6 browser – already outdated at the time, but still widely used – to break into the systems of Google China. From there they infiltrated its systems and sought the master keys for the e-mail servers so they could tap the communications of targeted users.

The reset

Google discovered the hack as part of its routine security monitoring. But for a company which relies on user trust, the idea that it had been hacked with such clear intention by a host nation was intolerable. Brin later called it 'the straw that broke the camel's back'[4].

The decision on what to do was a key moment in the relationship between the triumvirate at the top of the company. Arguably, it marked the point at which Brin and Page began to trust each other's instincts just that little bit more than they did Schmidt's, whose apparently trusting approach and 'adult supervision' – foisted on the duo by venture capitalists – was proved wrong. Brin's native suspicions were proved right. China, he told the *Wall Street Journal* in March 2010, had 'made great strides against poverty and whatnot' but 'with respect to censorship, with respect to surveillance of dissidents, I see the same earmarks of totalitarianism'. He said he found that 'personally quite troubling'. Schmidt insisted that they should stay on; that the benefits outweighed the downside. But Brin's view prevailed. Exiting China might hurt its search business, but being tarnished with complicity with the Chinese government's approach would hurt Google's reputation more in the long term.

Yet nothing had actually changed about Google vis-à-vis China; the company had simply established that its host had little respect for its property or rules. The morality of censorship hadn't altered; Brin had just gained sufficient extra leverage to make the case for exiting.

On 12 January 2010, Google began routing searches from the Chinese mainland to its search engine in Hong Kong, where it didn't have to self-censor. Searchers soon found that the Connection Had Been Reset.

But the reality was that Google had not anyway made much headway in the search market. When it exited for Hong Kong, its market share stood at about 12 per cent, compared to the indigenous Baidu.com, which had 77 per cent. By 2012, it was the same: Baidu at 78.6 per cent, Google at 15.6 per cent. By November 2013, Baidu had 63.6 per cent, '360' (a local rival) 21.8 per cent, and Google just 1.7 per cent.

Biting a chunk from Apple's reputation

As a company which needed to find contract manufacturers, Apple had more direct experience of dealing with Chinese businesses than either of its big rivals. By 2000, China had become essential to any company with a manufacturing supply chain involving electronics components. It was developing fast; but quality control was also extremely uneven. The creation of the iPod in 2001 relied almost exclusively on Chinese manufacturing for its assembly; a manufacturing fault in some of the prototypes meant they had to be thrown away and entirely new ones made.

Napoleon remarked that an army marches on its stomach; that is, you have to keep the troops fed for them to succeed, and your battle plan will count for nothing if you have failed at the logistics of feeding hundreds or thousands of men day after day while on the move. Modern-day Napoleons run supply chains in manufacturing, and are handsomely rewarded when they succeed. As John Sculley (whose leadership of Apple saw it struggle to control its supply chain) remarked, 'If you look at the state of the iPod, the supply chain going all the way over to iPod city in China – it is as sophisticated as the design of the product itself. The same standards of perfection are just as challenging for the supply chain as they are for the user design. It is an entirely different way of looking at things.'

According to Fred Vogelstein, writing in his book *Dogfight*, when Steve Jobs showed off the iPhone in January 2007, Apple didn't actually have a production line to make them. Supply chain experts looked at Apple's attempts to move into this new field with interest. They knew that – contrary to Steve Ballmer's pronouncements in late 2004 – Apple could handle volume: the success of the iPod nano, where it had cornered a huge chunk of the world supply of solid-state memory, and produced millions of devices perfectly timed for the Christmas rush, demonstrated that. But phones?

Thus they looked at the combination of the expense of the iPhone, and its relatively poor specifications – a two-megapixel camera, no 3G connectivity – and perceived necessary compromises.

Kevin Jefcoate had extensive experience sourcing components for manufacture; earlier in that decade he was sourcing parts in China for a line of MP3 players for Verbatim, a storage company, and discovering how primitive some of the production systems were. Then, he found boards being hand-soldered, instead of using automated surface-mount technology to insert components more quickly and reliably. When asked why, the factory's Chinese owner just snorted: SMT was 'too expensive and too unpredictable'.

Having a cheap, low-quality camera in the first iPhone was a smart move, Jefcoate explains. 'I think they were able to go to [a supplier] who had a load of those two-megapixel cameras, which were previous generation and so mass production, low cost, and basically buy them up as a job lot,' Jefcoate says. That meant there would be no supply constraint on the cameras, which had become an essential part of any mobile phone. Apple could thus concentrate on other parts of the chain, such as the capacitative touch screen.

'People think that there are just suppliers waiting out there to make anything you want,' Jefcoate says. 'It's not like that at all. You have to bid with them, and I've seen cases where suppliers would in effect be holding companies to ransom if they wanted something new.' Had Apple tried to go for a top-end camera to compete head-on with Nokia and Sony Ericsson, it would probably have been frozen out because it would want smaller volumes than those rivals.

Creating a new device and then moving it to industrial-scale assembly also requires careful timing, Jefcoate explains. 'Once you've committed to an order, say 2,000 of something, then you won't be able to vary it at will to 1,800 or 2,200.' Or at least, not without significant financial penalties.

Hardware companies that rely on software from another separate company will always have problems if the timetable for the software's release slips: a handset maker cannot ask the factory to reserve time on their production lines in the hope that the software company will iron out the bugs at some future date. That creates a natural tension in a horizontally-split ecosystem; while the companies such as Griffin's, making add-ons for Apple, could prepare themselves for product cycles because there were so few product lines and SKUs [stock-keeping units; a biologist would call them species] to watch, a handset maker waiting for new software from a separate company was totally hamstrung if the software timetable slipped. And in an horizontally-split ecosystem, the hardware manufacturer would have no comeback against the software company. If Windows is late, it hurts Microsoft, and its hurts OEM computer manufacturers; but the OEMs have to lump it.

'You wouldn't want to make a handset or a tablet in quantity without doing final testing of the software on it,' Jefcoate says. 'It's in the nature of software to have bugs. It's got errors.'

Benedict Evans, formerly a technology and telecoms analyst for Enders Analysis in London, suggests that the first iPhone was a 'minimum viable proposition' – a product which offers the most minimal specification that a company can get away with. For Apple, and the millions who bought the phone despite its lack of 3G, picture quality and indeed call quality, minimum was enough. And it gave Apple a position it could exploit with factories in China.

Nor was it just the factories in China which were interested in the iPhone. The growing capitalist element in China, and its budding sector of millionaires, meant that some Chinese saw it as essential to own an iPhone. The fact that it wasn't compatible with the data networks on their systems wasn't important. The iPhone, and the Apple logo, had cachet.

Killer fact

On July 26 2009, a month after the launch of the iPhone 3GS, a story appeared in the *New York Times* reporting[5] that Sun Danyong, a 25-year-old employee at Foxconn Technology, had jumped to his death from the 12th floor of its factory in China. What made the story unusual was that Sun, who worked in the logistics department had two weeks earlier been the subject of an investigation into the disappearance of a prototype iPhone – almost certainly the iPhone 4, which would not be released until September 2010. Sun had been given 16 prototype phones to deliver to research and development; he didn't report one missing until three days later. The company said later that Sun had had products go missing before, though he had always got them back.

In a note, Sun claimed to have been beaten up by the factory's security team. 'I ran into some problems,' Sun texted his girlfriend in a farewell message.

Foxconn also assembled products for Sony and Hewlett-Packard, the paper noted. But it was Apple which drew the attention; after all, it had been its phone that had gone missing. It issued a statement saying it was sorry at the 'tragic loss' and adding that, 'We require that our suppliers treat all workers with dignity and respect.' It wouldn't comment further.

It had never commented before on who its suppliers were; Cook kept those highly secret (though within the industry it was well known – through 'teardowns' – just where the parts in its products came from). Partly the aim was to avoid industrial espionage, and partly to keep the media from knowing what Apple's next product was going to be. The scale of China, where city-sized factories could exist side by side, with multiple lines, helped. But the growth of the iPhone production line, and the increasing value to rivals of knowing what was being tried, raised the stakes. For the assembly companies, terrified Apple might drop them if the wall of silence was breached, a hardline approach to employees – many of them part-time during the long summer breaks, just when production would ramp up to make devices which would be unveiled for Christmas sales – was only in everyone's best interests.

The media storm around the treatment of workers at Foxconn became a hurricane, with Apple at the centre. 'Why have suicides spiked at Apple iPad supplier Foxconn in China?' asked the *Christian Science Monitor* in May 2010. It cited nine deaths and two survivors of suicide attempts since the start of that year. By then Foxconn employed 400,000 people at its plant near the 13 million-strong city of Shenzhen in south-east China. 'It's a tough place to be and you have to be tough to survive,' said Geoffrey Crothall, speaking for the Hong Kong-based *China Labour Bulletin*, which monitored working conditions. In vain did Terry Gou, the Taiwanese founder of the parent company Hon Hai Precision Industry, insist that it was 'not a blood and sweat factory'. Media coverage had it as a death factory. National news outlets began picking up the story, using phrases like 'Orwellian control'. One quoted a 19-year-old who polished iBook computers saying: 'We need discipline because Apple products are expensive and there is no margin for mistakes.'

Together with separate coverage of Apple's patent rows with Samsung, which began at the same time, a picture began to be drawn of Apple as a corporate bully: one that brutalized its workers and tried to crush rivals through the courts, not the market. Now the stories from Foxconn presented Apple with a version of the famous question to which there is no 'right' answer – 'have you stopped beating your workers?'

The coverage grew and grew, and showed no sign of abating. There was, in effect, no respite for the company. On the one hand, in the West it charged premium prices for its products. On the other, it employed labour in China which by western standards was poorly paid.

Apple was, in effect, the victim of its own exceptionalism – and the PR image it had built of a brand where all was good. The idea of workers dying to make an iPhone jarred with its smooth lines in the adverts.

Steve Jobs did respond publicly in June 2010. He said that the suicide rate at Foxconn was lower than at other Chinese factories; responding to an e-mail from an Apple user, he said: 'Although every suicide is tragic, Foxconn's suicide rate is well below the China average. We are all over this.' Queried on whether that meant Apple was simply putting the deaths behind it, Jobs responded: 'We do more than any other company on the planet', and linked to Apple's 'supplier responsibility' document. And 'over this', he explained, was 'an American expression that means this has our full attention.'[6] Tim Cook visited Foxconn soon after, recommending the company hire psychological counsellors, install nets around roofs (to prevent people leaping to their death) and open a 24-hour care centre.

The coverage subsided a little. Then in October 2011, soon after Jobs's death, an American author and actor called Mike Daisey began a tour of his one-man production called 'The Agony and Ecstasy of Steve Jobs'. Daisey's production revolved around a mesmerising tale he told of having visited China, gone to factories making Apple products, and of encountering workers who had been poisoned by n-hexane – an acetone-like product used to polish glass and plastic – and underage workers. Another older man had a hand mangled from making iPads, Daisey said. In January 2012 an episode of PBS's widely-respected show *This American Life* featured part of Daisey's recounting of his performance. It was a powerful, withering description of abuse.

As chief executive, Cook, however, showed a different touch from Steve Jobs, who was never pictured or even reported visiting the huge factories where workers laboured under artificial light for hours on end making identical products for (mainly) western consumption. Cook flew over to China for a well-publicized visit and was photographed looking happy amid slightly puzzled workers on the assembly line. In February 2012, with the coverage of worker experiences ramping up again, Cook invited the Fair Labor Association to begin an audit of Apple's 'final assembly' suppliers: 'We believe that workers everywhere have the right to a safe and fair work environment, which is why we've asked the FLA to independently assess the performance of our largest suppliers,' said Cook in a statement widely circulated to the media.

Yet it wasn't Cook's visit so much as Daisey's tale – of an awful, exploitative company – that turned out to be the element which lanced the boil around the coverage of the treatment of workers in Apple's contractors. Another journalist who lived and worked in China, Rob Schmitz, became suspicious of Daisey's claims after the playwright appeared on *This American Life*, a National Public Radio (NPR) programme with a stellar reputation for accuracy and interest.

Schmitz began investigating, and discovered that Daisey's meetings and visits could not have taken place in the times he claimed. N-hexane poisoning had happened, but in a factory a thousand miles from the one Daisey said he had visited. And Schmitz tracked down the woman who had been Daisey's interpreter; she said that the meetings with underage workers and the man with the mangled hand just hadn't happened. Nor, she said, did the Foxconn guards carry guns (another Daisey claim); nor could he have seen the crowded dorm rooms that he described on the programme.

Ira Glass, the presenter of the programme, was appalled at having been misled into thinking that the play was truth. In a press release in March 2012, he said: 'Too many of the details about the people he says he met are in dispute for us to stand by the story. I suspect that many things that Mike Daisey claims to have experienced personally did not actually happen'.

The tenor of coverage in the US media shifted from Apple to Daisey; given a person to focus on, the news agenda stopped being about Apple's suppliers, and became instead about whether what was being said was strictly true. Were the workers really underage? Had someone's injury really come from working in the plant? Journalists discovered that China's vastness, and otherness, posed challenges for reporting. Sources were hard to track down. Stories were difficult to verify. Even so, it was clear that labourers in the factories worked under sometimes terrible conditions; and that those became worse over the summer as Apple ramped up its demands for new products to cope with Christmas volumes. Yet it was far from the only company that used Chinese factories. In time Samsung and Dell were accused of using contractors that employed underage staff, or inadequate safety measures. China was going through its own version of the Industrial Revolution. But unlike the one in Britain in the 18th century, this one was attended by a media able to transmit the stories around the world.

What was really different was the attention being paid to Apple. Nick Bilton of the *New York Times* noted in April 2012[7] that Hewlett-Packard, Samsung, Microsoft, Lenovo and others also used factories in China, and that there seemed to be little complaint about those companies – despite their giving no details at all about working conditions, and assembling more PCs, and the Xbox games console (assembled at Foxconn) being a well-known brand, especially in the United States.

Bilton sent queries to the companies, asking about their policies. The replies were generally unhelpful; Samsung didn't respond. HP had a two-year-old report on its website. From a PR point of view, though, it would do Apple no good at all to complain about double standards.

Apple pledged to provide a transparency report around its suppliers, with regular audits. By the middle of 2013, the storm had blown itself out; suppliers appeared to have improved their practices. And a new middle class was slowly being created in the factories of Shenzhen, paid with money siphoned from western consumers. Soon enough they would be consumers in their own right.

Smartphones and tablets

Once Apple, Google and Microsoft began to tussle with each other over smartphones (and later tablets), China's economic situation abruptly snapped into focus.

In September 2010, Niklas Savander, then executive vice-president and general manager of markets for Nokia (who had just helped fire its then chief executive Olli-Pekka Kallasvuo), insisted that the falling average selling price for handsets wasn't because Apple and Android were skimming off the top-end profits; it was because people in emerging markets such as India and China were buying their first phone (a Nokia, of course). 'They drive the average down,' he explained.

Apple's iPhones were popular as a status symbol among rich Chinese: few could afford them, and so being able to flaunt them meant owners could ignore the fact that they were incompatible with the data systems on the biggest network, China Mobile, which used its own 3G standards. Status, though, meant that the launch of each new iPhone was attended by lines of people, significant numbers of whom would buy lots of phones, pay with cash, head to a nearby side street and hand over their haul, and rejoin the back of the queue. The phones would head to other countries, part of a 'grey market' that existed only because of the Apple brand. Such unofficial imports helped spark demand in China and elsewhere.

The definition of 'open'

In 2010, even as it retreated back across the Hong Kong straits after the unpleasant experience of being hacked, Google hadn't finished with China. Android phones had begun to appear there. China offered a gigantic, untapped market for smartphones: China Mobile, the largest of four mobile carriers there, had 523 million 2G subscribers in January 2010, and nearly four million 3G users.

As a whole, the country had 11.5 million 3G users. Compared with the 35 million in the United States, that might have seemed puny.

But China was then adding about three million 3G subscribers per month – and the number was accelerating, with headroom of hundreds of millions more. Moreover, for the vast majority of Chinese, a smartphone would be the first computer they ever owned. Compared to PCs, the devices had the attractive combination of longer battery life, lower capital cost, and vastly greater mobility: you could use them in a field or a city street.

For Google, eager to monetize the mobile web, China was a mobile continent which Android's zero price and customisability could conquer. The Chinese government could ban Google from the desktop. What about mobile, though?

The Chinese government was wary of, and wise to, that prospect too. Mobile phones offering Google services could not be sold in China without a licence from the government. As soon as Google announced its withdrawal from the Chinese mainland for its search service, China Unicom, the second-largest mobile phone operator, said it would stop installing Google search functions on new handsets. Just as important, local rivals including Baidu saw that they could compete directly in the smartphone business by customising Android. Google had put the tools for that competition into its rivals' hands: the raw code for Android – AOSP, or Android Open Source Platform – was downloadable directly from Google's servers. In October 2010, Rubin's first tweet was to give his definition of 'open': it described the lines of coding needed to download the AOSP code from Google's servers.[8]

Chinese handset makers – less interested in competing in value than volume – took the AOSP code and ran with it. In 2010, AOSP phones were a tiny fraction of the world total. But their numbers grew fast, driven by 'white box' Chinese handset makers churning out products by the million to satisfy a fast-growing market which wanted something that could access the internet but was cheaper than a computer.

The first company to feel the effects was not Apple, or Google, but the existing giant – Nokia. After peaking in the first quarter of 2011 at 27 per cent of Nokia's mobile revenue, or €1.2 billion, and taking 22 per cent of all the handsets it sold during the period, all of Nokia's key metrics in Greater China – the number of handsets sold, the average selling price, total mobile revenue – began dwindling rapidly. By the fourth quarter of 2011, even as Nokia's mobile revenues had dwindled by a third from a year before, China was only 16 per cent of mobile revenues, and taking 13 per cent of handsets. By the third quarter of 2013, with Nokia's mobile division apparently having hit bottom and showing mild signs of growth, China was just 7 per cent of revenue, and taking 6 per cent of handsets – a mere 4 million of them compared to nearly 24 million at its height.

That the fall coincided with Stephen Elop's announcement that Nokia would kill off Symbian looks coincidental. The problem was more that Nokia's Symbian phones were suddenly competing against a much more capable rival which could also be 'skinned' to do anything that was needed. The iPhone had made Nokia look like an unclothed emperor in the West; now Android was doing the same in the world's biggest single market. Symbian's share contracted from over 40 per cent of sales at the start of 2011 to 19 per cent by the end of the same year, according to Analysys International.[9]

By June 2011 there were 80 million 3G subscribers across China; a year later it was 175 million, and the majority of phones being sold were 'smartphones' by the standard definition (internet-capable, able to run third-party apps, supported by an app store). By then, China's mobile networks were adding about 10 million new users per month, of whom more 9 million were buying smartphones, often with data plans. All the Android phones – the vast majority of those being sold – used AOSP, but none would count as 'activations' under Google's definition because they did not sign into Google's services. They still counted as 'Android' for the purposes of research company measurement, though. The handsets were cheap, but capable.

In Google's absence, a frenzied market for apps opened up. Dozens of competing app stores began offering Android app downloads. In some cases that meant malware; China became the principal source (and, in general, sink) for Android-based malware of all complexions – often surreptitiously sending premium text messages. But more generally, China became the market for fierce competition in the mobile web services market that the West could not be – because Google had won a monopoly in search, and annexed that with Android handsets tied to Google Play. In China, with no Google, and no monopoly player in app stores, a sort of Cambrian explosion of app stores occurred.

China's handset market was vibrant. Cheap smartphones – priced at up to $165 – made up half of all sales, according to data collected by Ben Bajarin, an analyst at Creative Strategies in the United States. Add in those selling at prices up to $250, and you had three-quarters of the market. (For those which cost over $500, they chose premium foreign brands – such as Apple and Samsung.) Chinese consumers also bought new phones much more often, for whatever reason: Bajarin's report noted a survey by Umeng, which found that 90 per cent of owners had bought a new handset in the previous 14 months – compared to two years or more in the West. A key driver was local vendors, who competed heavily to bring out new devices – often tied to local promotions, apps or large retailers.

Apple, meanwhile, saw China grow as a destination for its phones. The iPhone was formally launched on a single carrier – China Unicom – in October 2009 – but not on the largest, China Mobile. The carrier used its own TD-SCDMA standard for 3G, which required a different set of chips for data reception. To work on China Mobile, Apple would either have to make a completely different variant of the iPhone specifically for that carrier, or include extra chips in the standard version that would only ever be useful for those who roamed to China. Given the choice of adding expense to the basic phone, or to its production line, it chose to do neither. Nor could the two decide on a revenue split for phone and app sales – another key factor.

It didn't matter. By mid-2012 there were 15 million iPhone users on China Mobile's network, stuck on 2G services offering about 56 kilobit per second links. By September 2013 the number was estimated at 42 million. It was more important to be seen with an iPhone than to get 3G data on it.

Don't Dalai

For Apple, selling its phones in China posed the same problems of censorship that both Microsoft and Google had faced in turn. In its case, though, the problems arose through the App Store. Even though many Chinese consumers could not access the store directly, the Chinese version of the App Store still fell under Chinese government censorship. In December 2009 it became clear that inside China, you couldn't download apps from the App Store which related to the Dalai Lama, the exiled spiritual leader of Buddhist Tibet – and a figure banned by the Chinese authorities, which would sever diplomatic relations with countries which associated too closely with him. Google had already been obliged to block searches on the same topic; the hacking of its systems nearly a year later targeted e-mail accounts belonging to close associates of the Dalai Lama.

Trudy Miller, an Apple spokesperson, was quoted saying that: 'We continue to comply with local laws. Not all apps are available in every country.' For Apple, this was a fulsome comment: it as much as implied that the apps had been yanked at the government's orders. Compared to the company's usually brief responses, it said as much as Gates's silence to the Forbes reporter, or Sergey Brin's later repudiation of China and its 'earmarks of totalitarianism'.

Apple, though, had a faint advantage over Google and Microsoft in its desire to make money from China. It did not rely on software that could be pirated; nor did it rely on a web service that could be censored. Instead, it sold a device which was essentially a closed box. And while counterfeit iPhones (and lookalikes which on closer examination would turn out to be running Android) abounded, the cachet associated with having the real thing guaranteed those silent queuers in the West on iPhone launch days, and big queues outside Apple's stores in China. The stories that emerged were incredible: in 2012 the story emerged of a 22-year-old boy from Hunan province who sold one of his kidneys for $500 to buy his girlfriend an iPhone 4S – then the new model.

What made the iPhone attractive? It was expensive – which meant having one implied you were rich. And in a status-obsessed society like China, who wouldn't want to appear rich? And with China's male population outnumbering females (because of the one child per family rule, and families' preference for boys over girls leading to statistically significant levels of abortion), looking rich could help you hook a mate.

For Apple, it was all upside. From being just 8 per cent of its overall revenue in the Christmas quarter of 2011, China jumped in 2012 to between 12 per cent and 19 per cent of its total revenues – almost the reverse of Nokia's experience. It didn't break out country-by-country sales of iPhones or iPads, but in China they clearly numbered in the millions. Google and Microsoft had tried to break China and been rebuffed and attacked. Apple was just making its way.

Even so, the future for Apple is less than clear. The number of companies large and small pushing out handsets in China is astonishing. One in particular, Xiaomi, clearly has greater ambitions than simply serving the Chinese market. Lenovo, Huawei and ZTE had already pushed out of China to begin marketing in the broader world. Pieter Knook, Microsoft's former head of mobile, looked to a future where the competition that had already hurt Apple in the West would intensify.

'I wonder whether you'll see quite the same dynamic as you have on the PC, when a good enough PC is priced at half the level of a Macintosh, therefore Apple has 6 per cent market share, 7 per cent market share, whatever the number is,' Knook says. 'Clearly [Apple] has much higher market share on the phones today, but I'm not optimistic that they can maintain that if Google's onslaught – particularly with the Chinese focus – continues.'

He thinks that the Chinese handset makers could first pose a threat, though, to established companies which cannot lean on a world-famous brand. 'I think there's a scenario where you could quite easily argue that five years from now there won't be anybody like a Samsung or a Motorola left in that [Android] ecosystem, because they won't be able to compete with the gross profit margins that Huawei and ZTE are prepared to put up with,' Knook says. 'And if it's not Huawei or ZTE, it'll be the next Chinese company that has subsidized rent from the local Chinese province, that has a labour force that's paid in yuan in Chengdu, puts their parts together in a factory somewhere in a dirt cheap place and ships them across China – through beautiful infrastructure – and then across on a container, and they come in for $150.'

The world's largest market might turn out to be the one which also generates the greatest threat for the established businesses. But smartphones could change the climate of censorship. Speaking in January 2014, Schmidt said that connectedness would eventually overwhelm Chinese government censorship: 'You can't heavily censor that many people all the time. They don't understand the power of empowering a hundred million Chinese, no matter how brutal they're going to be with the bloggers.'

China, then, may be the future of huge change everywhere – enabled by smartphones.

Chapter Eight
2011

On 9 August 2011, Apple's market capitalization briefly rose to $341.5 billion, edging it just ahead of Exxon, until that morning the highest-valued company in the world. The company Steve Jobs had co-created putting together computers, the one that Michael Dell had suggested shutting down 14 years earlier because it had no future, was now worth more than any other. The stock fell back by the end of the day, but it had made its mark; the transformation of Apple from financial basket case to ruler was complete. At the end of the day it was worth $346.7 billion; Microsoft was worth $214.3 billion and Google $185.1 billion.

Compared to the end of 1998 (Apple $5.54 billion, Microsoft $344.6 billion, Google $10 million), the aggregate wealth of the companies had more than doubled. Microsoft, though, had shrunk by 40 per cent, after being outdistanced first in search, then in digital music and then in smartphones – in the latter category by both companies.

The companies had changed enormously. Google was soon to celebrate its 13th birthday, having roared from a three-person garage start-up to web giant; it was struggling too with having nearly 29,000 staff worldwide. Larry Page, once more the chief executive, was forcing the divisions to justify themselves, getting divisional heads to explain their projects in soundbite-length memos. His greatest concern was that Google was getting too big and slow to act: 'Large companies are their own worst enemy', he said in September. 'There are basically no companies that have good slow decisions. There are only companies that have good fast decisions.'[1]

Where Apple hadn't heard of Google 13 years before, now it had gone from having a common cause against Microsoft to being just a business acquaintance, and frequent opponent; Apple and Microsoft bid together against Google for patents covering the mobile business. Apple was seeking to disintermediate Google from search with the cloud-based voice search of its upcoming iPhone. And they were constantly niggling each other in smartphones and tablets. Even so, by September 2011 the majority of mobile search still came from iPhones, according to Google testimony at the US Senate.

Apple had changed. From just under 10,000 full- and part-time staff in September 1998,[2] it had grown to being 50,000-strong, though around 30,000 were in its retail store chain; the core of the company in Cupertino remained small and relatively tight-knit. The old enmity with Microsoft still flickered occasionally, but strategically they almost ignored each other. Apple's position in PCs was set at 5 per cent of the market. It had won in music. It didn't do search. Its position in phones and tablets had pushed Microsoft to playing catch-up; yet the Redmond company could rely on the sheer heft of 1.5 billion PC installations to ensure a stream of replacements and of new sales for Office. Apple's value, revenues and profits had all passed those of its old rival. Its reputation had been transformed from put-upon also-ran PC maker to world-spanning design brand. Cook's influence was visible in its inventory, whose value was equivalent to three days' hardware sales.

Microsoft, by contrast, had gone from world-beater to catch-up. The staff at Microsoft (90,000 worldwide, compared to 27,000 in summer 1998)[3] were a little battle-weary too. As Steve Ballmer, still the chief executive, spoke at the September 2011 all-hands company meeting in front of 20,000 employees, some simply got up and left, unhappy at the 'cloud computing' strategy, the stock's lack of movement, and the lack of excitement at their employer. The version of Windows that would truly work on tablets was still a year away. Microsoft seemed mired in its fabulously profitable past – not a leader or innovator in search or on mobiles or tablets or *anything*. People began whispering that Sinofsky, who had conquered internal politics and got the Windows team to grapple successfully with the future of tablets and chip architectures, might be chief executive material.

So it was Jobs who should have felt triumphant. Apple ruled. Companies and consultants had begun to try to distil and reproduce 'the Apple secret', the one that had forced Microsoft to alter direction not once but three times: over music players, then phone design and then tablet interface design. Like Archimedes understanding the physics of levers and commenting that, given a place to stand on, he could move the Earth, Apple had moved the computer industry – and industries beyond it. The music business, the phone manufacturing business, the mobile carrier business, the computer tablet business: all had been transformed. The idea that the horizontal model was the 'best' was no longer taken as read. The idea that you might want to build a company that would design the hardware and write the software too wasn't nonsense. When Google had bought Motorola Mobility in August, many thought the purpose was to mimic Apple, and create its own vertically integrated smartphone and tablet business. Amazon, the internet retailer that is a geographical companion to Microsoft, had followed Apple into the vertical model by designing its own Kindle e-reader, and then following that with its own tablet (based, ironically, on its own version of Android uncertified by Google) late in September 2011. In tablets, Amazon already looked the likely most successful rival to Apple.

But the success was bittersweet. Jobs was dying. He had been on medical leave since January, when his letter to Apple staff, released to the media, said that he would 'focus on my health' – and added that 'I love Apple so much and hope to be back as soon as I can.' Even that showed his meticulous attention to detail and the ability to rouse emotion: the use of 'love' sounds like a boyfriend being sundered from his first crush.

Though he had popped up a few times through the year in public – launching the iPad 2, introducing the next version of iOS, finally in June lobbying Cupertino town council over Apple's proposed new headquarters – paparazzi photos in August had suggested he was losing muscle mass rapidly to cancer. Yet he would not be hurried; once again he managed the moment perfectly, releasing a statement to the board later that month saying that 'I have always said if there ever came a day when I could no longer meet my duties and expectations as Apple's CEO, I would be the first to let you know. Unfortunately, that day has come.' He 'strongly recommended' that the board 'execute our succession plan and name Tim Cook as CEO of Apple'. That Apple had a succession plan came as a surprise to analysts and shareholders who had repeatedly asked the company to specify what, if any, plans there were if Jobs were to fall under a bus, and been rebuffed. He asked to be made chairman (a role largely seen inside Apple as a sinecure). The board acquiesced to all his demands.

'I believe Apple's brightest and most innovative days are ahead of it,' Jobs wrote. 'And I look forward to watching and contributing to its success in a new role. I have made some of the best friends of my life at Apple, and I thank you all for the many years of being able to work alongside you.'

No self-pity; no self-regard; no self-congratulation. Once more Jobs offered a glimpse of the focus that fuelled his success.

The tributes poured in, from people who had known him a little or a lot. Many of course thought it must be the immediate precursor to his death. It wasn't. But there was a sense that the world of technology, and of business, would not see his like again. The questions began: would Apple be able to spot the ideas with real potential and turn them into hits as it had? Would the gestalt of Cook, Schiller, Forstall and Ive add up to the ubermensch of Jobs?

Paul Griffin, whose accessory business thrived as he rode the slipstream of the company's success, told me he thought the outcome was, in time, assured:

> If you look at the bigger picture, I think that Jobs has had it right all along. Controlling both the hardware and the software has turned out to be the better model than someone who just

did the software and let everyone build hardware. If you do that, you end up with a lot of products that just don't all work together very well... I think Apple has done themselves a service by controlling both.

He pauses. 'Certainly has worked out well for them,' he said with a smile.

Jobs was a one-off; yet so much of what he did could be copied – if you had the will and the nerve to copy it. Barely anyone did. Receiving and answering customer e-mails directly (to know what the customer is thinking). Cutting out intermediaries. Focusing on the eventual user as the most important element in the chain. Throwing away preconceptions in order to embrace the new. Being unafraid to kill existing products to replace them with better ones before your rivals do. Stripping out what is unnecessary, and improving what is left to the best possible. Even before Jobs left, Apple had an enormous internal project, called the Apple University, to educate its staff in how the most effective traits of the company could be promulgated, refined and reproduced. Even without Jobs, his spirit would still live on inside the company.

As John Gruber put it, as he pondered the Apple co-founder's goodbye, 'Jobs's greatest creation isn't any Apple product. It is Apple itself.'

On 5 October, Jobs's death was announced. Bill Gates was among the first to offer his condolences, and praise his long-time friend's legacy: 'The world rarely sees someone who has had the profound impact Steve has had, the effects of which will be felt for many generations to come. For those of us lucky enough to get to work with him, it's been an insanely great honour. I will miss Steve immensely.' At Google, Page agreed: 'He always seemed to be able to say in very few words what you actually should have been thinking before you thought it. His focus on the user experience above all else has always been an inspiration to me.' Brin, too, felt the loss keenly: 'From the earliest days of Google, whenever Larry and I sought inspiration for vision and leadership, we needed to look no farther than Cupertino.'

It was the visionary element that now looks so hard to reproduce. Once, after the introduction of yet another set of iPods, I asked Jobs whether he had been able to foresee how the market would develop – from iTunes to the iPod to the Music Store. Most people couldn't get that sort of visibility over the technology horizon. Had it really been clear how they would follow from one another?

Schiller, beside him, gave a quick grin. Jobs gazed at me through his round glasses, his expression a mixture of patience and amusement. He smiled a little.

'Of course,' he said, and then lifted his hands slightly, with the palms upturned. 'Of course we did.'

Steve Jobs always knew he could win. He just needed to find the right battlefield.

Epilogue
The age of uncertainty

Steve Jobs was dead; that much was certain. But at the start of 2014, over two years after he had died, the certainties of the technology business seemed to be in upheaval.

In 1998, when Google became a company, the three companies – Microsoft, Apple and Google – had appeared to be on utterly different trajectories. Microsoft licensed software, but didn't make hardware (apart from some dabbling with the Xbox games console), and didn't offer services. Apple made computers and wrote the software to power them. It barely had an internet presence, and didn't offer web services, though it had had an online store since 1997. Google was entirely online; but all it did was offer a search service where it aimed to direct visitors away from its site as rapidly as possible.

Fifteen years later, Microsoft was a hardware maker – offering its own Surface line of tablets – and had announced that it would buy the mobile handset business from Nokia, in a deal to close early in 2014. It had desktop and mobile app stores. It offered free webmail and a public search engine, and web services through its Azure cloud system which would let individuals or businesses set up virtual machines online. And of course it still offered its Windows desktop software and Windows Phone mobile software, which it was happy to license. It also offered users a map service, Bing Maps.

Apple, meanwhile, offered desktop computers, tablet computers, and smartphones, and wrote the software for all of them. It offered web services through all of those, such as its iCloud document synchronization service, and free email. It had a gigantic app store for mobile and desktop. It had a mapping service. It had a productivity software suite for creating spreadsheets, presentations and documents – like Microsoft's Office.

And Google still had its search engine, but also offered software for tablets and smartphones (which it was happy to license, for free), as well as a desktop OS (ChromeOS, for its 'Chromebook' line). It had a world-beating mapping service. It offered web services where individuals and businesses could set up virtual machines. It owned an office productivity suite, QuickOffice, compatible with Microsoft's Office. It had a globe-spanning app store for desktop and mobile. It also owned a mobile handset company, Motorola, which turned out new products. Even as it planned to sell that, it bought Nest, a maker of home monitoring systems.

The more one looked at the companies, the more they seemed the same; all that differed was the principal source of their revenues and profits. Microsoft still made its from licensing software (and, increasingly, patents, where the tithes from Android device makers were heading towards $2 billion per year). Apple generated almost all of its revenues from hardware. Google made its money through advertising, largely linked to its search engine. In that sense, none had really changed in 15 years.

There were other similarities: only Google retained the same chief executive. Jobs had been replaced by Tim Cook. Ballmer was on his way out, the victim of a board-level putsch led by activist shareholders unhappy that Microsoft's stock value had barely risen for a decade. His replacement, Satya Nadella, 46, had a background in enterprise and cloud services – and 22 years at the company.

The certainties of the past – that the horizontal model must always succeed – were less clear. Android had so far won the battle to be the most-used smartphone platform; though with global use of smartphones estimated at just 20 per cent by the end of 2013 (because there are so many in the developing world which had not yet been catered for) the possibility remained that another 'open' OS – such as FirefoxOS, from the Mozilla foundation – could rise up and serve the next few billion buyers.

What did look clear was that the three companies which had tangled so viciously in the past would now continue to do so. What is less clear is which of the many fronts on which their battles are being fought will be essential. Are web services such as document sharing the key measure? Is it the size of an app store that matters, or the customizability of the platform on which it will be used? Or is it the sheer amount of marketing money that can be put behind each ecosystem by its partners?

To the average user, the answer doesn't matter. What does matter, though, is how large the toll that any eventual winner will exact for access.

With Apple, the toll is principally paid upfront in the cost of the device – but that is essentially the end of it. As Apple said in a November 2013 statement about government data requests, 'our business does not depend on collecting personal data. We have no interest in amassing personal information about our customers.' It looked very like a dig at Google – whose business is very much built on amassing data about people, to the extent of setting up a 'social network', Google+, with the unstated aim of tying peoples' broader web activity to a single identity.

With Google, the toll is paid in lack of anonymity, and being 'known' – so that adverts on a particular topic seem to follow you around the web, the search results you see are nudged in favour of your previous interests, and you are offered information before you might expect to see it. (Some people don't see this as a cost at all.)

With Microsoft, the costs of the software licensing are absorbed into the cost of devices and services, and barely visible upfront. Its essence is scale: as long as enough people buy the software, its incremental cost to the company falls essentially to zero, and huge profits result.

The keepers of the toll bridges onto the internet all take their payments in different ways. But they all take them; in that way they are identical.

Notes

Chapter One   1998

[1] Ken Auletta (2009) *Googled: The end of the world as we know it*, Virgin Books, London.

[2] http://gladwell.com/outliers

[3] http://www.wired.com/wired/archive/4.02/jobs_pr.html

[4] http://www.cultofmac.com/john-sculley-on-steve-jobs-the-full-interview-transcript/63295

[5] Alan Deutschman (2000) *The Second Coming of Steve Jobs*, Broadway Books, New York.

[6] http://onstartups.com/tabid/3339/bid/58082/16-Brilliant-Insights-From-Steve-Jobs-Keynote-Circa-1997.aspx

[7] http://www.zdnet.com/news/jobs-apple-still-on-right-track/99946

[8] http://news.cnet.com/Dell-Apple-should-close-shop/2100-1001_3-203937.html

[9] http://money.cnn.com/2008/11/09/technology/cook_apple.fortune/index.htm

[10] http://www.industryweek.com/articles/whats_really_driving_apples_recovery_325.aspx

[11] http://www.cringely.com/2010/04/masters-tournament

[12] http://www.wired.com/wired/archive/4.02/jobs_pr.html

[13] http://blog.tomevslin.com/2005/02/att_lessons_fro.html

[14] http://frozennorth.org/C509291565/E668712860/index.html

[15] http://ilpubs.stanford.edu:8090/422/

Chapter Two   Microsoft antitrust

[1] Private e-mail.

[2] Private e-mail.

Chapter Three
Search: Google versus Microsoft

1 http://news.cnet.com/2100-1023-204390.html

2 http://searchenginewatch.com/2165701

3 http://www.cs.cornell.edu/home/kleinber/auth.pdf

4 Douglas Edwards (2011) *I'm Feeling Lucky: The confessions of Google employee number 59*, Allen Lane, London.

5 https://web.archive.org/web/19990821060408/http://www.salon.com/21st/rose/1998/12/21straight.html

6 Edwards, *I'm Feeling Lucky.*

7 Private e-mail.

8 Edwards, *I'm Feeling Lucky.*

9 http://stopdesign.com/archive/2009/03/20/goodbye-google.html

10 http://news.cnet.com/AltaVista-In-search-of-a-turning-point/2100-1023_3-270869.html

11 John Battelle (2005) *The Search: How Google and its rivals rewrote the rules of business and transformed our culture*, Nicholas Brealey, London.

12 http://www.microsoft.com/presspass/features/2000/jul00/07-17belluzzo.mspx

13 http://www.businessinsider.com/in-2000-business-week-wondered-how-google-will-ever-make-money-2009-3

14 Amy K Gilligan (2001) Googling is the newest date thing, *Telegraph Herald*, Dubuque, Iowa, 14 January.

15 http://www.nytimes.com/2001/08/29/opinion/liberties-the-manolo-moochers.html

16 http://en.wikipedia.org/wiki/Stac_Electronics#Microsoft_lawsuit

17 Ken Auletta (2009) *Googled: The end of the world as we know it*, Virgin Books, London.

18 http://www.wired.com/epicenter/2007/04/my_other_interv/

19 http://www.wired.com/epicenter/2007/04/my_other_interv/

20 Private e-mail.

21 Private conversation with Joel Spolsky.

22 Battelle, *The Search.*

[23] Private e-mail.

[24] http://blogs.ft.com/fttechhub/2011/03/where-microsoft-went-wrong-by-paul-allen/

[25] https://research.google.com/archive/bigtable.html

[26] http://techcrunch.com/2010/08/29/bubble-blinders-the-untold-story-of-the-search-business-model/

[27] Private conversation with Gayle Laakmann.

[28] http://www.wired.com/epicenter/2007/04/my_other_interv/

[29] http://www.microsoft.com/presspass/press/2004/nov04/11-11searchbetalaunchpr.mspx

[30] http://www.businessweek.com/technology/content/nov2004/tc20041112_7986_tc119.htm

[31] http://money.cnn.com/magazines/fortune/fortune_archive/2005/05/02/8258478/index.htm

[32] Private conversation with Pieter Knook.

[33] http://www.zdnet.com/blog/web2explorer/leaked-documents-from-bill-gates-and-ray-ozzie/52

[34] http://www.nytimes.com/2006/12/09/technology/09msn.html

[35] http://www.nytimes.com/2009/03/01/business/01marissa.html?pagewanted=all

[36] http://www.strategy-business.com/article/06202?gko=c650b&tid=27782251&pg=all

[37] https://research.google.com/archive/bigtable-osdi06.pdf

[38] http://www.bing.com/community/blogs/search/archive/2010/06/04/a-farewell-to-bing-cashback.aspx

[39] http://ftc.gov/opa/2013/01/google.shtm

[40] http://googleblog.blogspot.com/2011/03/update-on-buzz.html

[41] https://web.archive.org/web/20110917222446/http://www.livemint.com/articles/2009/01/19210503/Microsoft-bid-to-beat-Google-b.html?atype=tp

[42] http://www.businessinsider.com/microsoft-bing-losing-billions-2011-4

[43] http://www.businessinsider.com/henry-blodget-bing-revisited-still-toast-but-slightly-less-burnt-2010-3

[44] http://press.nokia.com/2011/04/21/nokia-and-microsoft-sign-definitive-agreement-ahead-of-schedule/

45 http://money.cnn.com/magazines/fortune/fortune_archive/
2005/05/02/8258478/index.htm

46 http://www.nytimes.com/2006/12/09/technology/09msn.html

Chapter Four
Digital music: Apple versus Microsoft

1 http://www.theregister.co.uk/2000/12/06/apple_to_fall_into/

2 Walter Isaacson (2011) *Steve Jobs*, Little, Brown, London.

3 Private conversation with Gayle Laakmann.

4 http://www.wired.com/gadgets/mac/commentary/cultofmac/2006/
10/71956?currentPage=all

5 http://www.youtube.com/watch?v=kN0SVBCJqLs

6 http://slashdot.org/story/01/10/23/1816257/Apple-releases-iPod

7 http://news.cnet.com/Apples-iPod-spurs-mixed-
reactions/2100-1040_3-274821.html

8 Private conversation with Paul Griffin.

9 http://www.apple.com/pr/library/2002/jan/16results.html

10 Private conversation with Bob Ohlweiler.

11 http://www.wired.com/wired/archive/4.02/jobs_pr.html

12 http://www.macobserver.com/tmo/article/A_Few_Of_Her_Favorite_
Things_Oprah_Gives_iPods_To_Everyone_In_Audience/

13 Private conversation with Don Norman.

14 http://www.thesun.co.uk/sol/homepage/showbiz/bizarre/165843/
iCant-believe-Geri-hasntBRgot-an-iPod.html

15 http://money.cnn.com/magazines/fortune/fortune_archive/
2003/05/12/342289/index.htm

16 http://www.microsoft.com/presspass/features/2003/oct03/
10-15MusicServices.mspx

17 http://www.guardian.co.uk/uk/2003/dec/14/gadgets.christmas

18 http://www.youtube.com/watch?v=3dxwopXL3fs

19 http://www.businessweek.com/magazine/content/04_05/b3868001_
mz001.htm

20 http://www.psfk.com/2004/06/iPod_Launches_i.html

21 http://www.guardian.co.uk/technology/blog/2004/oct/04/whatsteveball

22 Private e-mail.

23 http://www.ifoapplestore.com/stores/risd_johnson.html

24 http://www.nytimes.com/2004/09/02/technology/circuits/02vide.html

25 http://www.businessweek.com/stories/2004-11-14/
the-music-mess-advantage-microsoft

26 http://www.zunethoughts.com/news/show/224/here-s-why-the-
zune-isn-t-playsforsure.html

27 http://news.teamxbox.com/xbox/7427/CES-2005-Bill-Gates-
Keynote-Summary/

28 http://www.nytimes.com/2006/02/03/technology/03ipod.html

29 http://web.archive.org/web/20051102043509/http://weblogs.
jupiterresearch.com/analysts/gartenberg/archives/010172.html

30 http://arstechnica.com/apple/reviews/2005/09/nano.ars/3

31 http://news.bbc.co.uk/1/hi/technology/4286294.stm

32 http://www.washingtonpost.com/wp-dyn/content/article/2005/09/27/
AR2005092701701.html

33 http://tech.slashdot.org/story/06/08/25/203226/
Microsoft-leaks-Zune-Details-in-FCC-filing

34 http://www.youtube.com/watch?v=SGqK6kP-AzM

35 http://www.engadget.com/2006/11/29/
Zune-takes-2-spot-in-retail-launch-week/

36 http://www.cultofmac.com/john-sculley-on-steve-jobs-the-full-interview-
transcript/63295

37 http://macdailynews.com/2007/01/17/
microsoft_ceo_ballmer_laughs_at_apple_iphone/

38 Private conversation with Paul Griffin.

39 http://seekingalpha.com/article/150291-apple-f3q09-qtr-end-6-27-09-
earnings-call-transcript

40 Private e-mail.

Chapter Five   Smartphones

1 Private conversation with Pieter Knook.

2 http://media.corporate-ir.net/media_files/irol/10/107224/reports/
Q4_2006_earnings_release.pdf

3   http://news.cnet.com/Palms-tale-of-Treo-intrigue/2100-1047_
3-5883320.html

4   http://news.cnet.com/Palm-does-Windows/2100-1041_3-5882674.html

5   http://www.computerweekly.com/Articles/2006/02/21/214278/
Microsoft39s-improved-Windows-Mobile-5.0-will-boost-applications-
choice-for.htm

6   http://www.gartner.com/press_releases/asset_132473_11.html

7   http://www.wired.com/wired/archive/13.11/phone_pr.html

8   http://www.niallkennedy.com/blog/2004/06/walt-mossberg-i.html

9   http://www.infoworld.com/%5Bprimary-term-alias-prefix%5D/
%5Bprimary-term%5D/zander-recalls-tearful-first-days-motorola-460

10   http://www.wired.com/gadgets/wireless/magazine/16-02/
ff_iphone?currentPage=all

11   http://web.archive.org/web/20061229171906/
http://www.mercurynews.com/mld/mercurynews/news/
columnists/16057579.htm

12   Private conversation with Horace Dediu.

13   http://www.businessweek.com/magazine/scott-forstall-the-
sorcerers-apprentice-at-apple-10122011.html

14   http://www.wired.com/gadgets/wireless/magazine/16-02/
ff_iphone?currentPage=all

15   http://web.archive.org/web/20080807123457/http://www.
martybarret.com/2007/01/ces-2007.html

16   http://www.european-rhetoric.com/analyses/ikeynote-analysis-
iphone/transcript-2007/

17   http://www.engadget.com/2007/01/09/live-from-macworld-2007-
steve-jobs-keynote/

18   Private conversation with Matt Drance.

19   http://www.theaustralian.com.au/australian-it/exec-tech/is-this-the-
future-of-mobiles/story-e6frgazf-1111113870501

20   http://library.corporate-ir.net/library/10/107/107224/items/228168/
Q406.pdf

21   http://communities-dominate.blogs.com/brands/2007/06/
crunching-numbe.html

22   http://www.asymco.com/2009/07/07/assessing-nokias-competitive-
response/

23 http://www.bloomberg.com/apps/news?pid=newsarchive&sid=aRelVKWbMAv0

24 Private conversation with Don Norman.

25 http://abcnews.go.com/Technology/PCWorld/story?id=3334228

26 http://www.theaustralian.com.au/australian-it/exec-tech/is-this-the-future-of-mobiles/story-e6frgazf-1111113870501

27 http://itmanagement.earthweb.com/article.php/3685616

28 http://www.nytimes.com/2007/09/07/technology/07apple.html

29 http://www.apple.com/hotnews/openiphoneletter/

30 http://www.nytimes.com/2007/07/30/technology/30gates.html?pagewanted=2&_r=1&ref=business

31 http://macdailynews.com/2007/01/11/newsweeks_levy_interviews_apple_ceo_steve_jobs_about_iphone/

32 Private conversation with Matt Drance.

33 http://www.youtube.com/watch?v=vKKISOnOCaw, from 0:50.

34 http://daringfireball.net/2007/06/wwdc_2007_keynote

35 http://daringfireball.net/misc/2007/10/third-party-apps-on-iphone.text

36 http://radar.oreilly.com/2007/11/what-does-googles-open-handset.html

37 http://news.cnet.com/Googles-Android-has-long-road-ahead/2100-1038_3-6217131.html

38 http://www.pcworld.com/businesscenter/article/139421/google_android_just_a_press_release_says_ballmer.html

39 Private conversation with Mary Jo Foley.

40 http://www.microsoft.com/presspass/exec/rbach/MWC08.mspx

41 http://daringfireball.net/2008/03/one_app_at_a_time

42 http://daringfireball.net/2008/02/flash_iphone_calculus

43 http://mattgemmell.com/2011/07/22/apps-vs-the-web/

44 http://www.mikechambers.com/blog/2011/11/11/clarifications-on-flash-player-for-mobile-browsers-the-flash-platform-and-the-future-of-flash/

45 http://www.asymco.com/2011/06/02/does-the-phone-market-forgive-failure/

46 http://online.wsj.com/article/SB10001424052748703561604576150502994792270.html

47 Walter Isaacson (2011) *Steve Jobs*, Little, Brown, London.

48 http://techcrunch.com/2011/09/28/microsoft-samsung-extortion-google/

49 http://www.sec.gov/Archives/edgar/data/1495569/
000119312511246952/d224940dprem14a.htm#tx224940_40

50 http://www.engadget.com/2011/08/09/motorola-ceo-sanjay-
jha-talks-ice-cream-sandwich-future-tablets/

51 Nomura daily technology analyst briefing, 16 August 2011.

52 http://blogs.forbes.com/greatspeculations/2011/07/11/android-
could-be-a-billion-dollar-business-for-microsoft/

53 http://on.wsj.com/fLXPIR

54 Private conversation with Paul Griffin.

55 http://www.tanzaniagateway.org/docs/
LivelihoodChangesEnabledbyMobilePhones.pdf

Chapter Six   Tablets

1 http://www.nytimes.com/1999/08/30/business/microsoft-brings-in-
top-talent-to-pursue-old-goal-the-tablet.
html?pagewanted=all&src=pm

2 http://www.businessweek.com/archives/2000/b3675033.arc.htm

3 http://www.nytimes.com/2010/02/04/opinion/04brass.
html?_r=1&pagewanted=print

4 Walter Isaacson (2011) *Steve Jobs*, Little, Brown, London.

5 http://daringfireball.net/2010/01/the_original_tablet

6 http://www.fool.com/investing/general/2010/03/11/hp-and-friends-
will-kill-the-ipad.aspx

7 http://news.cnet.com/8301-10805_3-20128045-75/how-windows-
8-kod-the-innovative-courier-tablet/

8 http://msftkitchen.com/2010/06/windows-8-plans-leaked-numerous-
details-revealed.html

9 http://blogs.msdn.com/b/techtalk/archive/2005/08/18/453492.aspx

10 http://allthingsd.com/20110602/adobe-ceo-android-will-overtake-ipad-
just-like-it-did-the-iphone-video/

11 http://www.businessinsider.com/why-windows-8-is-not-
fundamentally-flawed-as-a-response-to-the-ipad-2011-6

12 http://www.youtube.com/watch?v=il47b3a9cEI

13 http://blogs.wsj.com/tech-europe/2010/11/19/intel-microprocessor-
business-doomed-claims-arm-co-founder/

[14] http://www.engadget.com/2011/03/02/live-from-apples-ipad-2-event/, at 11.12 am.

[15] http://blogs.msdn.com/b/b8/archive/2011/09/14/metro-style-browsing-and-plug-in-free-html5.aspx

[16] http://www.gartner.com/it/page.jsp?id=1800514

Chapter Seven   China

[1] http://money.cnn.com/magazines/fortune/fortune_archive/2007/07/23/100134488/

[2] http://www.nytimes.com/2009/10/19/business/global/19iht-windows.html

[3] http://searchenginewatch.com/article/2064256/Chinas-Great-Wall-Against-Google-And-AltaVista

[4] http://online.wsj.com/article/SB10001424052748704266504575141064259998090.html

[5] http://www.nytimes.com/2009/07/27/technology/companies/27apple.html?_r=0

[6] http://appadvice.com/appnn/2010/06/steves-email-foxconn-suicides

[7] http://bits.blogs.nytimes.com/2012/04/08/disruptions-on-worker-conditions-apples-rivals-are-silent/?_r=0

[8] https://twitter.com/Arubin/status/27808662429

[9] http://english.analysys.com.cn/article.php?aid=127990

Chapter Eight   2011

[1] http://searchengineland.com/larry-page-biggest-threat-to-google-google-94588

[2] http://investor.apple.com/secfiling.cfm?filingID=1047469-98-44981&CIK=320193

[3] http://www.sec.gov/Archives/edgar/data/789019/000132210-98-001067.txt

References and further reading

Auletta, Ken (2009) *Googled: The end of the world as we know it*, Virgin Books, London

Battelle, John (2005) *The Search: How Google and its rivals rewrote the rules of business and transformed our culture*, Nicholas Brealey, London

Deutschman, Alan (2000) *The Second Coming of Steve Jobs*, Broadway Books, New York

Edwards, Douglas (2011) *I'm Feeling Lucky: The confessions of Google employee number 59*, Allen Lane, London

Elliot, Jay (2011) *The Steve Jobs Way: iLeadership for a new generation*, Vanguard Press, New York

Foley, Mary Jo (2008) *Microsoft 2.0: How Microsoft plans to stay relevant in the post-Gates era*, John Wiley, Hoboken, NJ

Isaacson, Walter (2011) *Steve Jobs*, Little, Brown, London

Kirkpatrick, David (2010) *The Facebook Effect: The inside story of the company that is connecting the world*, Simon & Schuster, New York

Levis, Kieran (2009) *Winners and Losers: Creators and casualties of the age of the internet*, Atlantic Books, London

Levy, Steven (2006) *The Perfect Thing: How the iPod became the defining object of the 21st century*, Ebury Press, London

Levy, Steven (2011) *In the Plex: How Google thinks, works and shapes our lives*, Simon & Schuster, New York

Lewis, Michael (1999) *The New New Thing: A Silicon Valley story*, Hodder & Stoughton, London

Norman, Donald A (2004) *Emotional Design: Why we love (or hate) everyday things*, Basic Books, New York

Wu, Tim (2011) *The Master Switch: The rise and fall of information empires*, Atlantic Books, London

Acknowledgements

First mention must go to Susannah Lear, who e-mailed me out of the blue with the Velcro-covered idea of a book about these three companies and their interactions. Nothing could shake it out of my head, and what you're reading is the result of it.

Thanks to the many sources, named, unnamed and unnameable, who were so helpful.

Nicholas Radcliffe, who put forward the suggestion that Apple behaves most like a band with a charismatic frontman.

Jim Boke Tomlin, who put off going to bed in California to goog... to search for early instances of 'google' used as a verb.

Kogan Page, who put up with me.

Keith Blount for originally writing Scrivener, a formidable piece of software that actually enabled me to write a book. Believe me, nothing else could have made it happen except the quiet tyranny of a single screen for everything.

Last.fm, Sonos and Elbow for the soundtrack.

I wrote this book on an Apple MacBook, did a lot of the searching using Google's search engine, and made many, many phone calls using (Microsoft-owned) Skype. For listening to music I'd use an iPod Touch and for mobile calls a Google Nexus S smartphone. (I couldn't balance it with a Zune, because Microsoft never sold them in Europe.) I hope that will suffice for balance.

And of course to my marvellous wife, Jojo, who actually does write books again and again, and to Saskia, Harry and Lockie, all inspirational in their own way.

Trademarks

Due to the exceptionally high number of registered and unregistered trademarks referred to in this publication, the ® and ™ symbols have not been applied throughout. Instead the publisher refers readers to the online information available from many companies governing the use of trademarks. Below is a brief selection. The publisher supports the unequivocal reference to trademarks and fully recognizes their legal status.

APPLE http://www.apple.com/legal/trademark/appletmlist.html

MICROSOFT http://www.microsoft.com/About/Legal/EN/US/IntellectualProperty/Trademarks/Usage/General.aspx

GOOGLE http://www.google.com/permissions/guidelines.html

ARM http://www.arm.com/about/trademark-usage-guidelines.php

ADOBE http://www.adobe.com/misc/trade.html

Index

NB: page numbers in *italic* indicate figures or tables